AF581316

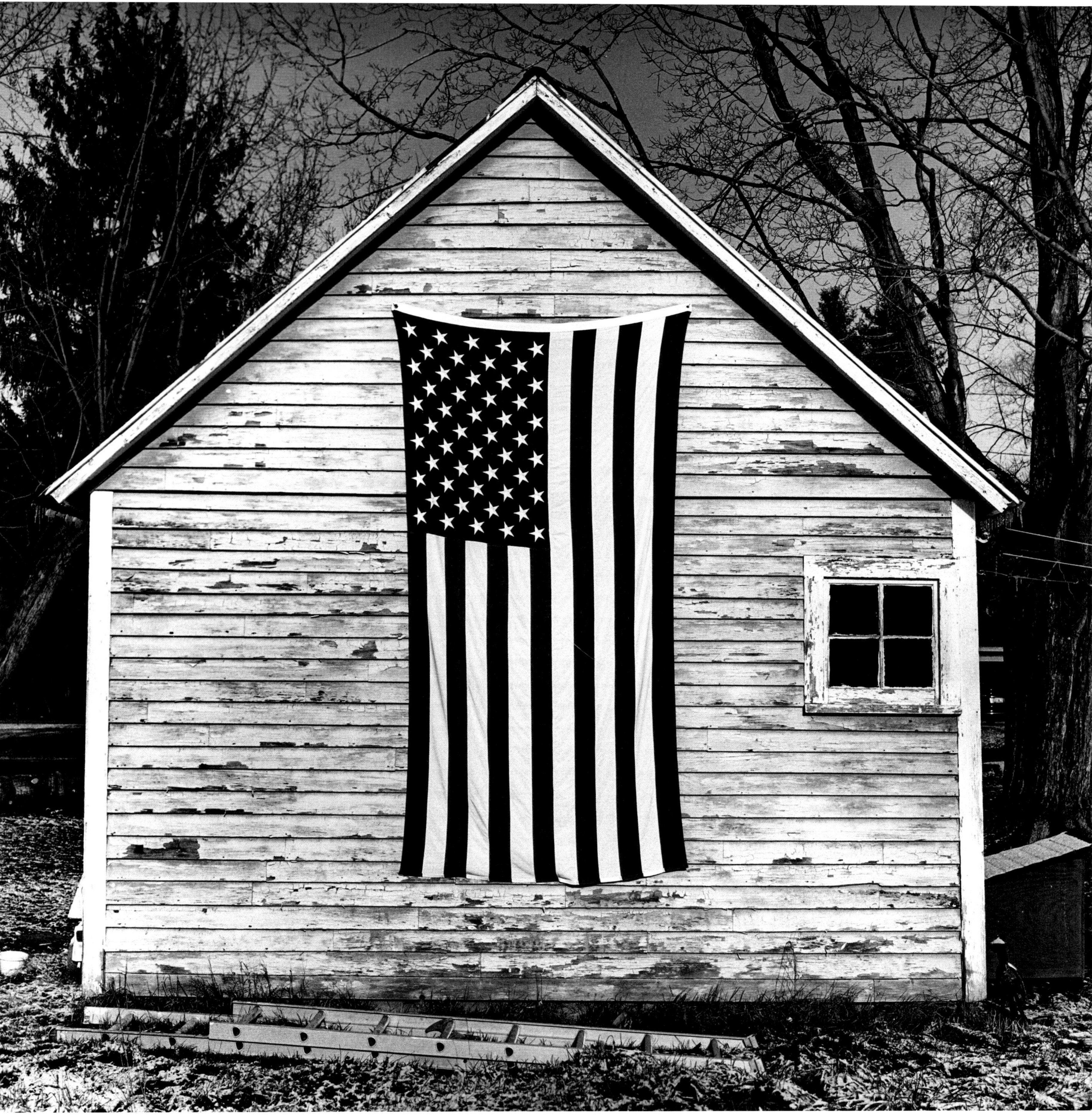

Our Voices, Our Streets

American Protests 2001–2011

Photographs by Kevin Bubriski

Foreword by Lucy McKeon
Afterword by Howard Zinn

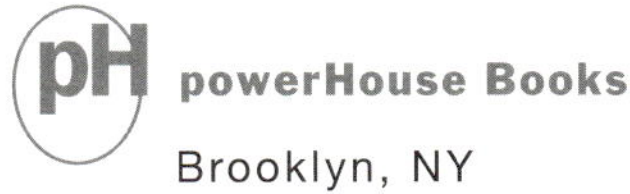

powerHouse Books
Brooklyn, NY

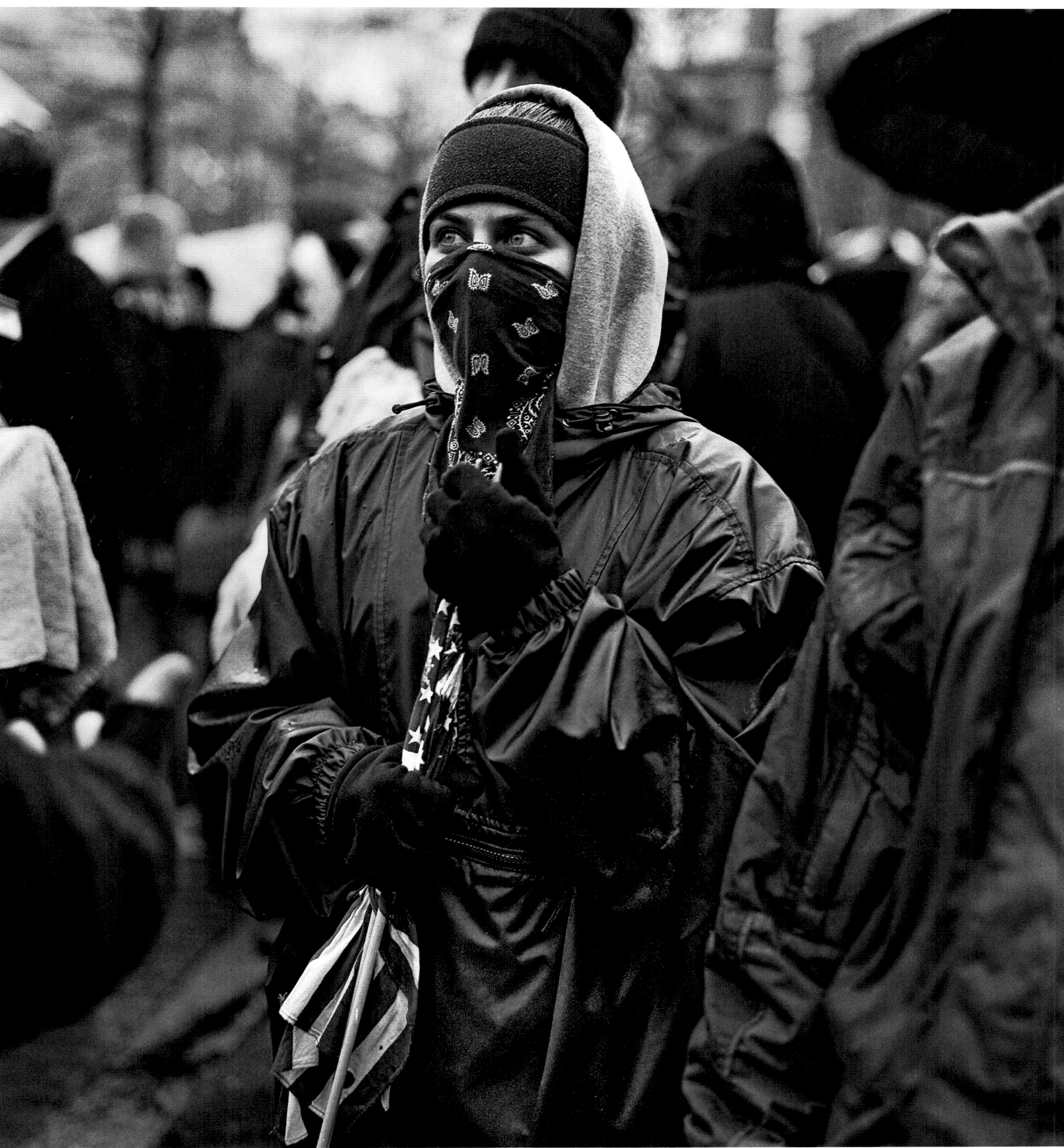

Contents

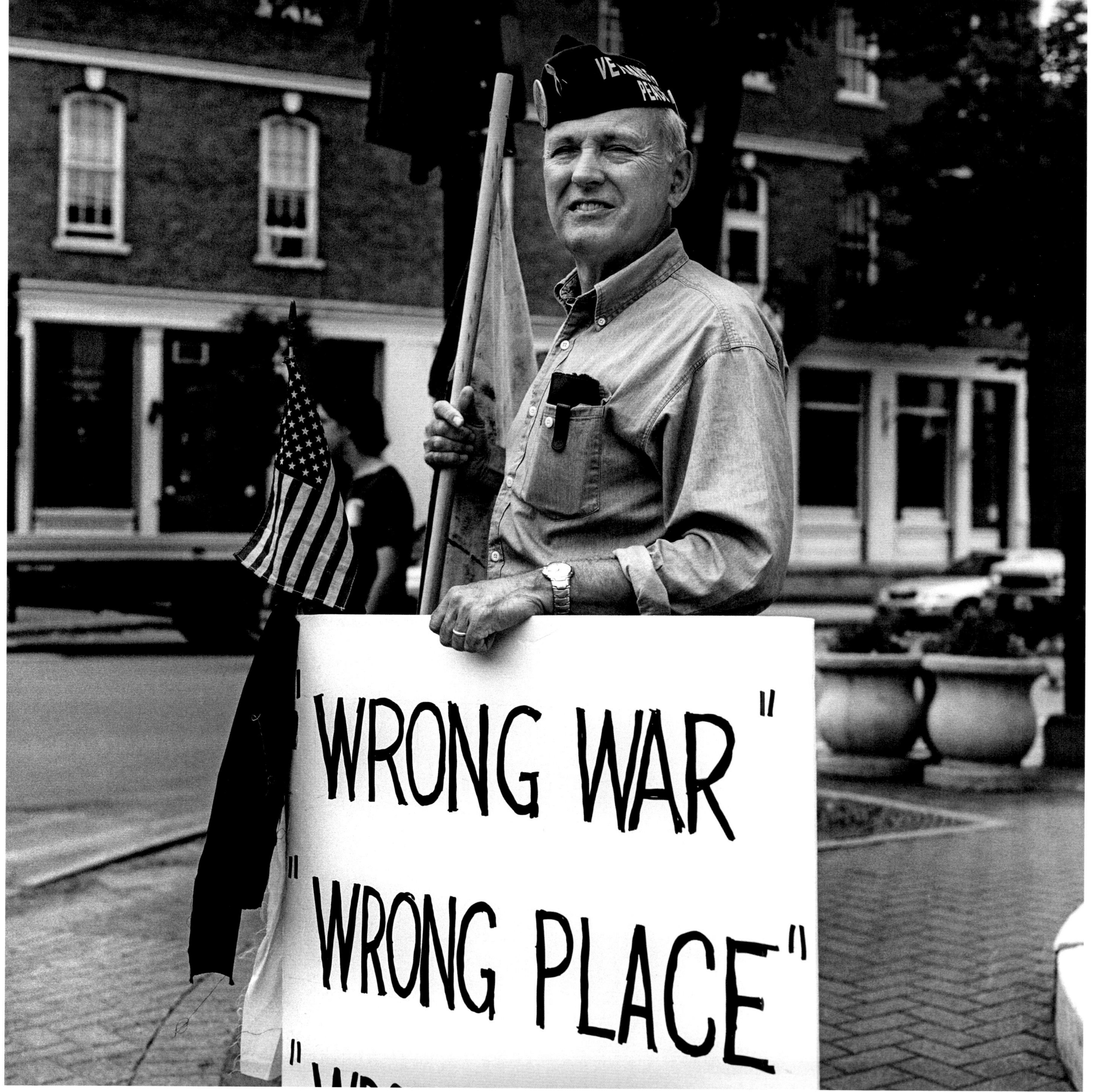
"WRONG WAR"
"WRONG PLACE"

Foreword

LUCY McKEON

I had recently moved to New York City when Occupy Wall Street erupted in lower Manhattan. I remember walking south to Zuccotti Park from the West 12th Street apartment where I was staying temporarily—home for many decades to my cousin Tony, a veteran writer for *Sesame Street*, and his wife Phyllis—while their executor prepared the apartment to be sold. Looking through Tony and Phyllis's things, I came across a photograph of the Twin Towers, taken from their living room window. A decade after the towers had fallen, I looked down at the photograph, then up again at the skyline where, minutes before, I hadn't felt their absence.

In *Our Voices, Our Streets: American Protests 2001–2011*, Kevin Bubriski documents the first decade of the new millennium with protest portraits, from demonstrations against George W. Bush's inauguration in 2001—and the gatherings at ground zero and anti-war marches that followed—to Occupy Wall Street in 2011. The images in this book, the most recent of which were taken only five years before the 2016 election, are a kind of time capsule. Like many rediscoveries, they offer a sense of continuity while also revealing the distance between now and then. More than one slogan on the homemade protest signs Bubriski captured—"Republicans for a sensible foreign policy"—is unquestionably of another era; 2001's "Democracy Dies Today" sounds almost quaint.

Occupy Wall Street—the movement that began in a public park in Manhattan's financial district, organized to unite a "99 percent" around issues like unaffordable health care, compromised democracy, unrelenting student debt, and other effects of neoliberal global capitalism—may feel particularly remote now, perhaps in part because its influence has been so thoroughly metabolized by the contemporary left. It's difficult to remember a time when its major ideas weren't taken for granted. In one of Bubriski's photos, a twentysomething holds a sign itemizing a "Wall Street 'To Do' List," which includes buying the presidency and the Supreme Court and owning all media; in another photograph from Zuccotti Park, a young man with an Afro-mohawk and bandana looks on with a slight smile, while three of his fingers rest across his neck as if lazily taking his own pulse.

I grew up with Bubriski's images. His photographs of Nepal, Morocco, Brazil, and Syria hang in my parents' house; the gesture of two holy men bending in a kiss, the impossible blues of Marrakech alleyways, are as familiar as a family portrait or the faded wallpaper of my childhood. But the very American scenes of *Our Voices, Our Streets* were new to me, and familiar in a different way. The images invoke atrocities around which the people pictured gather—war, corruption, injustice—but these events are not themselves the subjects of the photographs.

Photography criticism has, understandably, spent more time on images of atrocity than on images of the movements organized against it. But the terms of debate might be similar. To borrow Susan Sontag's famous criticism of war photography, that an image of protest—like that of suffering—has the capacity to move us (people are in the streets, I should join them!) or to inure us (people are already in the streets, why join them?) exemplifies the predicament particular to the artform, the dual responsibility of documentation, of "bearing witness," and of having an aesthetic, as art.

That photographs necessarily have a perspective is by now conventional wisdom, and Bubriski's point of view distinctively emphasizes the individuals who make up a crowd. But considering how continuously media are evolving, the effect that images have on our perceptions and habits seems to demand frequent reassessment. In our era of smartphones and social media (Instagram launched just a year before Occupy), of Black Lives Matter and the Climate Strike, of the Mueller Report and, now, impeachment proceedings, *Our Voices, Our Streets* puts a face—many different, striking faces—to the notable evolution of photography over the last twenty years.

Some faces are particularly memorable: an older white woman holds a sign reading, "President Bush, You Killed My Son," at an anti-war march at the 2004 Republican National Convention, her face mostly obscured by a hat and sunglasses, her mouth set as a man stoops down to speak to her. A black teenager wearing a *Washington Times* smock and holding the paper announcing Bush's second inauguration delivers a side-eye; the gaze of the president floats, disembodied and smug, his face folded just below the nose. A reverent trinity of profiles, two men in baseball caps and a woman with platinum hair, all face the same way at the World Trade Center site on the tenth anniversary of September 11.

Moments of determination, fury, and grief are complemented by those of celebration and commemoration, like the thrilling hope captured at Obama's 2008 inauguration, or the pensive pride at Bennington's Veterans Day Parade. Policemen point and wield their batons. Counterprotesters hold their own signs and views. Bubriski's portraits include people with different, opposing, politics. There is a funeral for one Iraq War soldier and a welcoming parade for another.

And though these images are of specific times and places, all protest photographs seem to refer to one another, despite the differences in their causes, fashions, slogans, and aesthetics. A little girl at an anti-war demonstration in Bennington, her face painted over with an American flag, her hands raised in peace signs, makes me think of images of Vietnam War protests. I'm reminded, too, of the young man at a Selma to Montgomery march, his face painted white save for the word "VOTE," which stands out across his forehead, the American flag behind him, photographed in 1965 by Bruce Davidson. Another of Bubriski's images—three black men in exquisite composition at the 2002 anti-war march in D.C., stylish in all-black with leather, berets, and sunglasses—recalls portraits of the Black Panthers by Stephen Shames. Bubriski's photos from a demonstration in solidarity with Palestinian rights, potentially the largest ever in the U.S. as of 2002, bring to mind the history and continuation of this long conflict. *Our Voices, Our Streets* reminds us how far back our present political ideals go, and how far they may yet have to travel.

America since its founding has been a place of extreme tension, violence, and turmoil. Each decade inherits those that preceded it, and while the future looks no less extreme, we continue to gather together. Today, young people are leading movements—from the activists who founded Black Lives Matter in 2013 to the 2018 student-led March for Our Lives against gun violence; from the youth-driven proliferation of socialist ideas in politics to the organizing of 14-year-old clean-water activist Autumn Peltier and 16-year-old climate activists Isra Hirsi and Greta Thunberg. As their voices and others' are heard, and as people continue to take to the streets, I imagine Bubriski there, making images to help us remember as clearly as possible this next chapter in American history.

Washington, D.C., January 20, 2001

Inauguration of George W. Bush

In spite of the bitter-cold rain and wind on inauguration day, there were large numbers of spectators and demonstrators present. The disputed election two months earlier between George W. Bush and Al Gore was settled with a Supreme Court ruling that the presidency would go to Bush. Security was tight, with long lines and bottlenecks at checkpoints for guests attending Bush's official inauguration event. Meanwhile the streets were lively with protestors chanting and wielding signs—both angry and comedic—facing off against riot police in body armor. Estimates later put the number of protestors at 20,000.

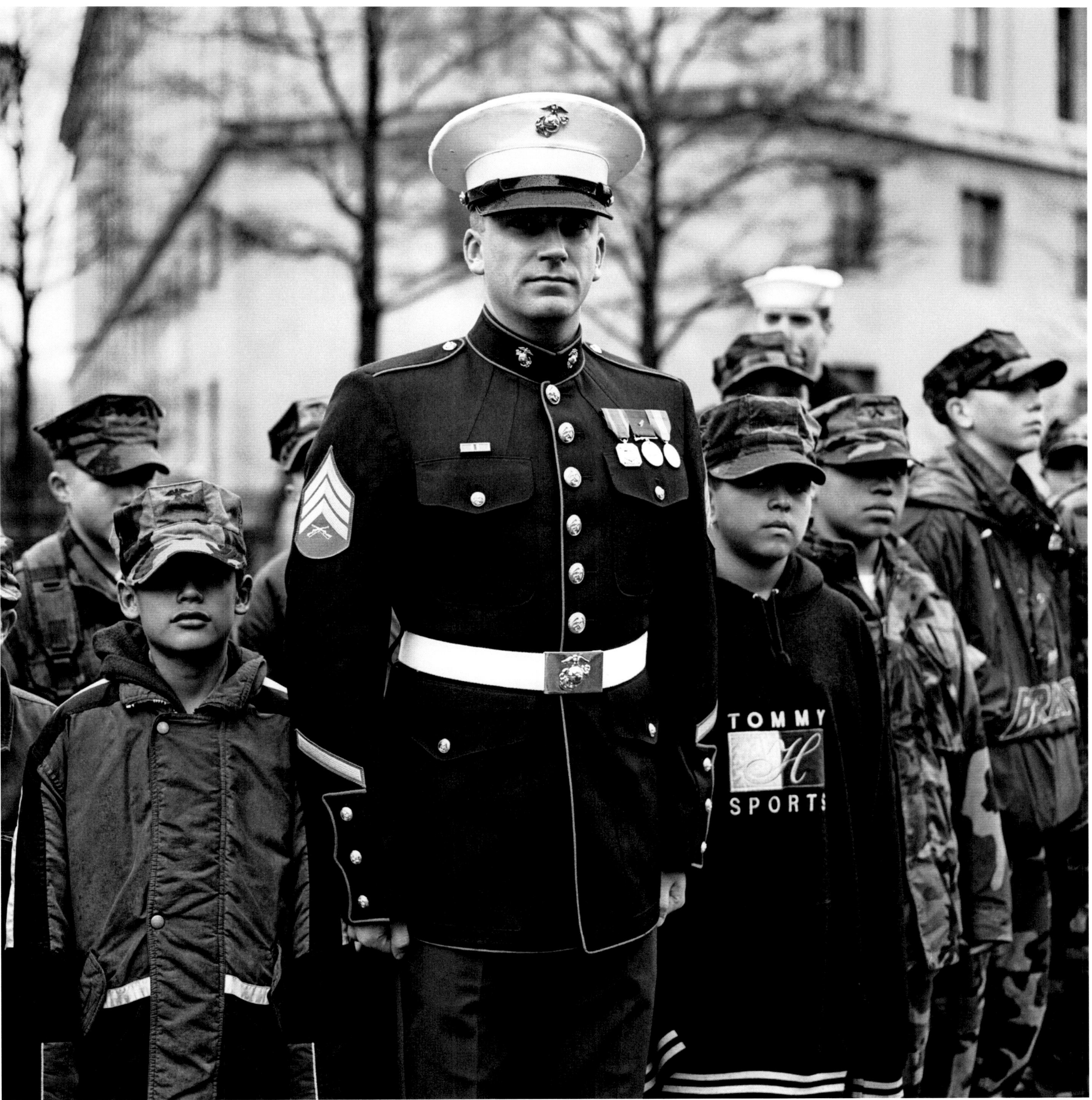
TOMMY
SPORTS

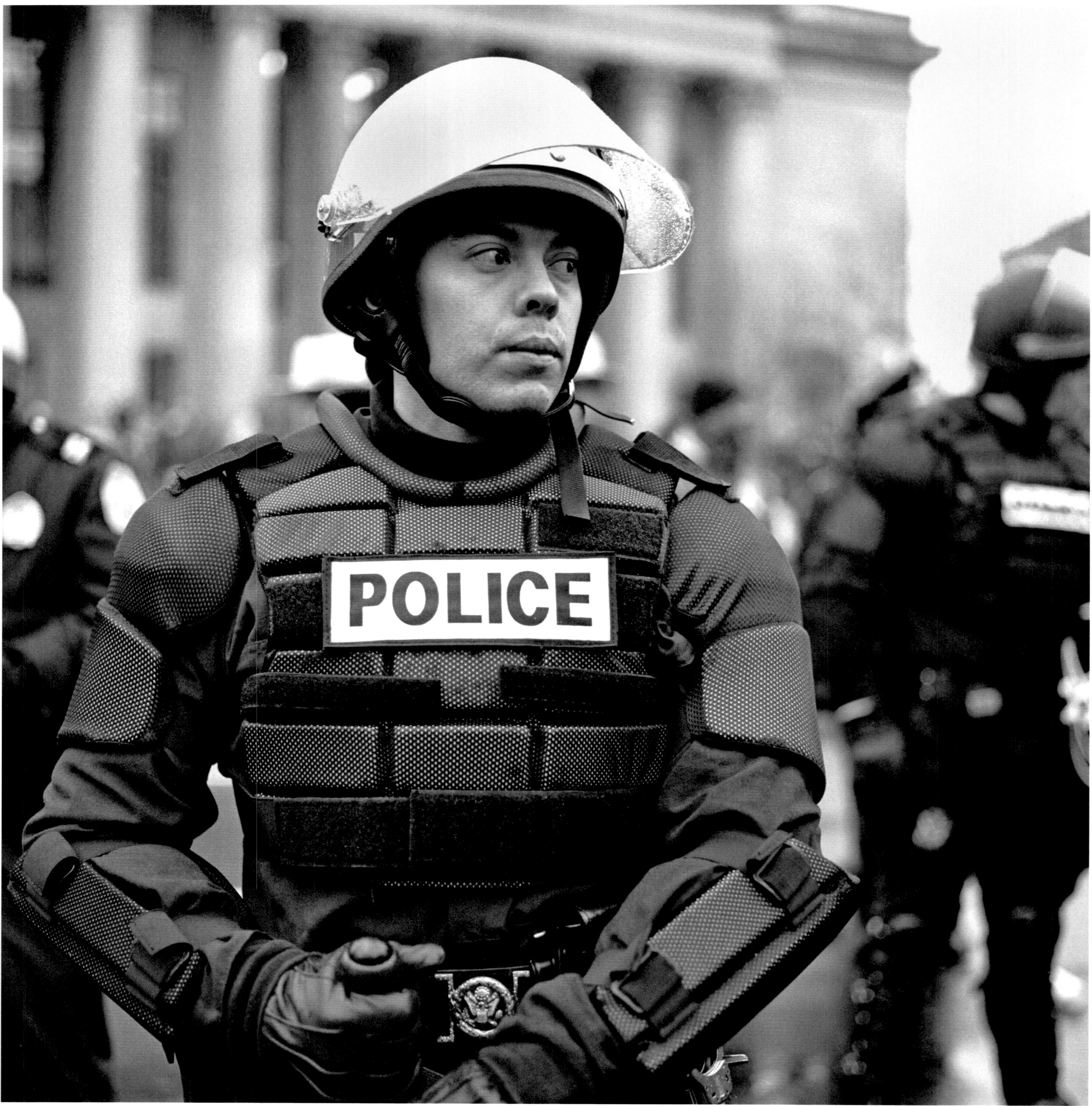
POLICE

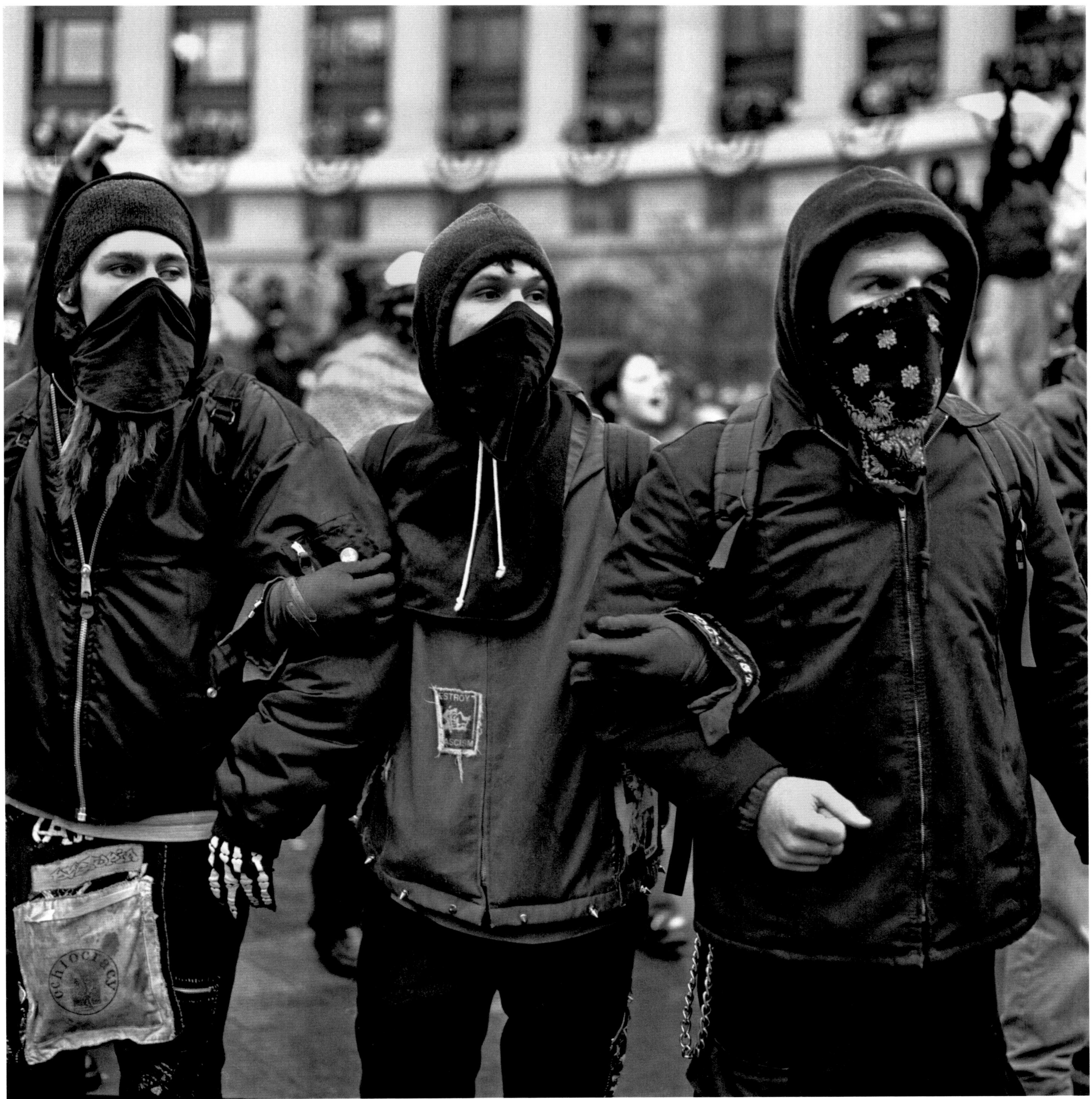

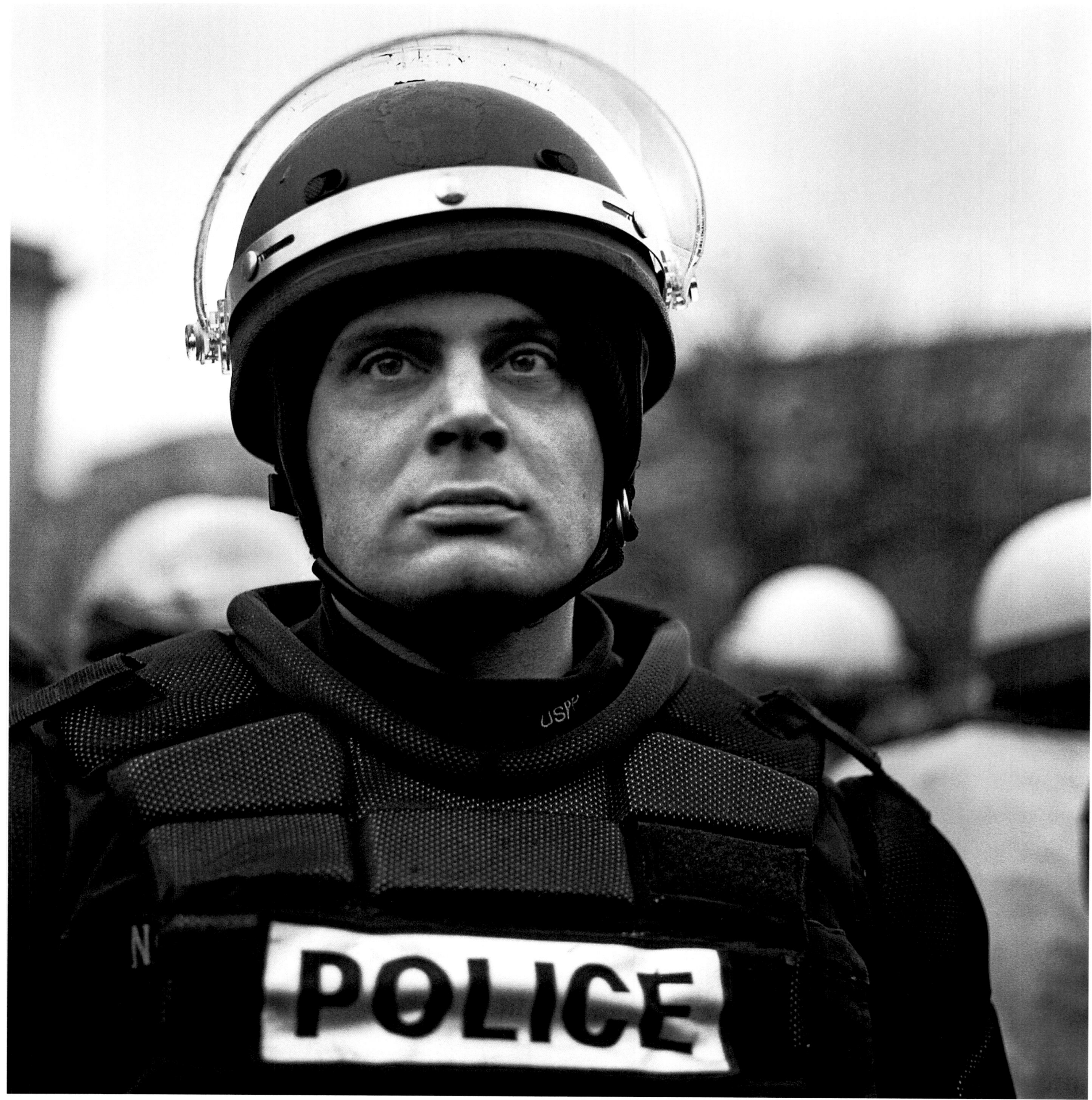
USPP
POLICE

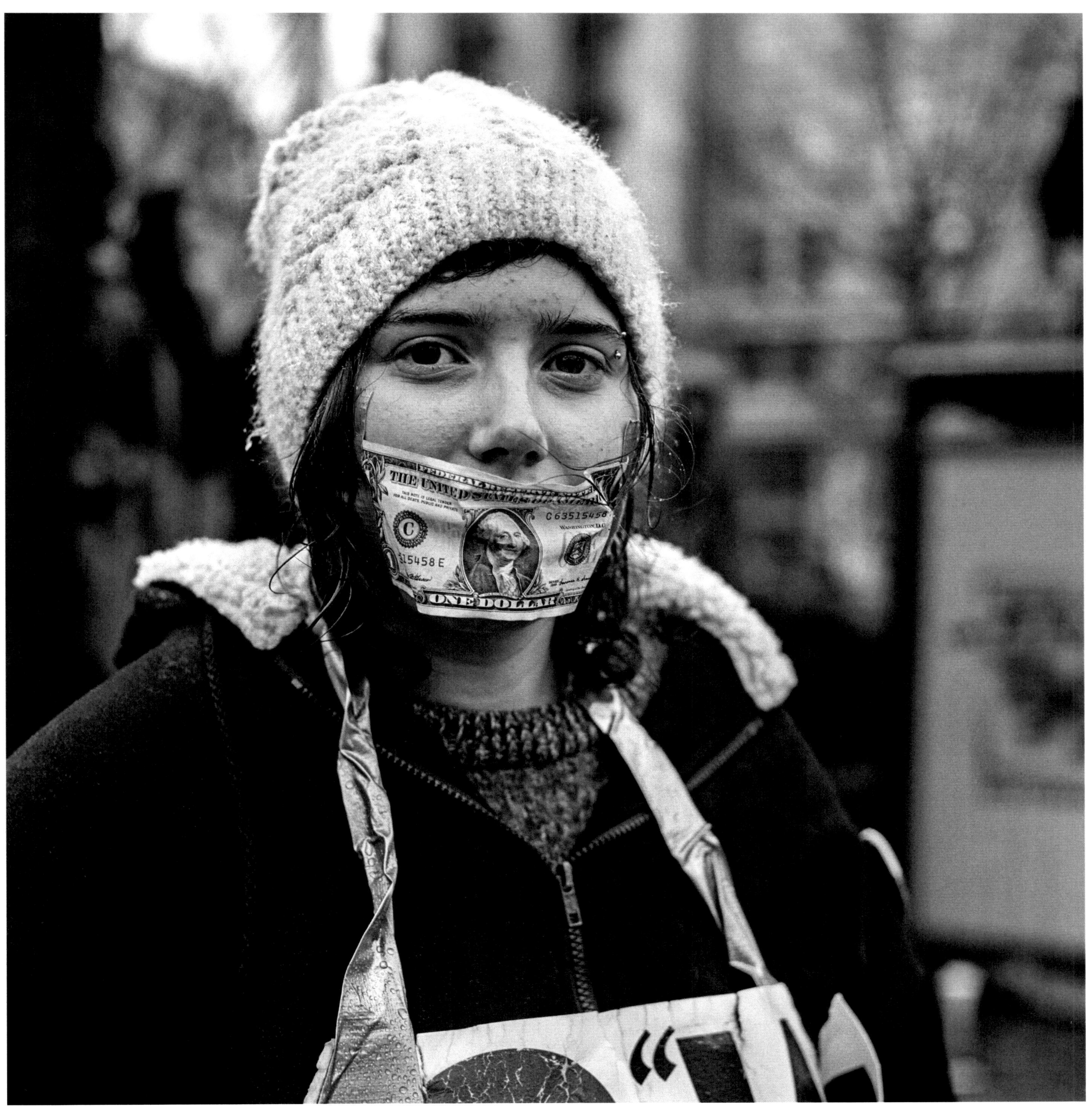
ONE DOLLAR
C63515458
515458 E

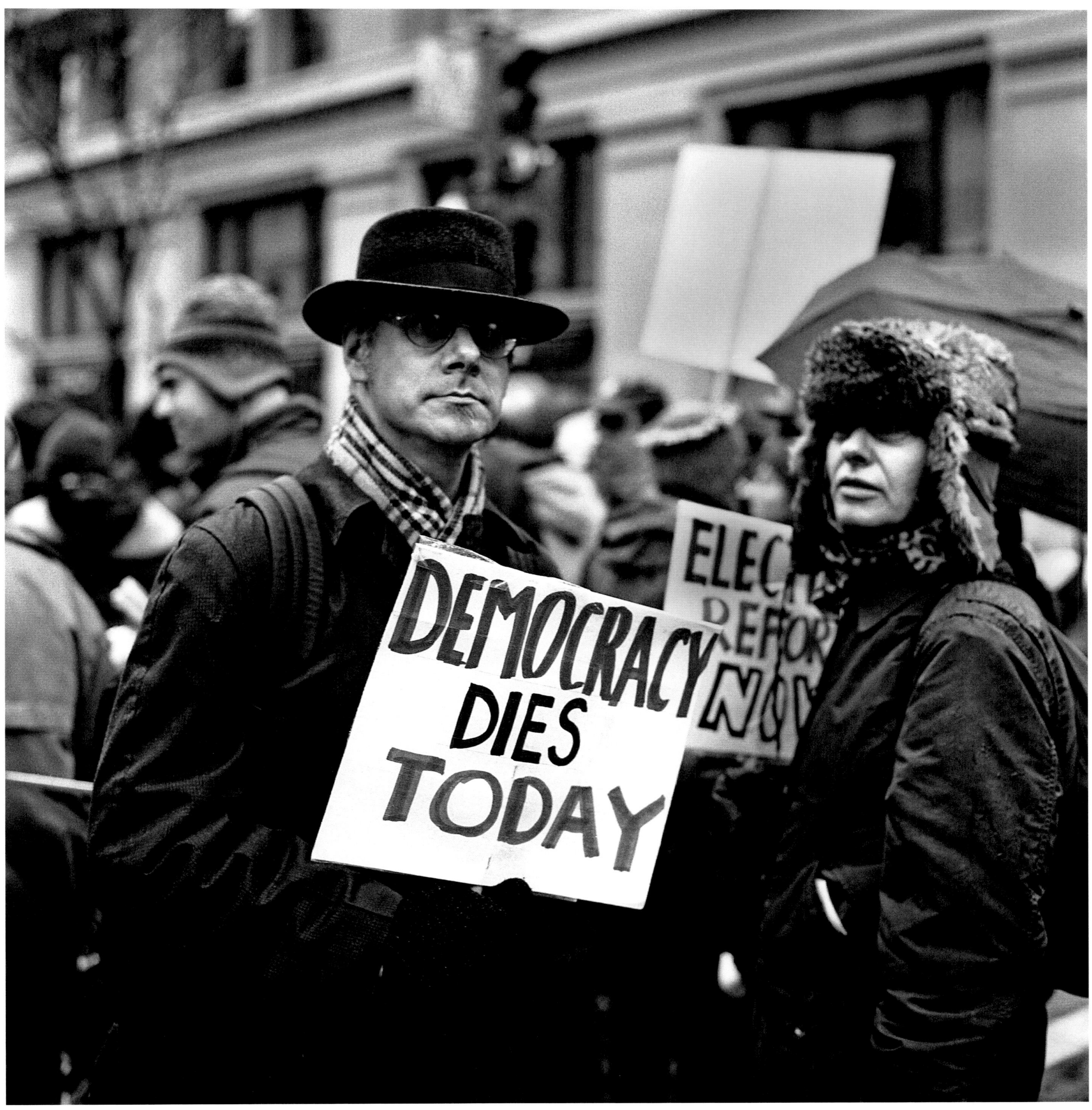
DEMOCRACY
DIES
TODAY

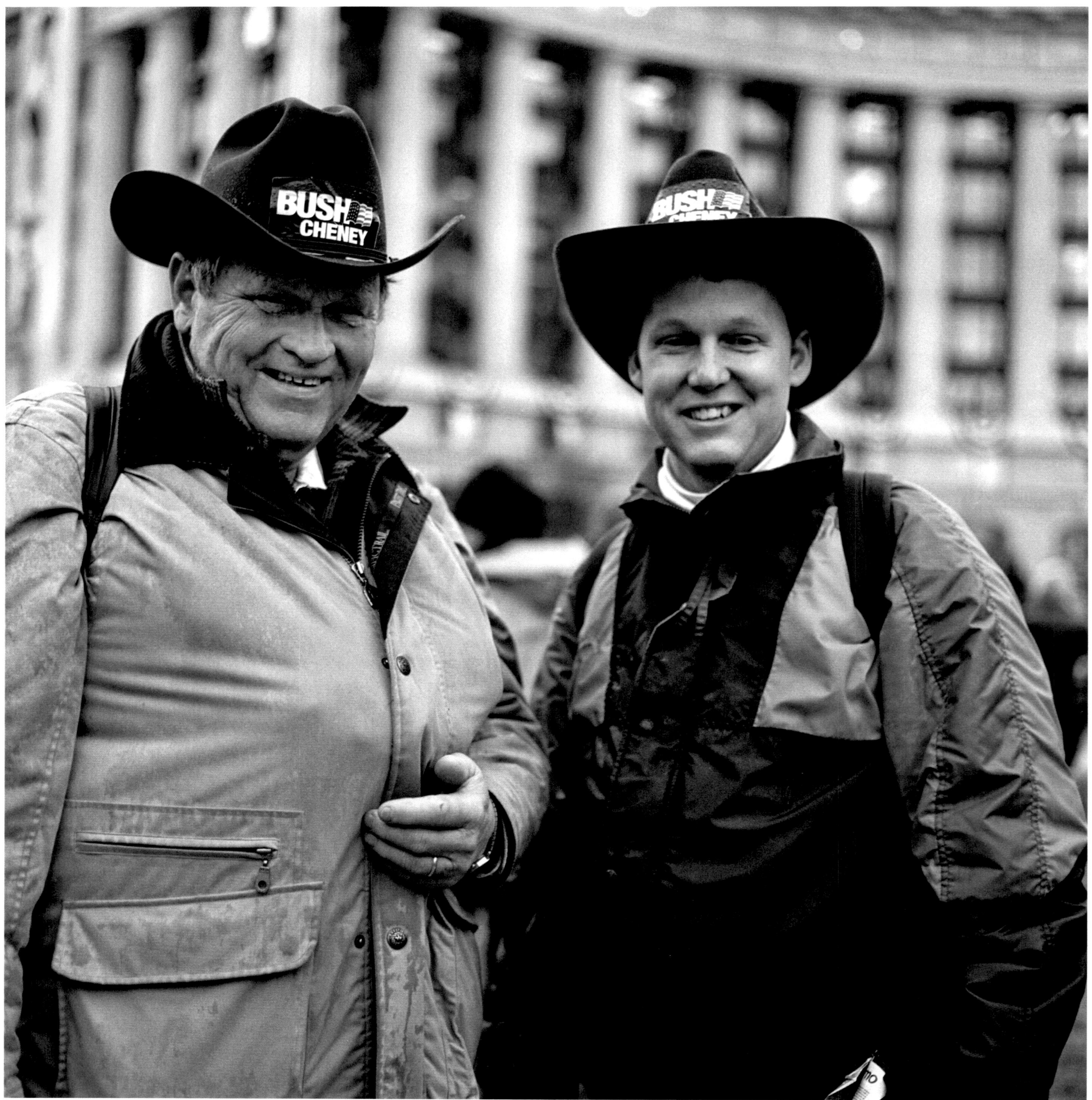
BUSH
CHENEY

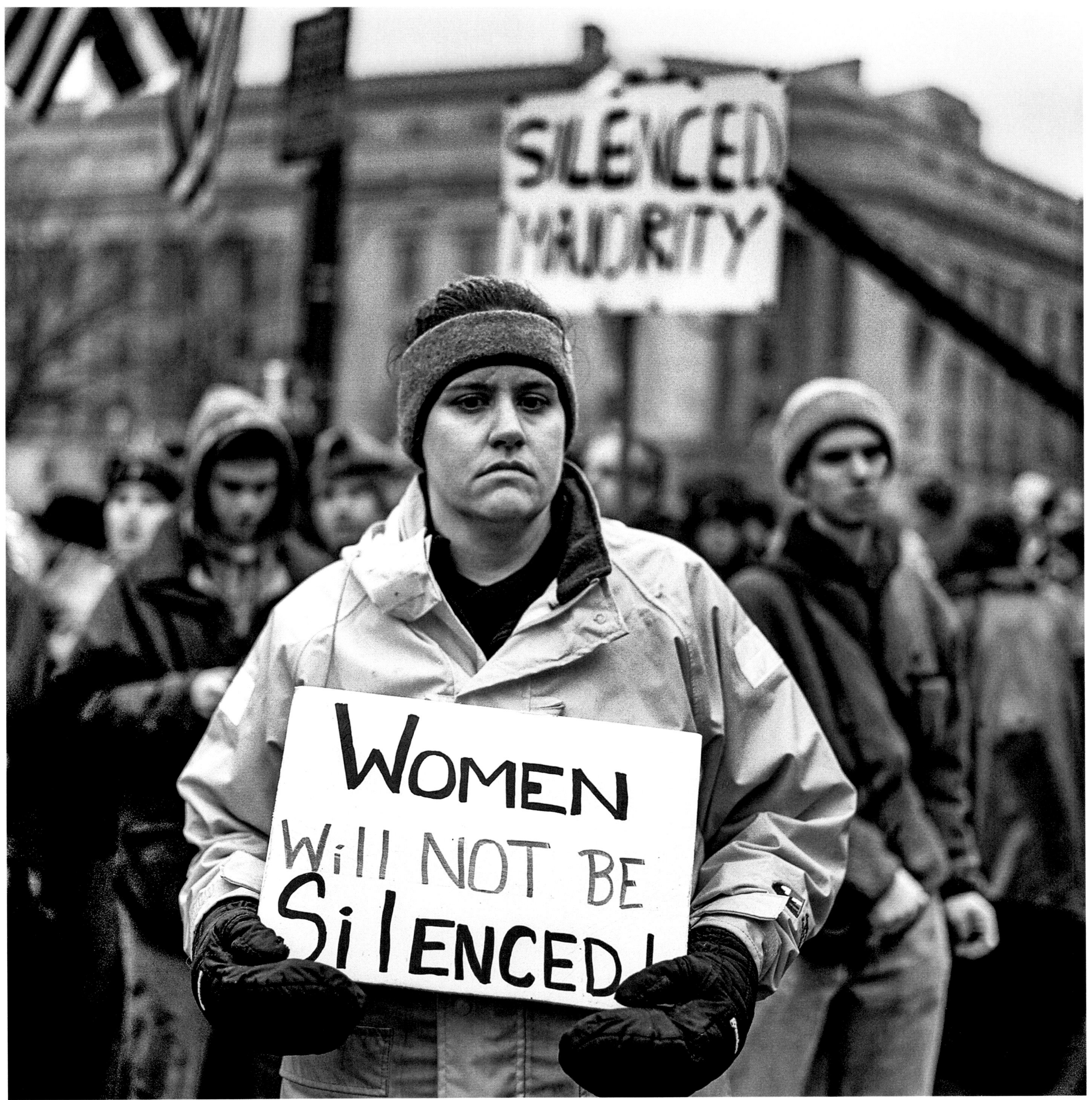
SILENCED MAJORITY
WOMEN
Will NOT BE
SilENCED!

Bennington, Vermont, November 11, 2001

Veterans Day Parade

Following the September 11 attacks in New York City, Washington, D.C., and Shanksville, Pennsylvania, President George W. Bush initiated attacks against suspected al-Qaeda positions in Afghanistan, on October 7, beginning a war that would continue through both his and Obama's presidencies. Veterans Day 2001 was a day to honor our military, but, with this new war, it was also a reminder that our servicemen and women were in danger. In the New England town of Bennington, Vermont, locals stood in the cold to honor their hometown veterans and remember those who never came home.

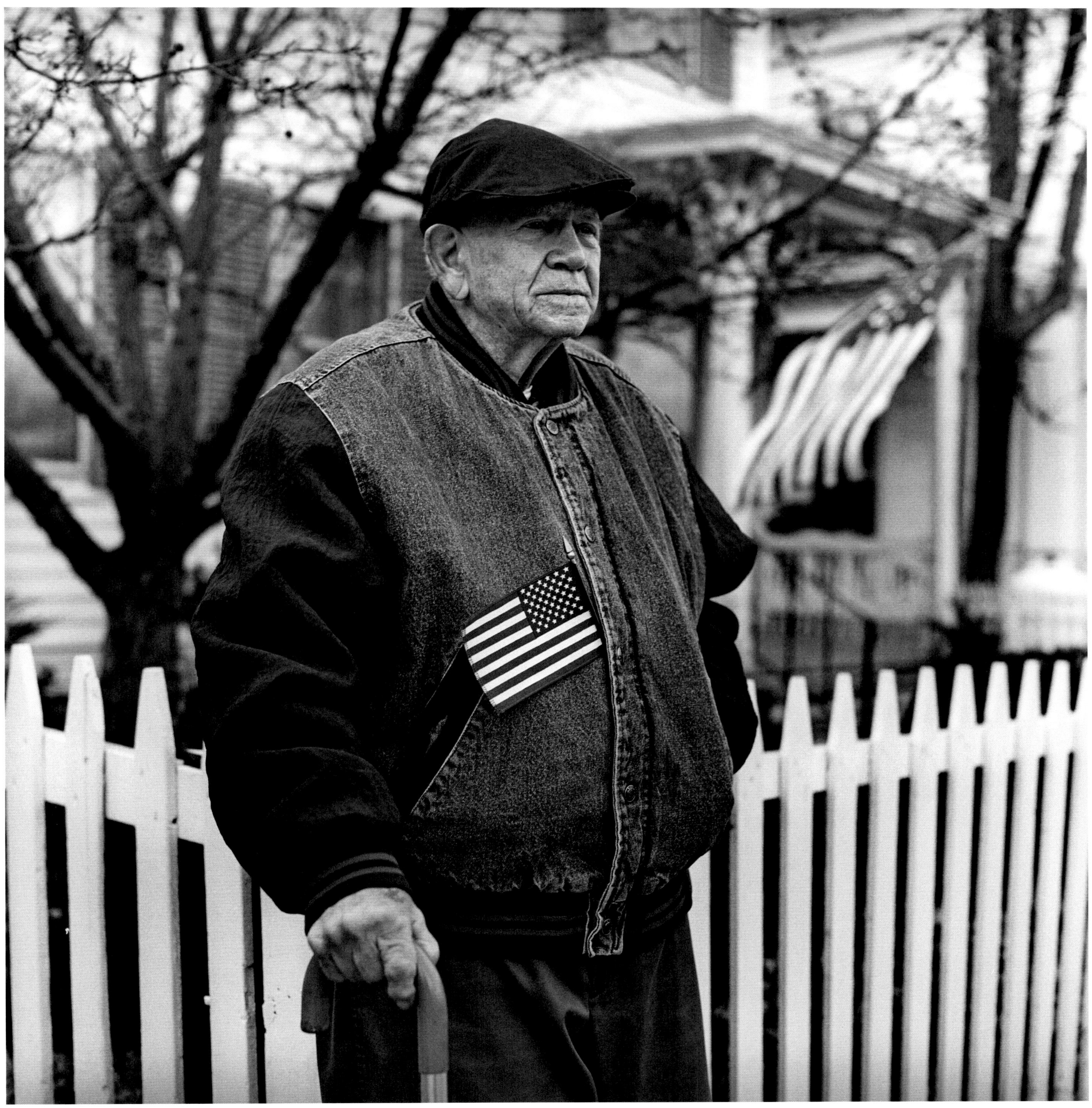

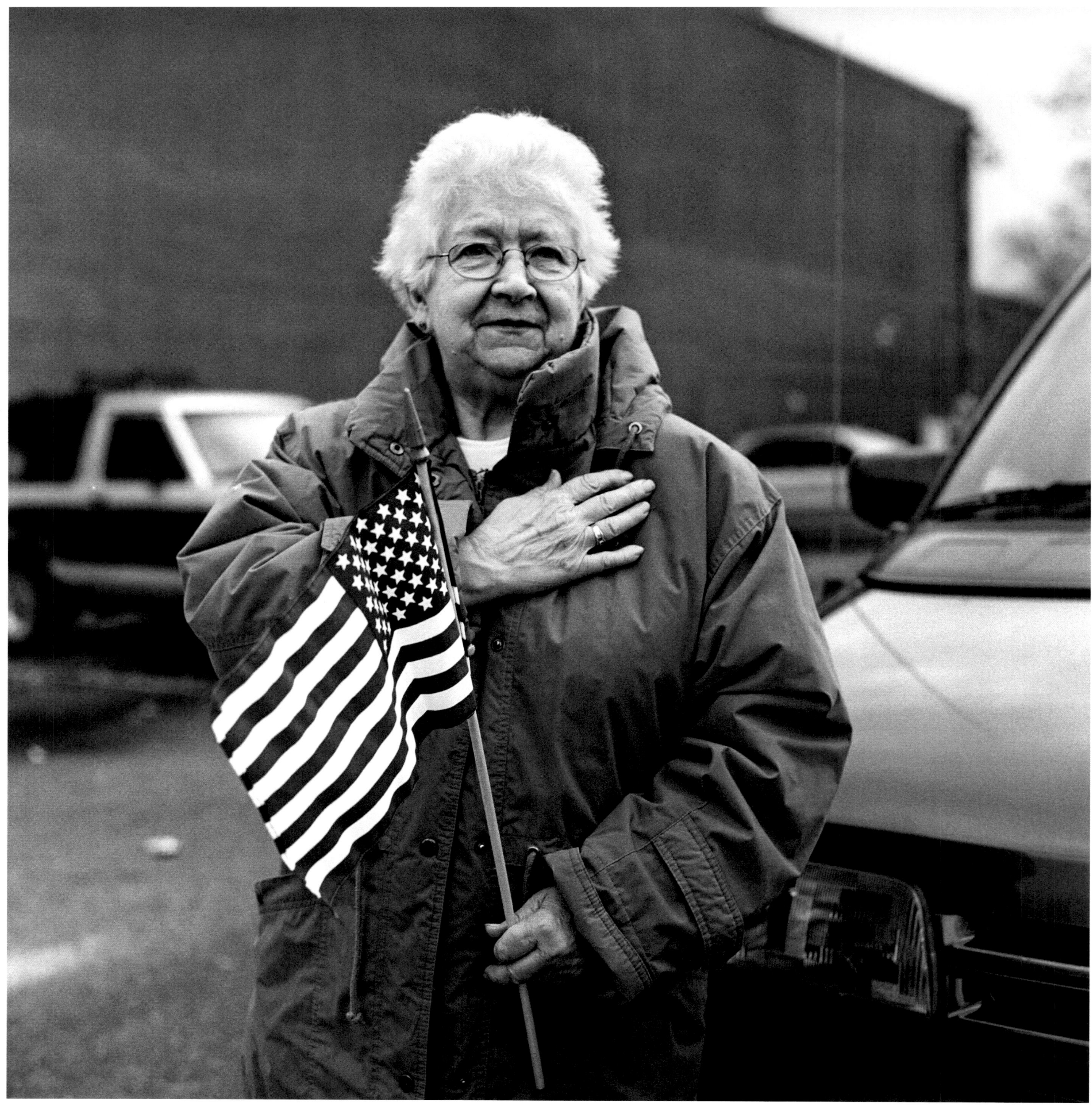

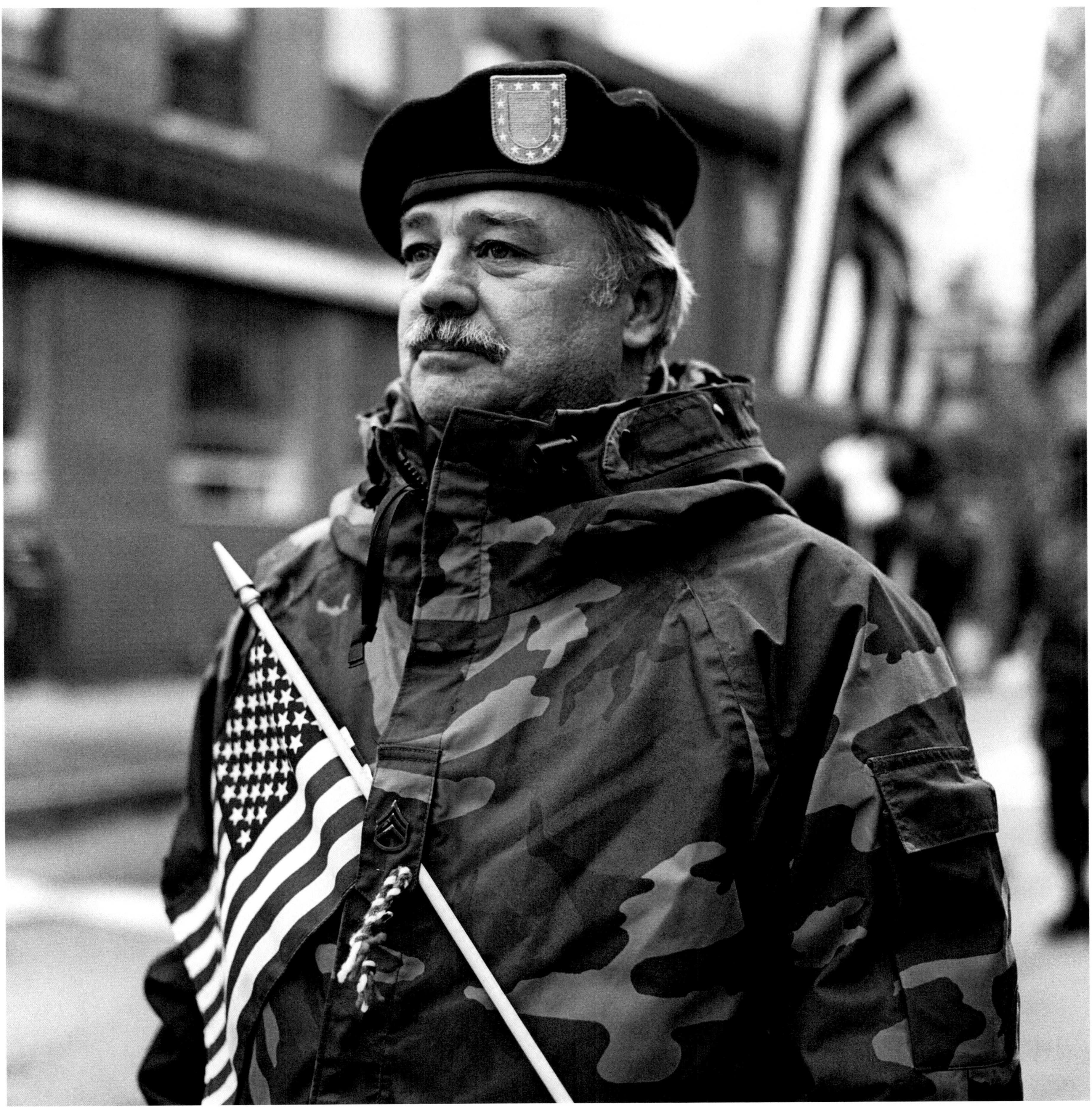

New York City, February 2, 2002

World Economic Forum Protest

Below the towering skyscrapers of midtown Manhattan, the streets were transformed into a maze of metal barricades to thwart the movement of the thousands who had congregated to oppose the meeting of the World Economic Forum. It was a challenge for protestors to even get to the demonstrations. The security barricades and numerous police personnel gave the streets of New York City, usually open and welcome-feeling, an oppressive and forbidding air.

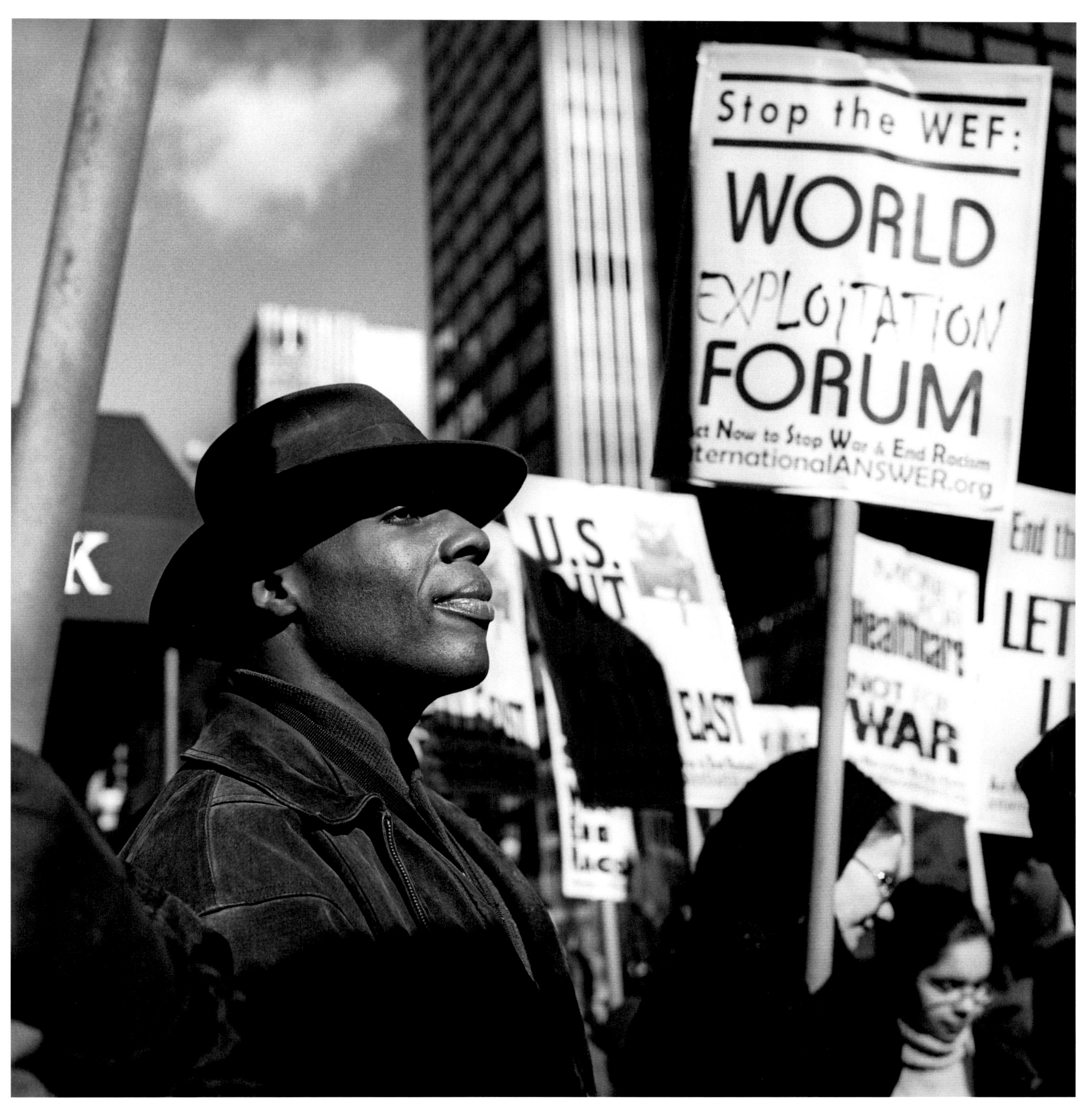
Stop the WEF:
WORLD
EXPLOITATION
FORUM
ct Now to Stop War & End Racism
ternationalANSWER.org
U.S.
EAST
Healthcare
NOT FOR
WAR

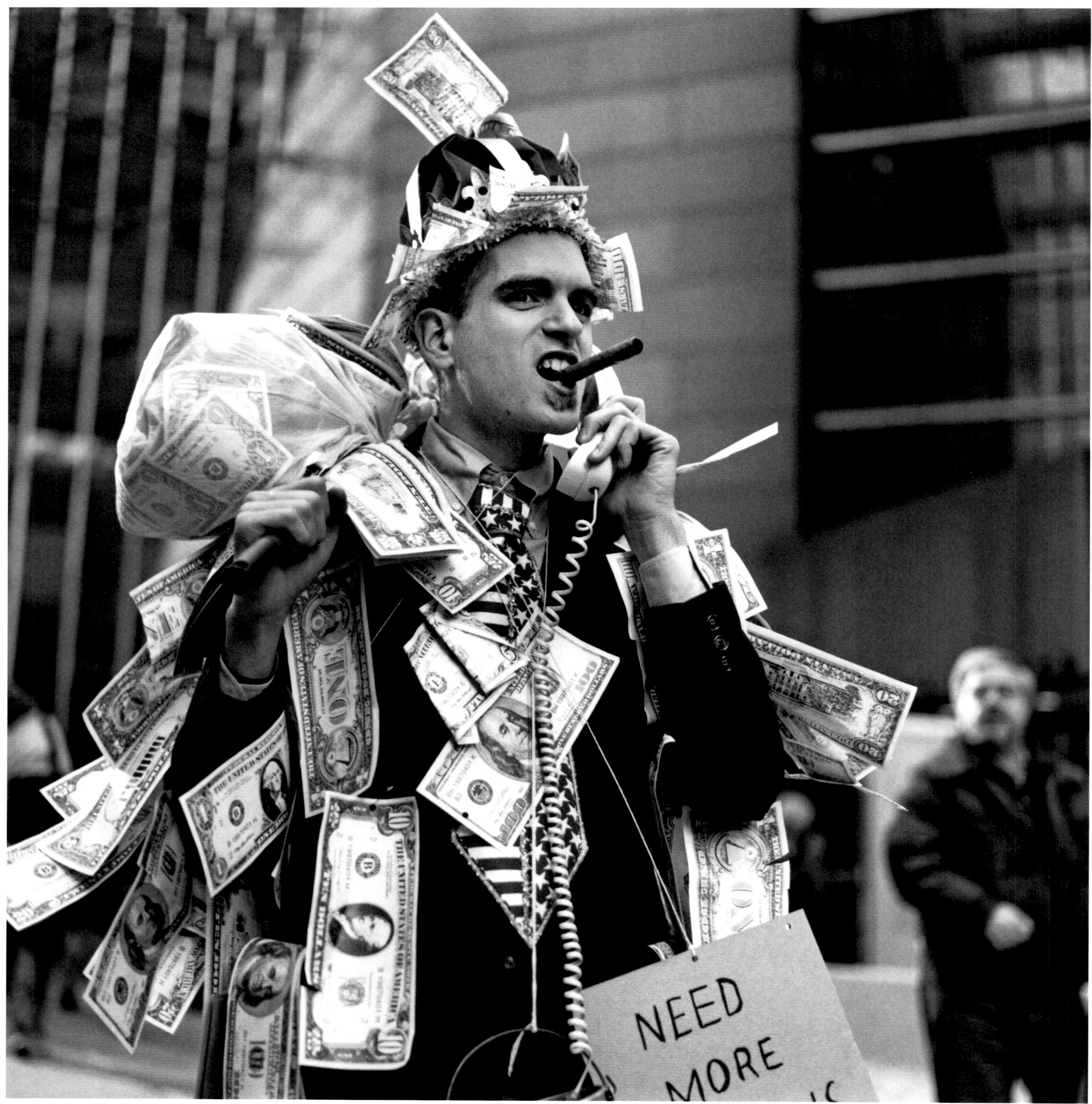
NEED
MORE

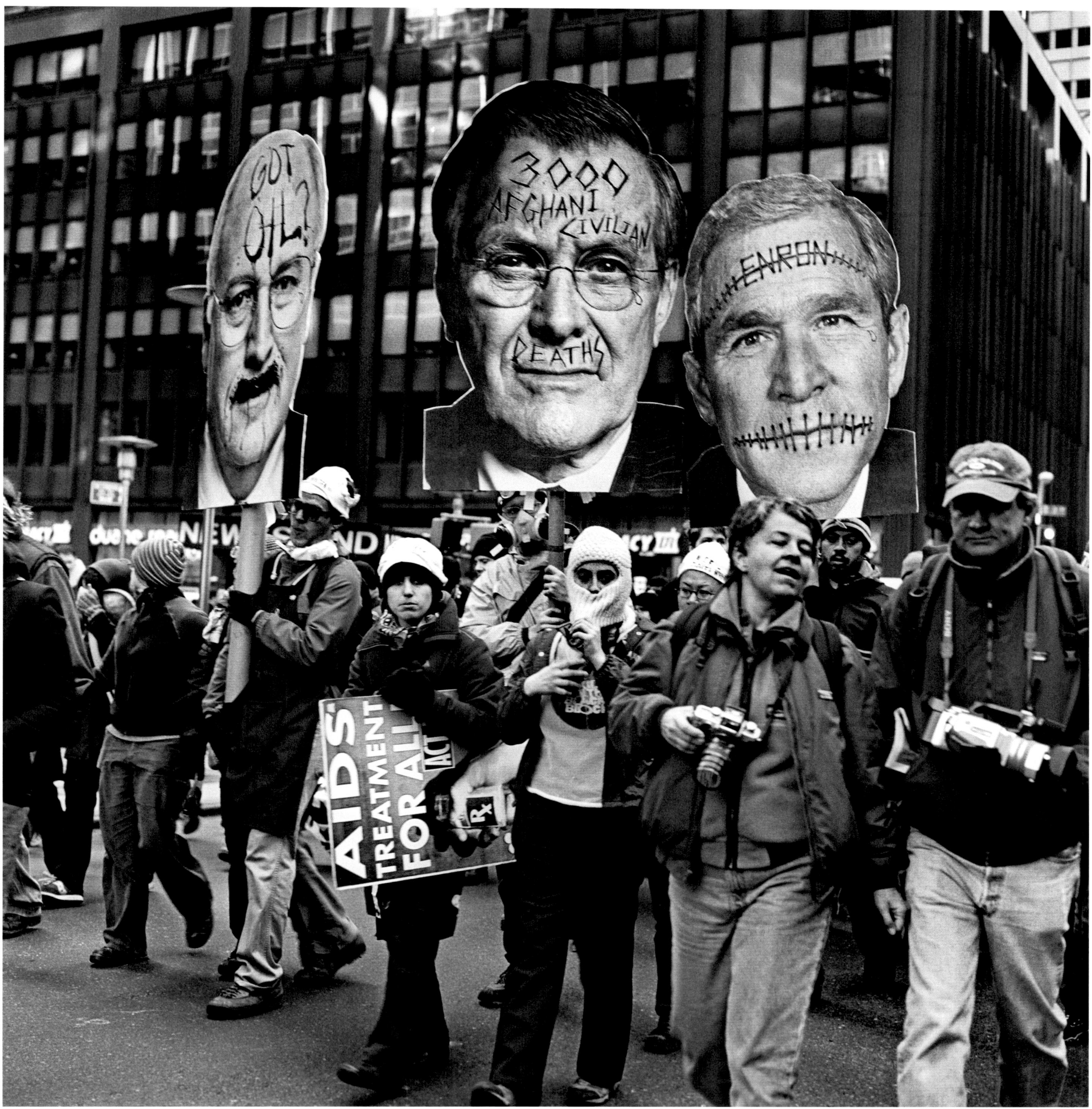
GOT OIL?
3000
AFGHANI
CIVILIAN
DEATHS
ENRON
AIDS
TREATMENT
FOR ALL

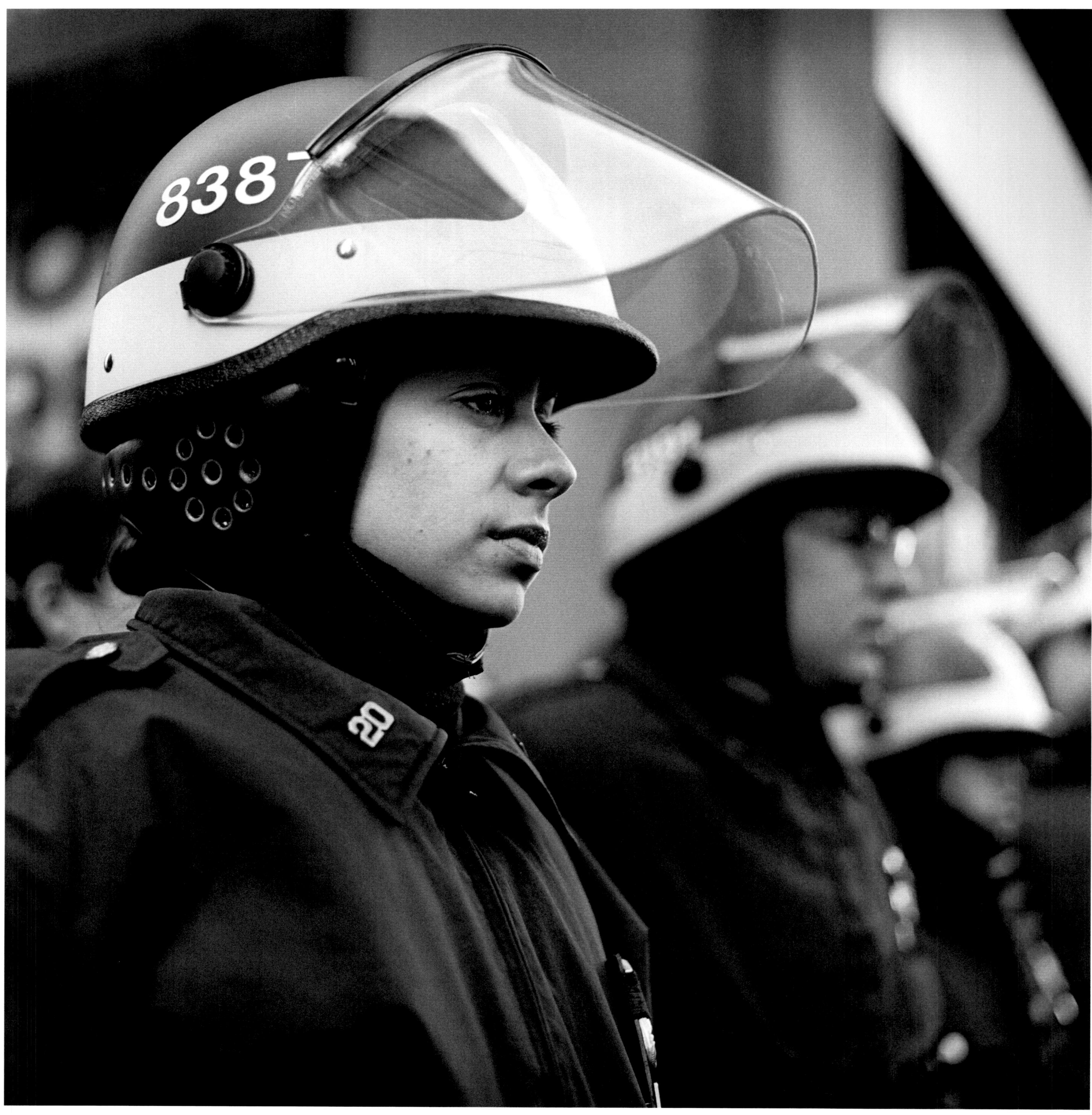
838
20

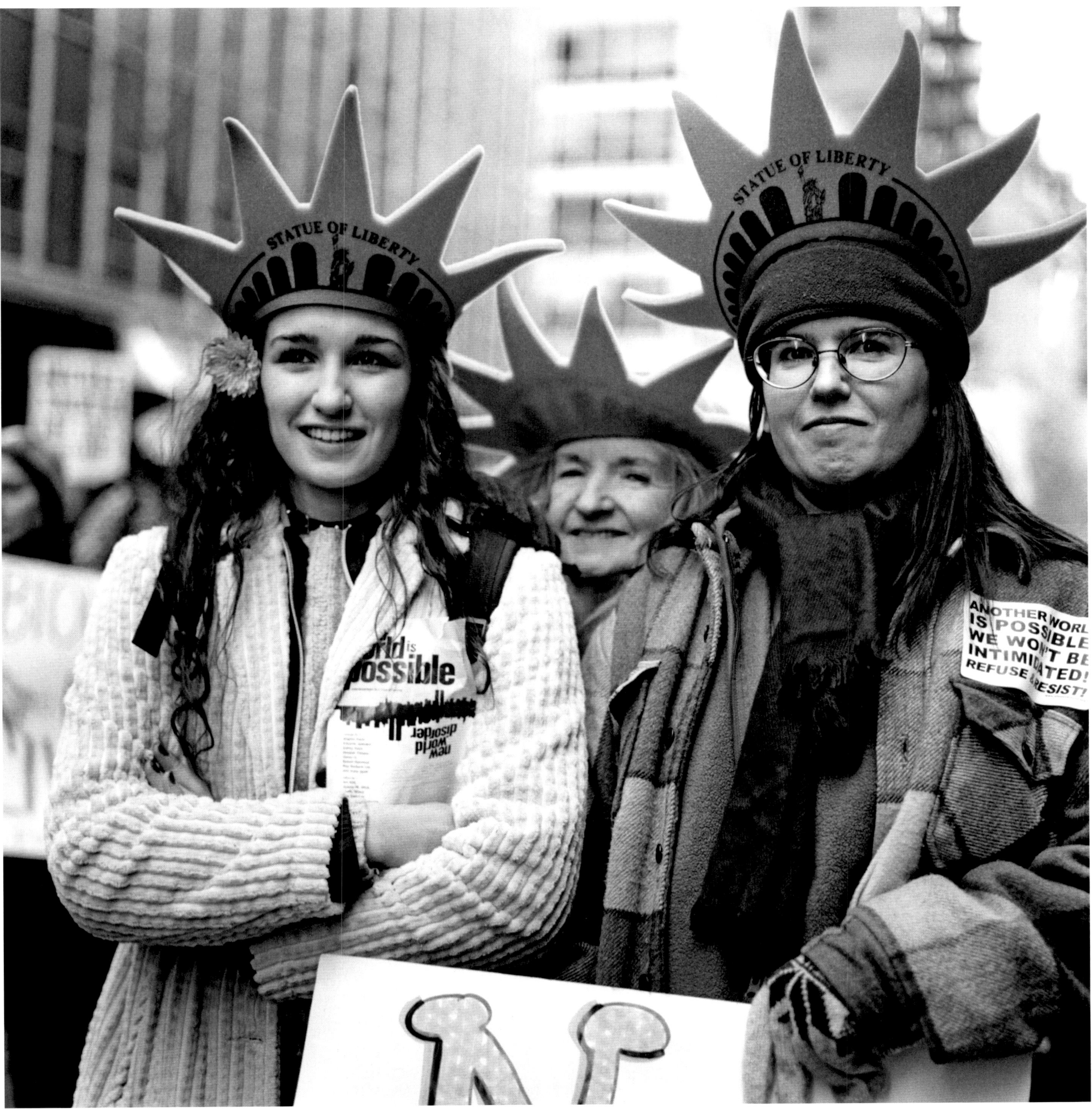
STATUE OF LIBERTY
STATUE OF LIBERTY
rld is
ossible
ANOTHER WORL
IS POSSIBLE
WE WON'T BE
INTIMI ATED!
REFUSE RESIST!

Washington, D.C., April 20–21, 2002

Palestinian Solidarity March

On this warm, sunny Saturday morning, Washington, D.C. was crowded with families, students, and people from all walks of life gathering to march in solidarity with Palestinians calling for peace and self-determination in the Middle East. Caravans of buses from states as far away as Michigan and Ohio had arrived filled with supporters, making this the largest demonstration for Muslim and Palestinian rights in America's history at the time, according to one organizer. They marched and chanted slogans for human rights, and carried signs that said "Free Palestine," "No War in Iraq," and "Don't Fund Israel Killing." After hours of marching, many families settled on the grassy Mall and Ellipse behind the White House for picnics.

The next day, another group of demonstrators, including large numbers of young people wearing masks and black bandanas, gathered for an economic justice rally at the World Bank headquarters demanding economic justice for all. From there, they marched peacefully to the Washington Monument.

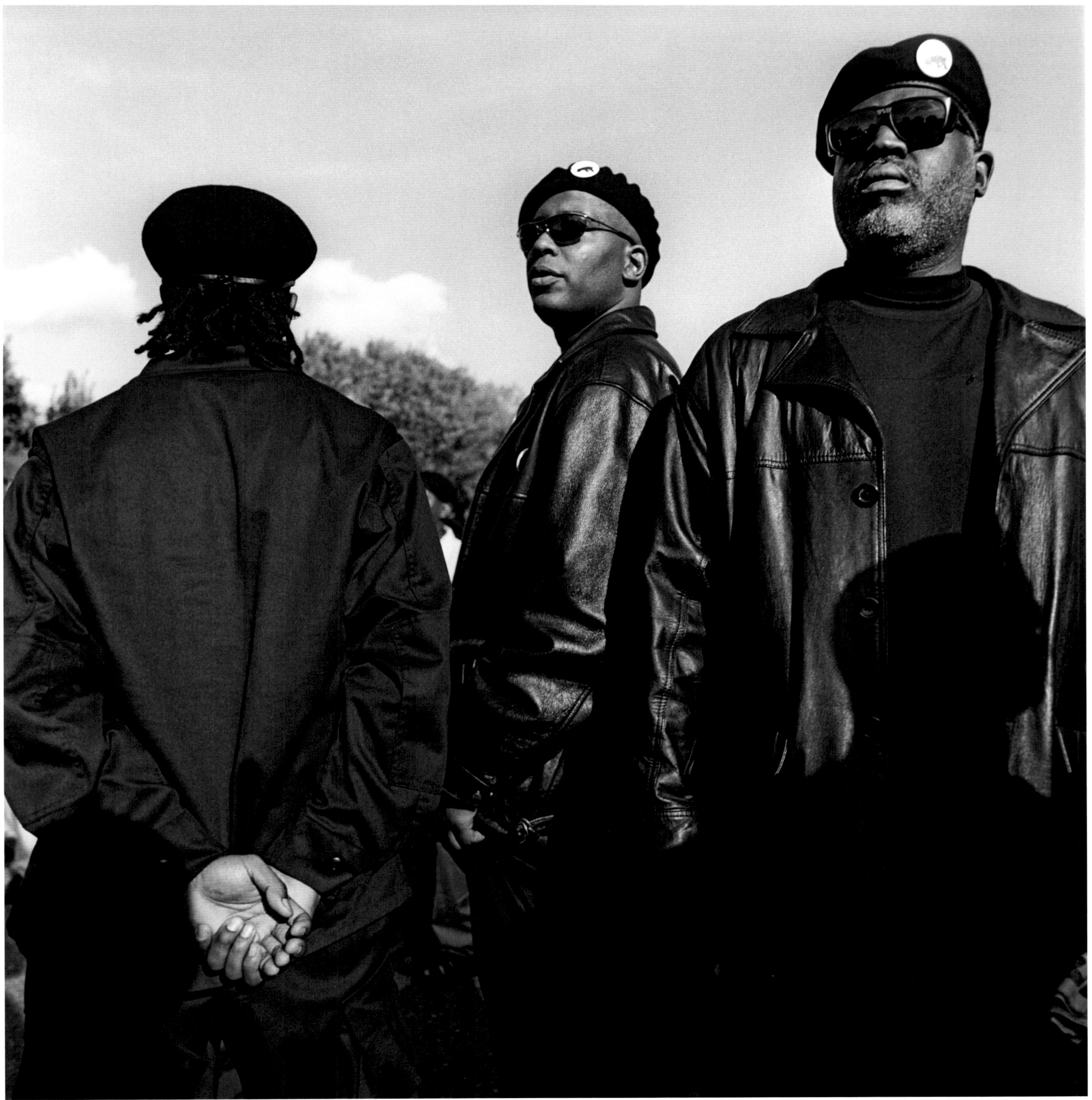

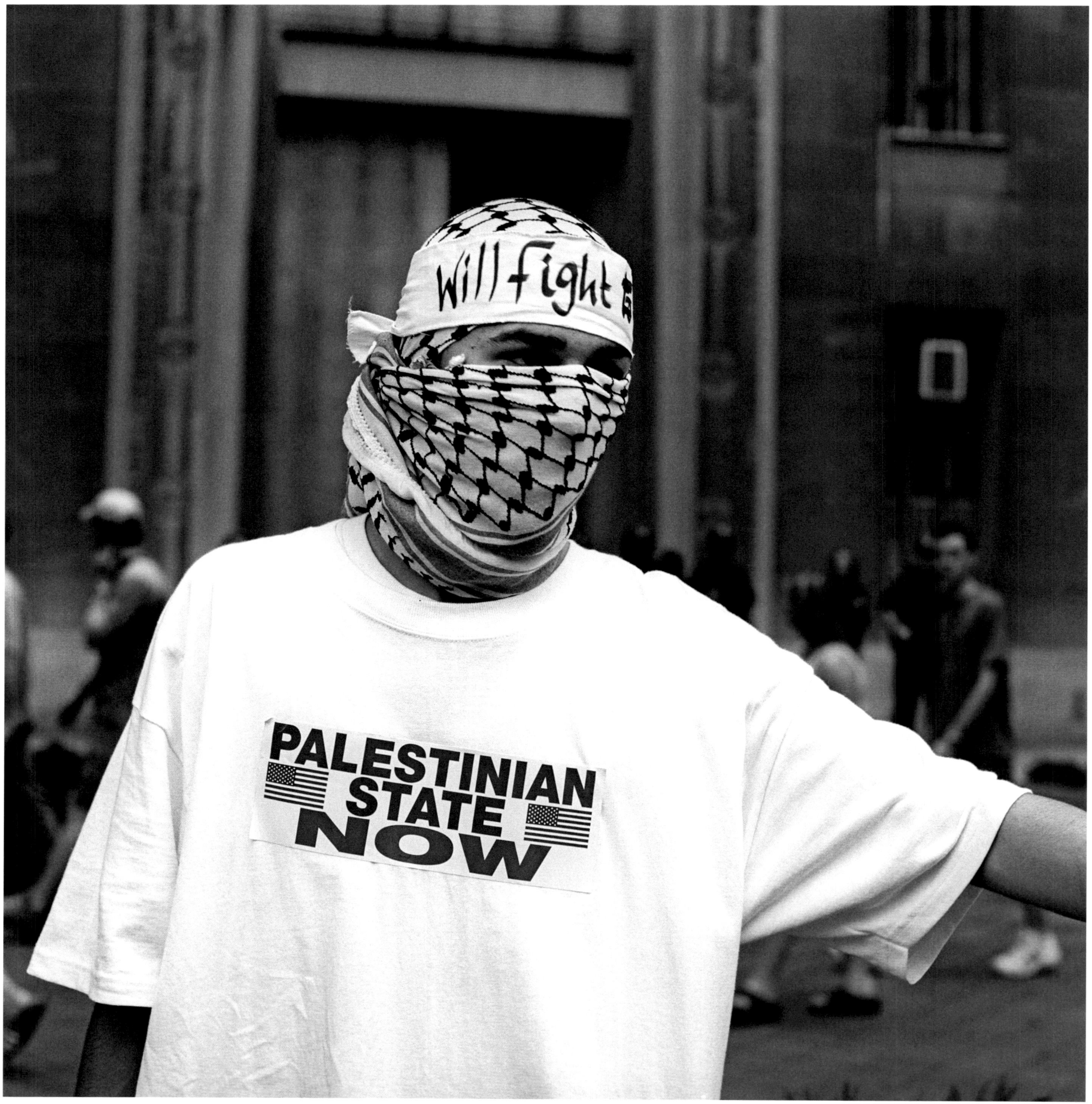
Will fight
PALESTINIAN
STATE
NOW

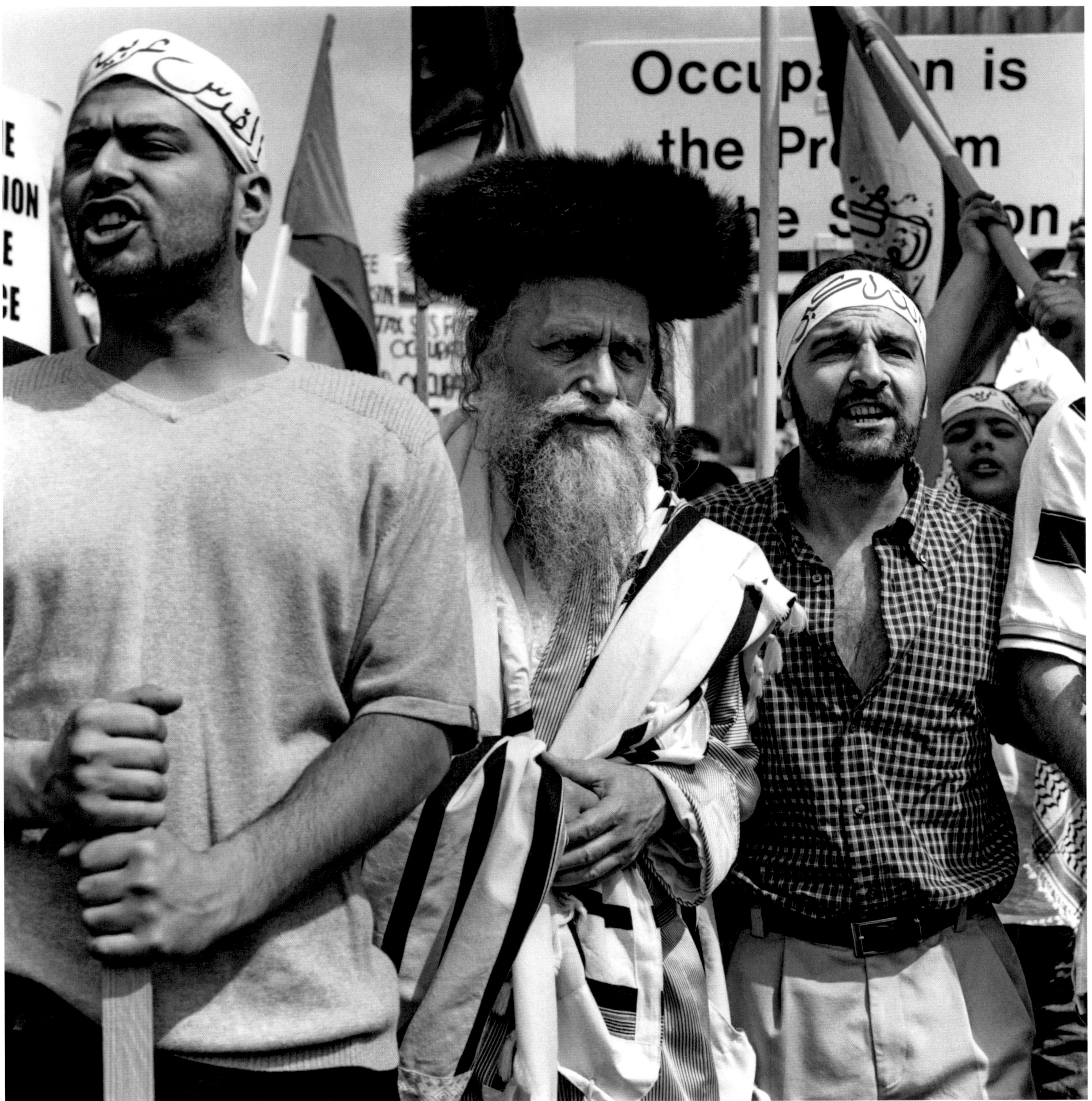
Occu pa n is
the Pr m
he S on

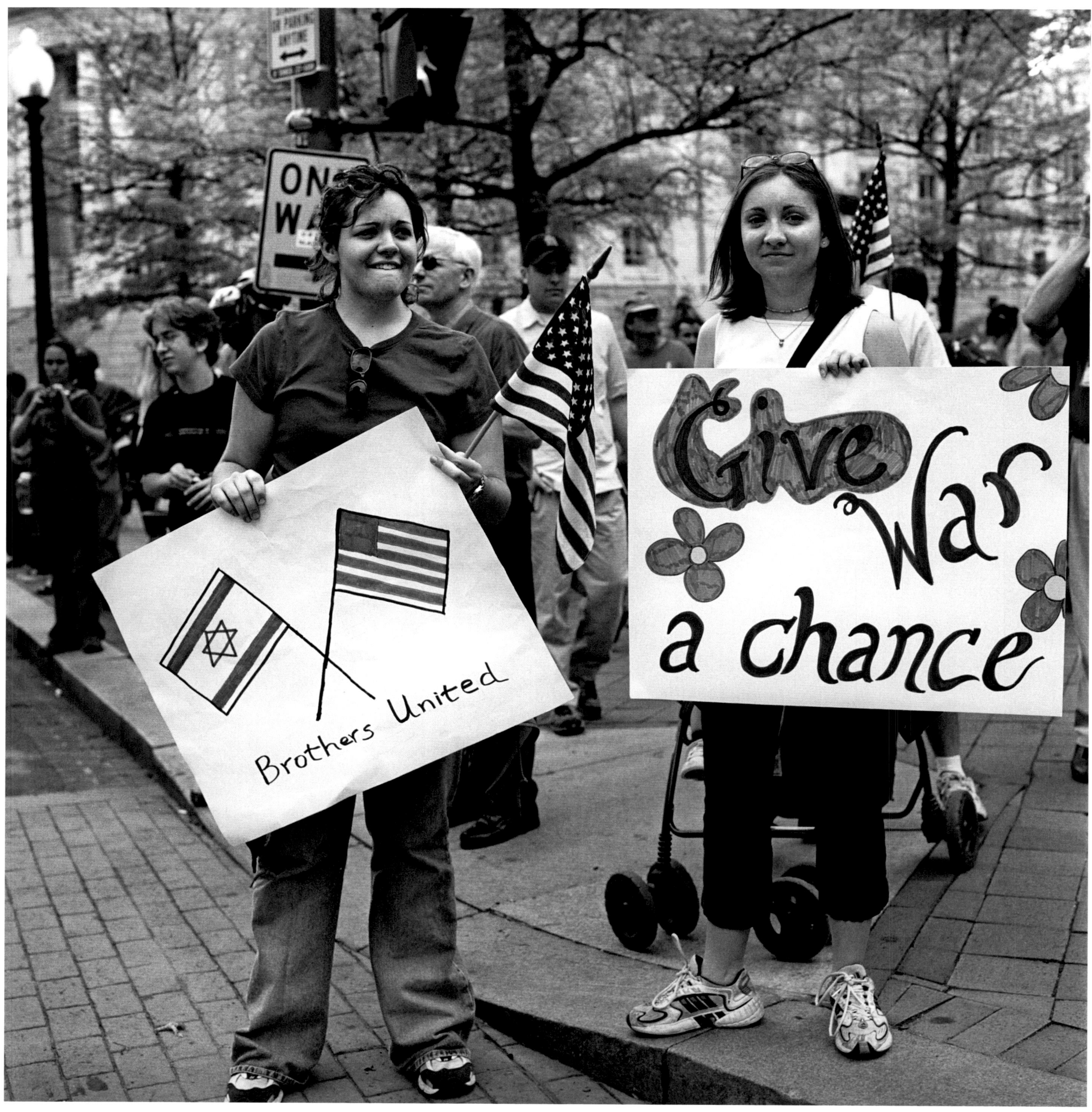
ONE WAY
Brothers United
Give War a chance

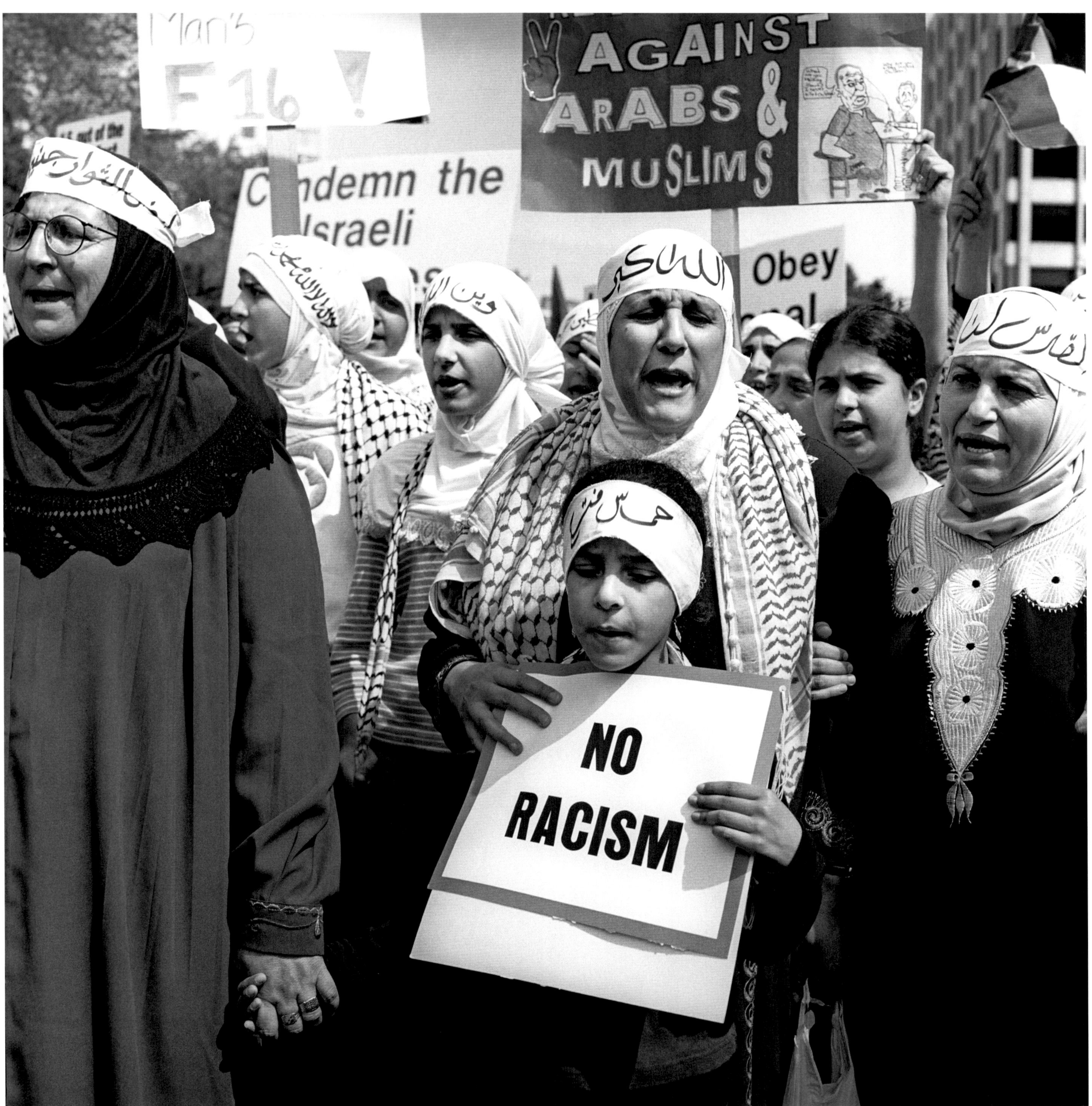
Man's
F16 !
AGAINST
ARABS &
MUSLIMS
Israeli
Obey
NO
RACISM

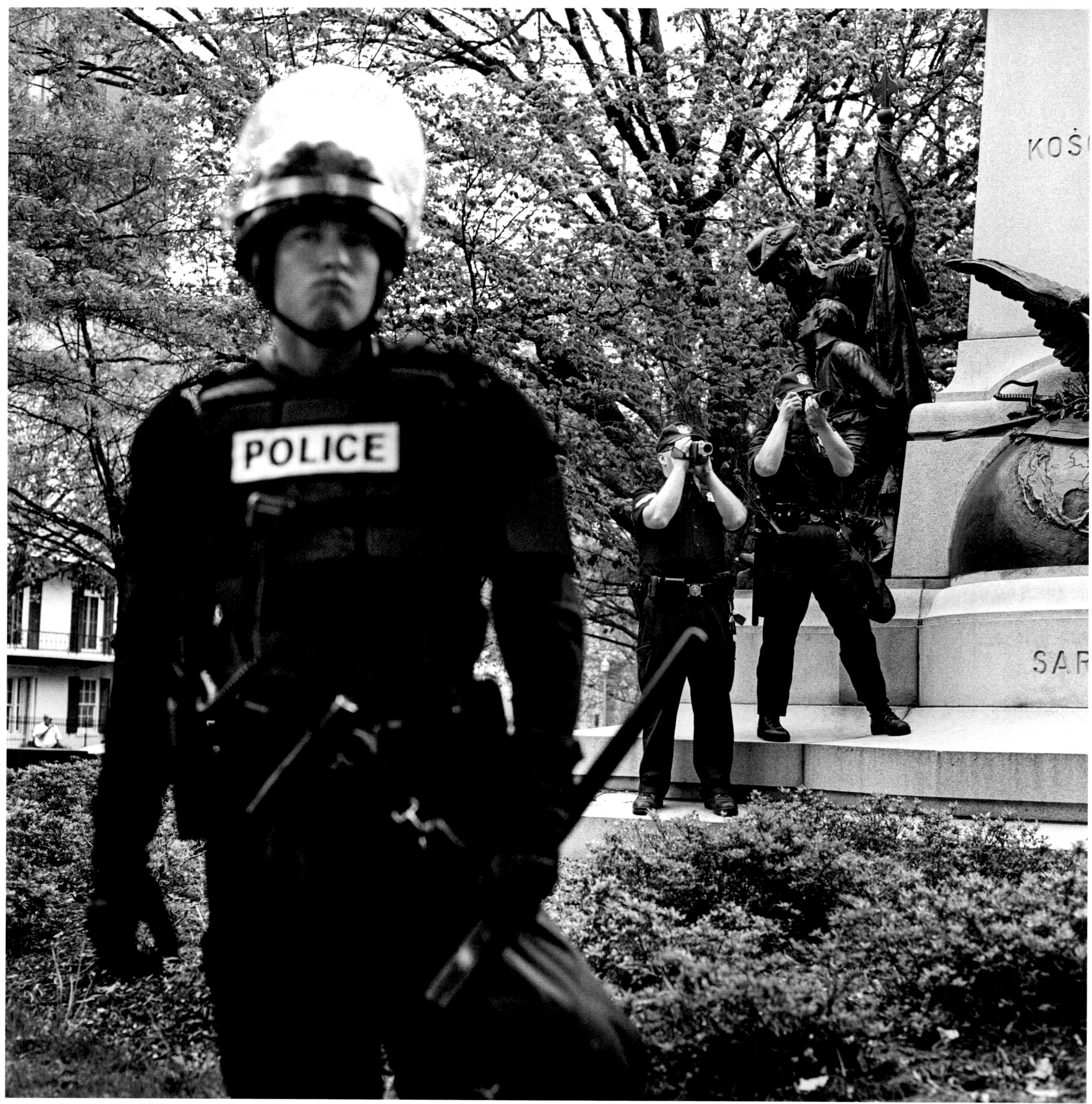
POLICE

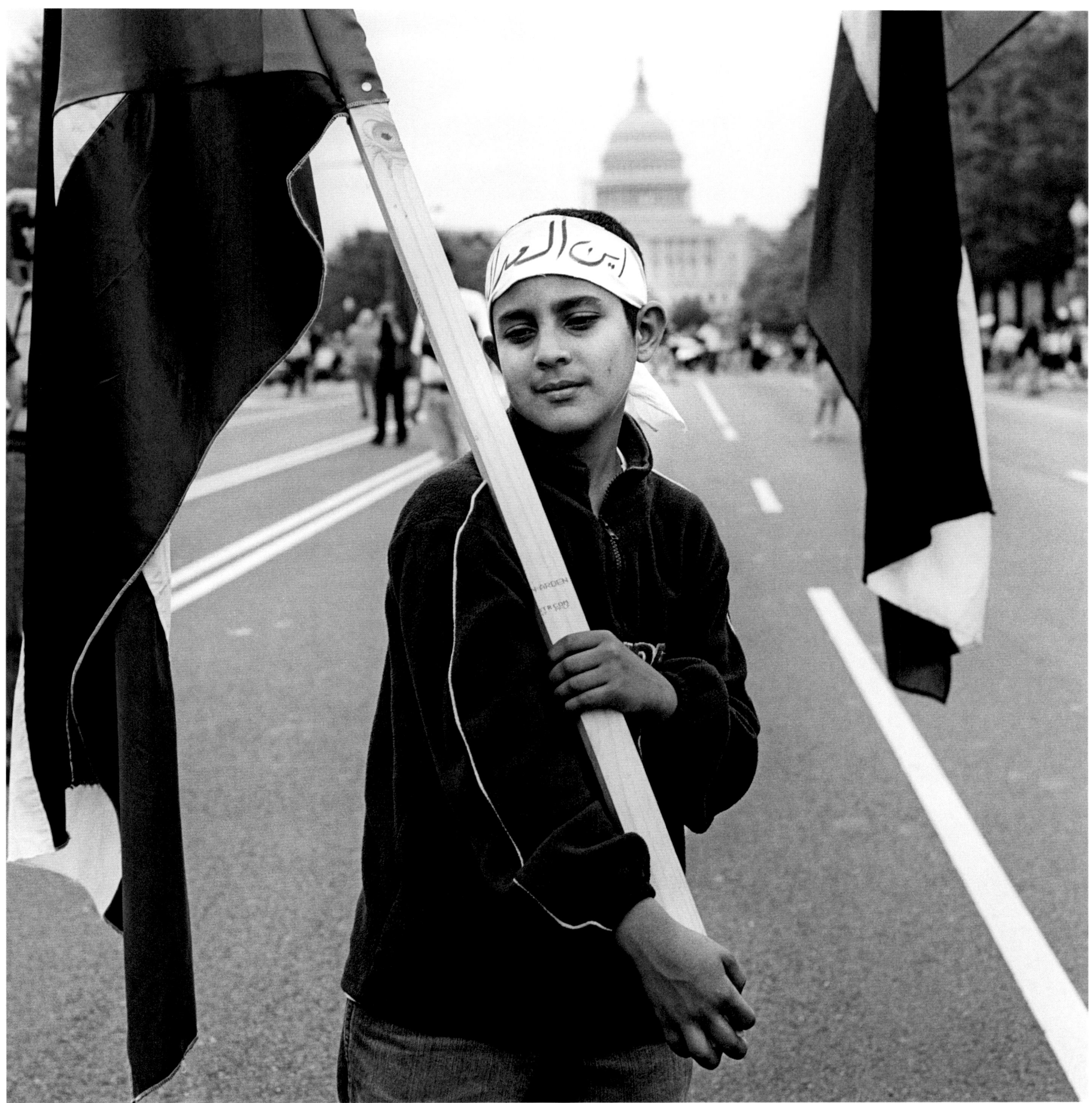

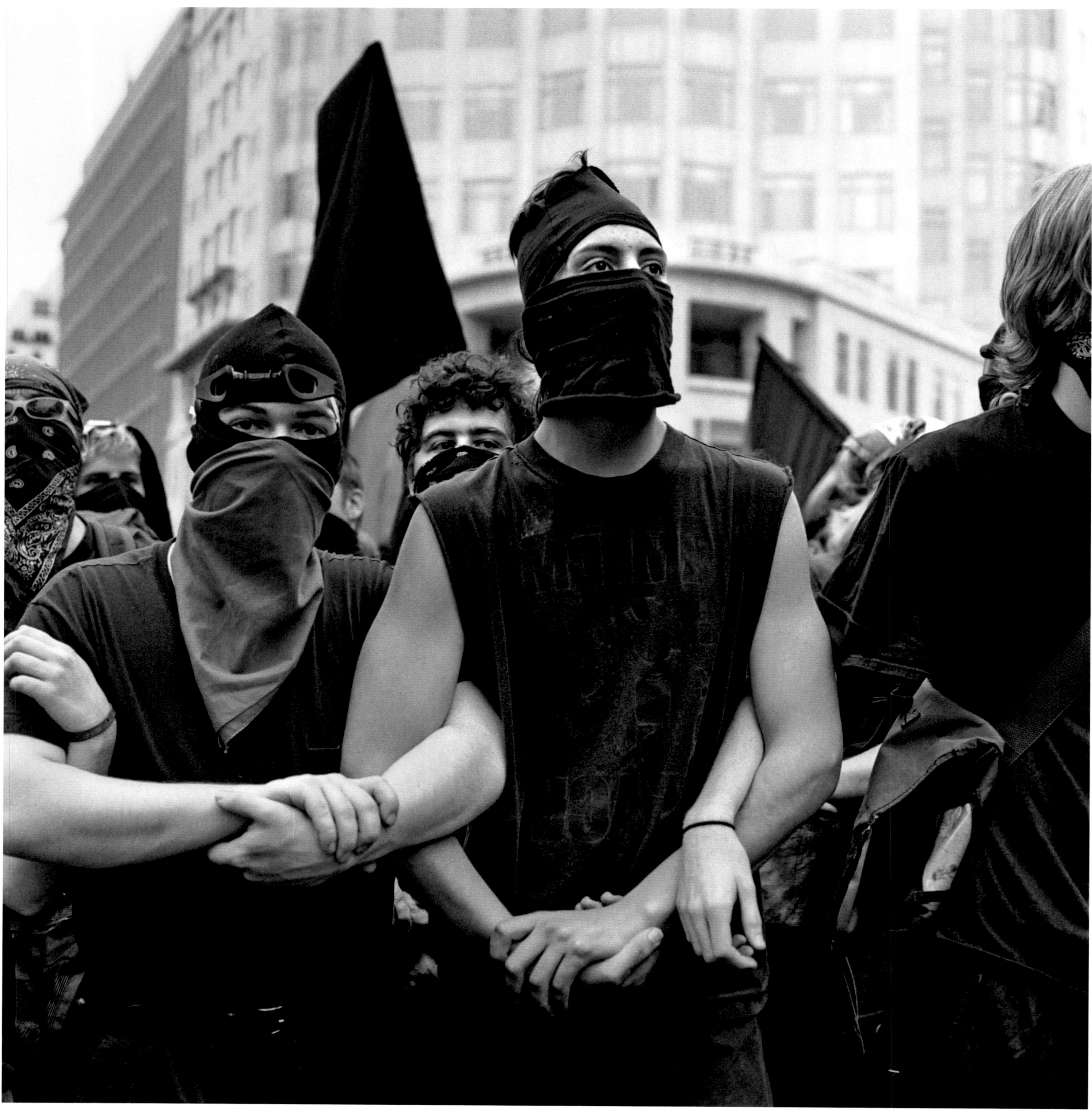

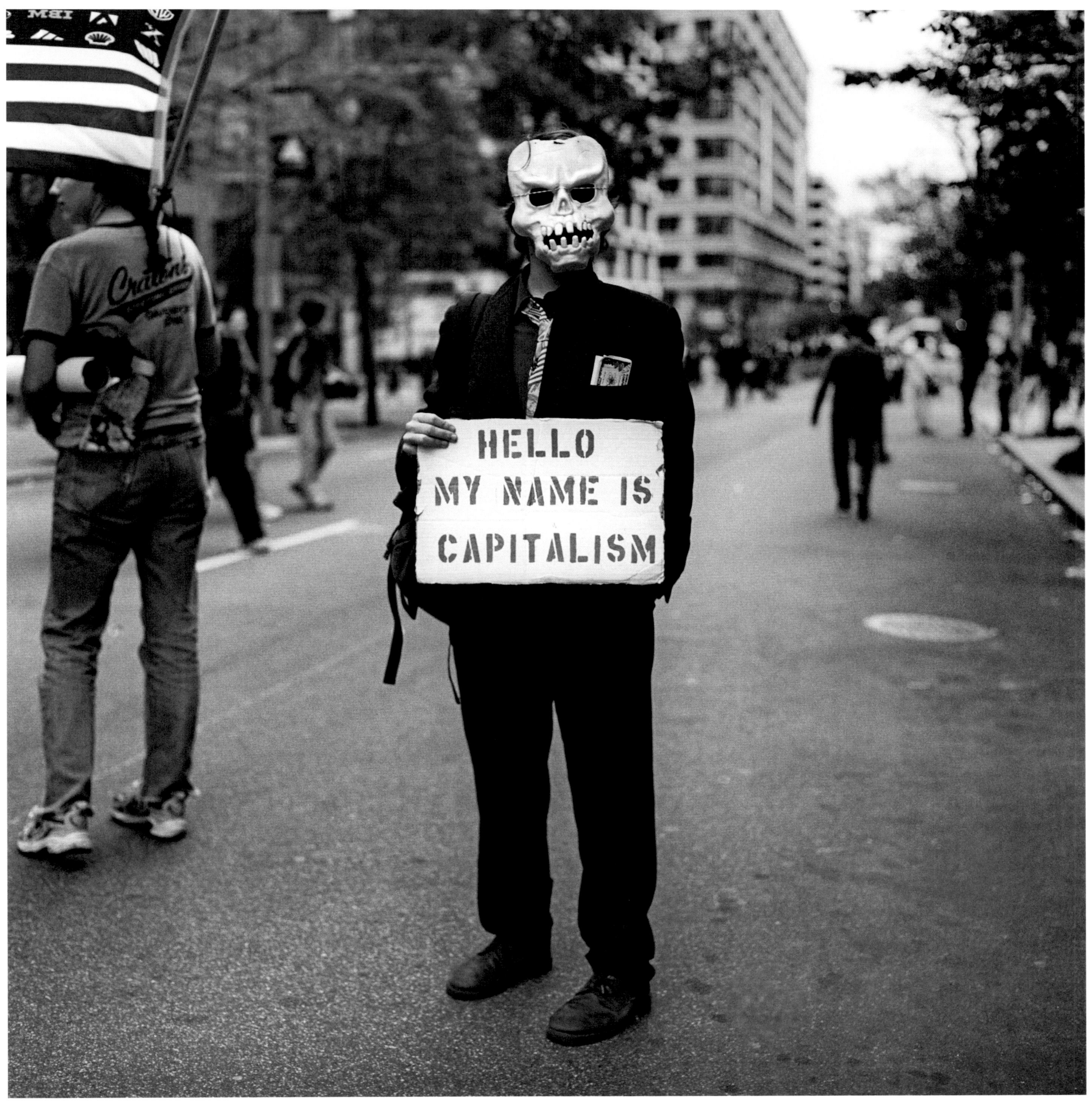
HELLO
MY NAME IS
CAPITALISM

Bennington, Vermont, April 27, 2002

Peace March

Gathering under the organizational leadership of the Greater Bennington Peace & Justice Center, local community elders, teachers, school children, and their parents marched from the public middle school on the east end of Main Street to Bennington's Four Corners intersection. The community group proudly held American flags, posters, and banners displaying messages of peace. They stood at the corners of the intersection, out of the way of passing motorists, some of whom honked their horns in appreciation as they went by. Many of the demonstrators could trace their political convictions to personal connections or meaningful memories.

"One of my earliest memories in life," Nathan Wallace-Senft, a local resident said, "was going with my father, a Lutheran minister and ardent pacifist, to visit with a young man who refused to serve in the military and was under house arrest. It still boggles my mind to realize how easily so many people join in enterprises with the purpose of killing other human beings if they don't do what you tell them to do. I firmly believe that the basic human impulse is to treat other people the way you would like to be treated."

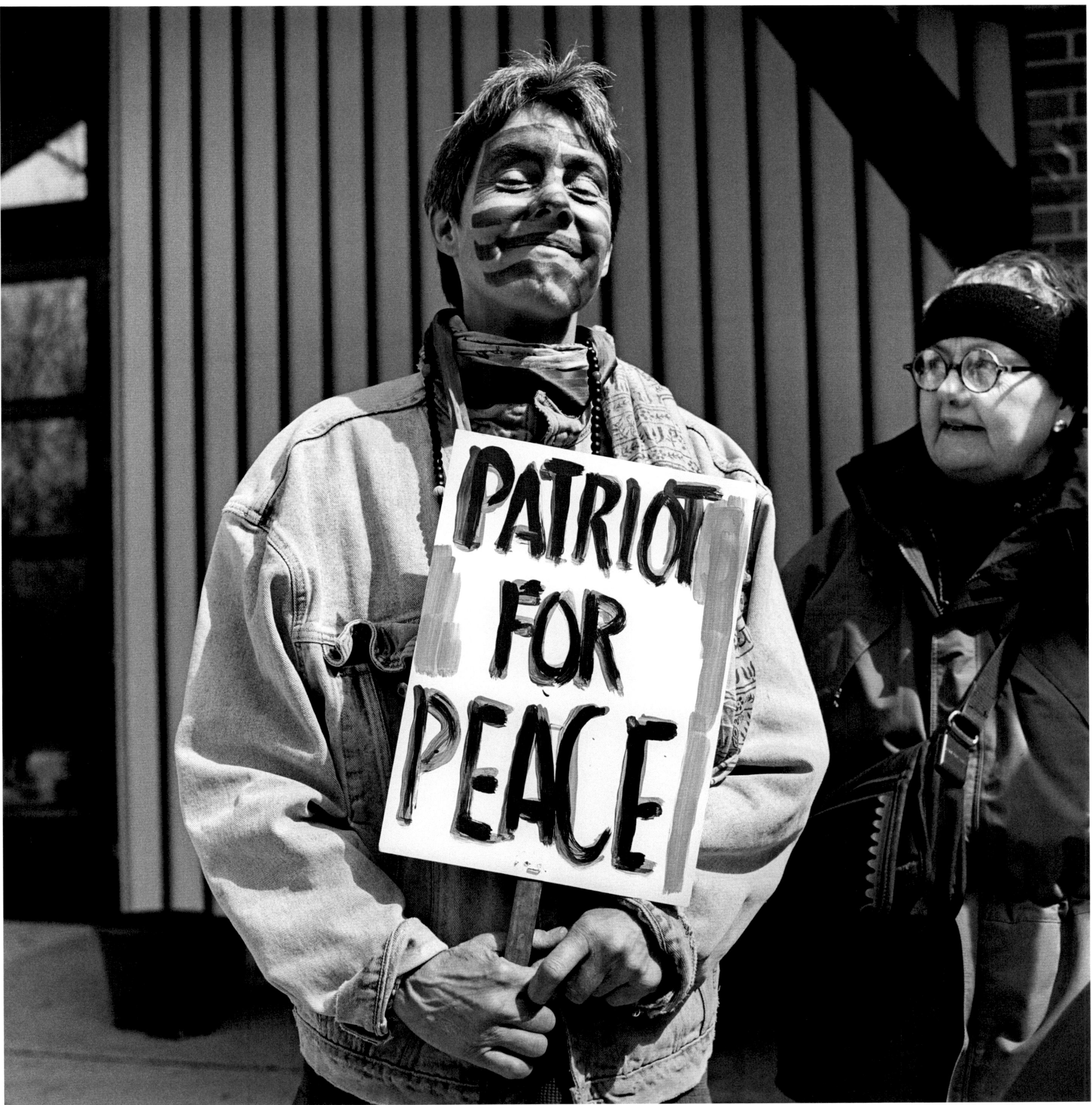
PATRIOT
FOR
PEACE

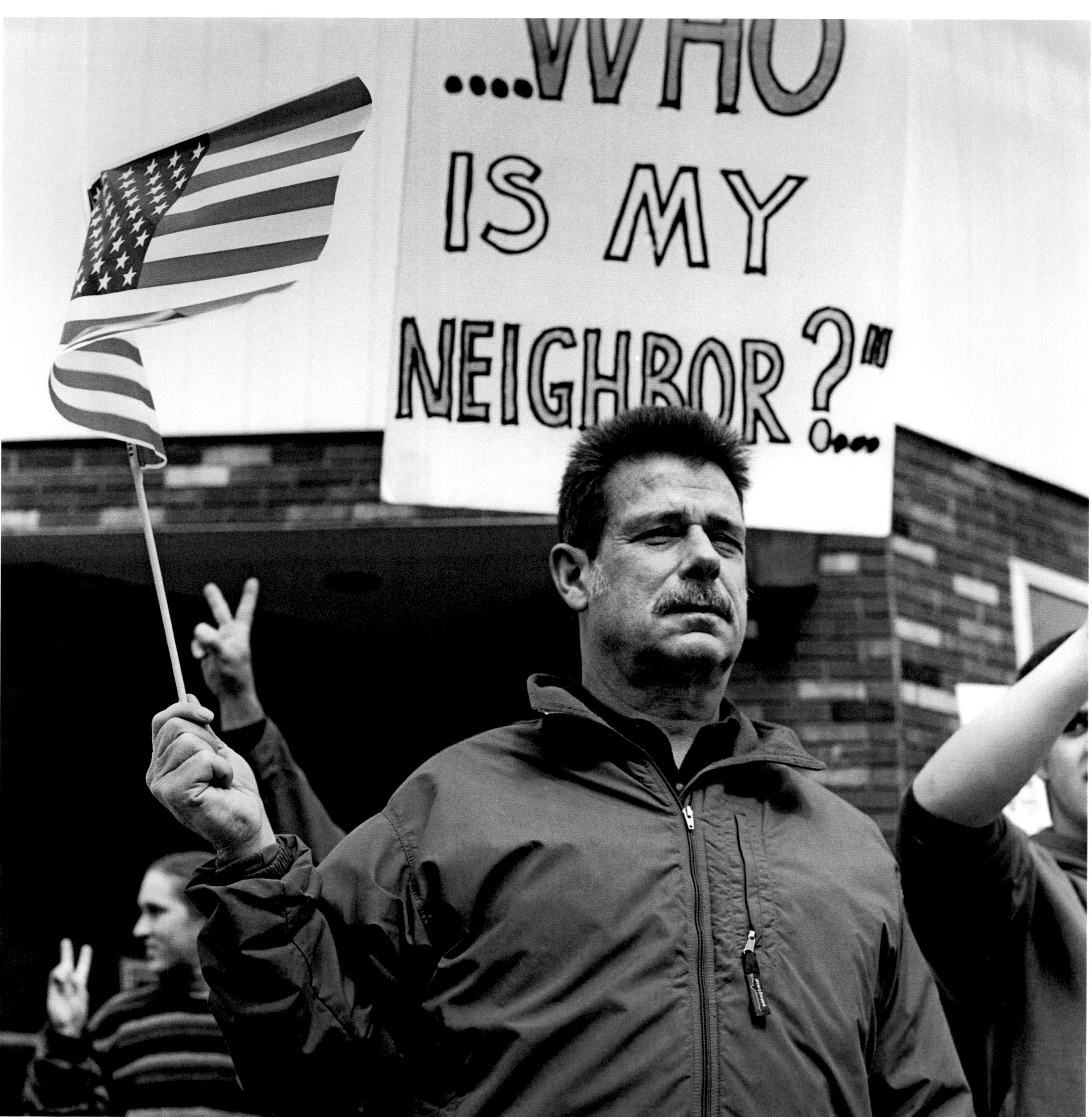
"...WHO
IS MY
NEIGHBOR?"...

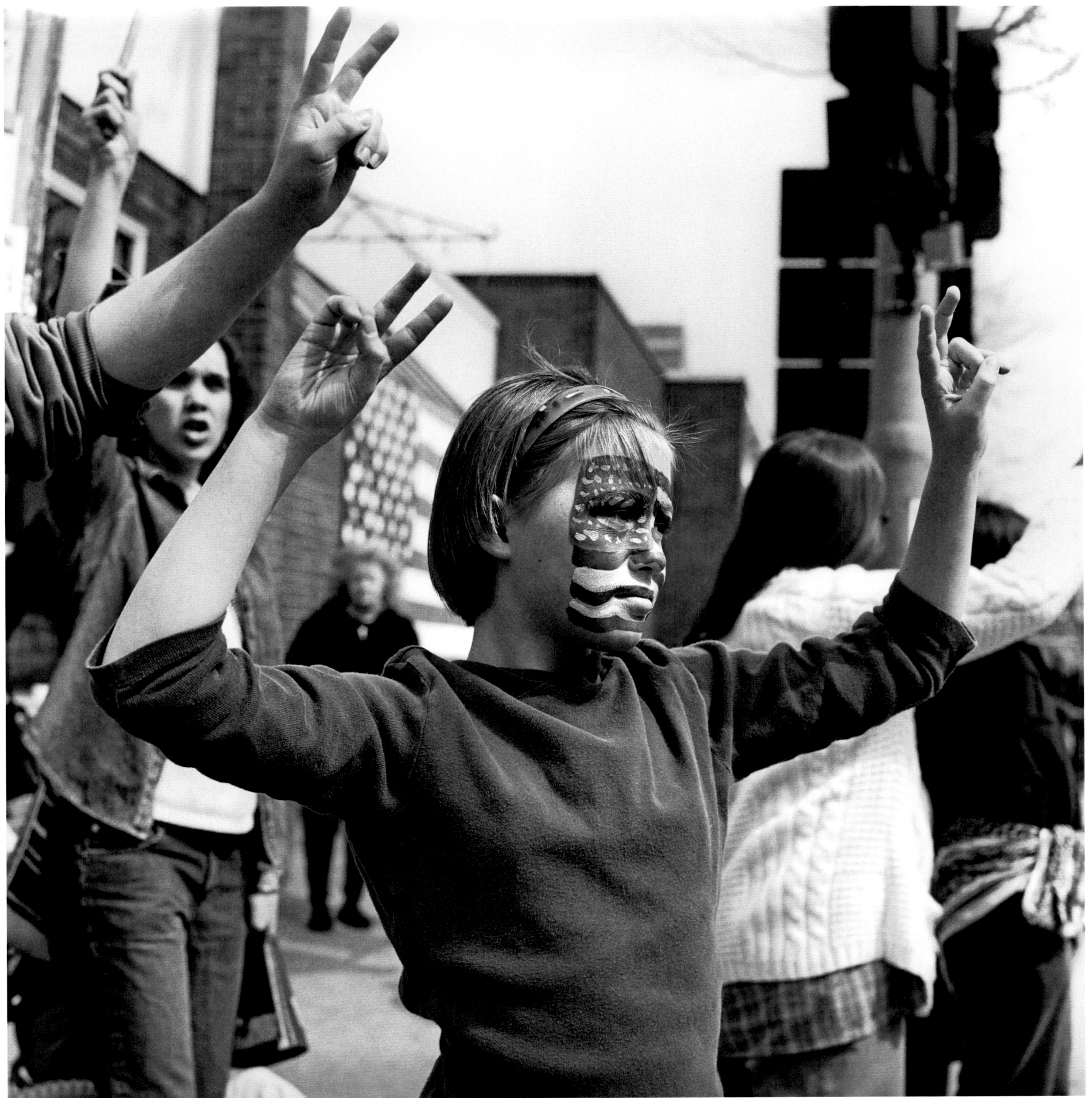

New York City, September 11, 2002

September 11 Anniversary Ceremony

By 9:00 a.m., a year to the day after the attacks on September 11, 2001 the ground zero site where the World Trade Center towers once stood was absolutely silent, all movement frozen. Families of the victims, survivors, visitors from abroad, fire fighters, and construction workers all packed into the plaza, sharing in their grief. Deep inside the empty cavity left by the absence of the buildings, a ceremony was conducted. Everyone in attendance was brought together by the powerful memories of the tragedy. Tears and silence marked the morning.

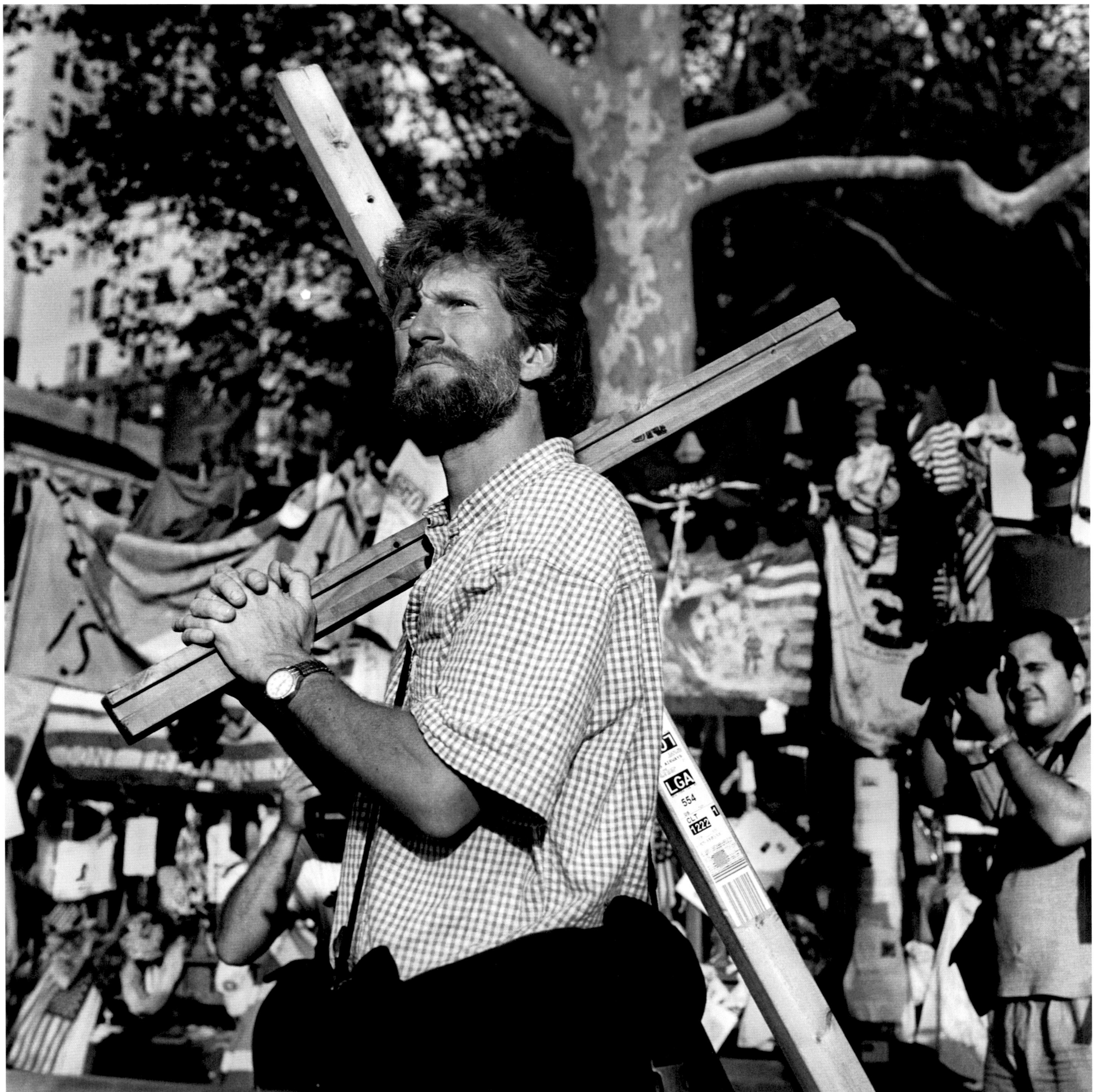
LGA
554
CLT
1222

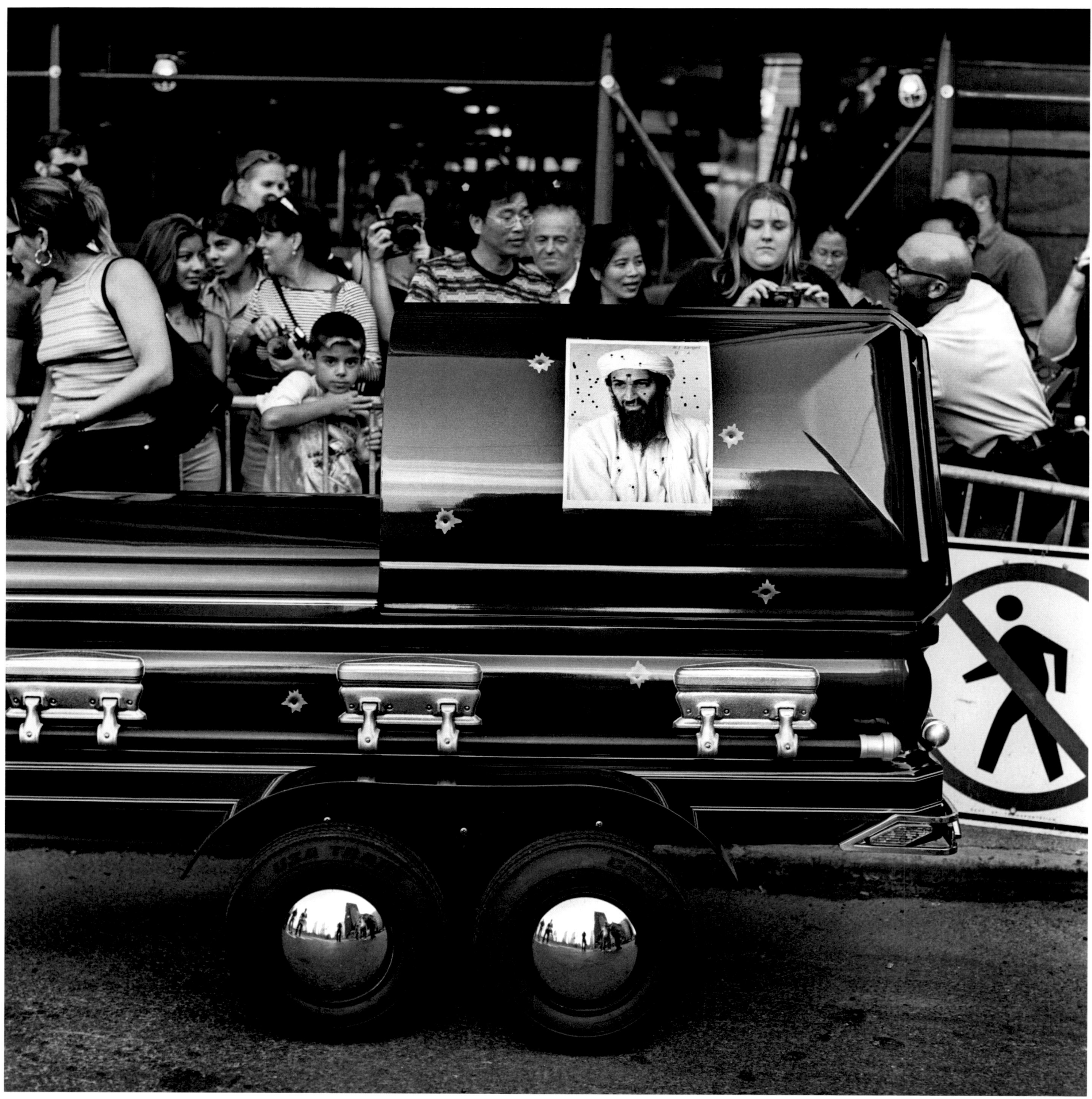

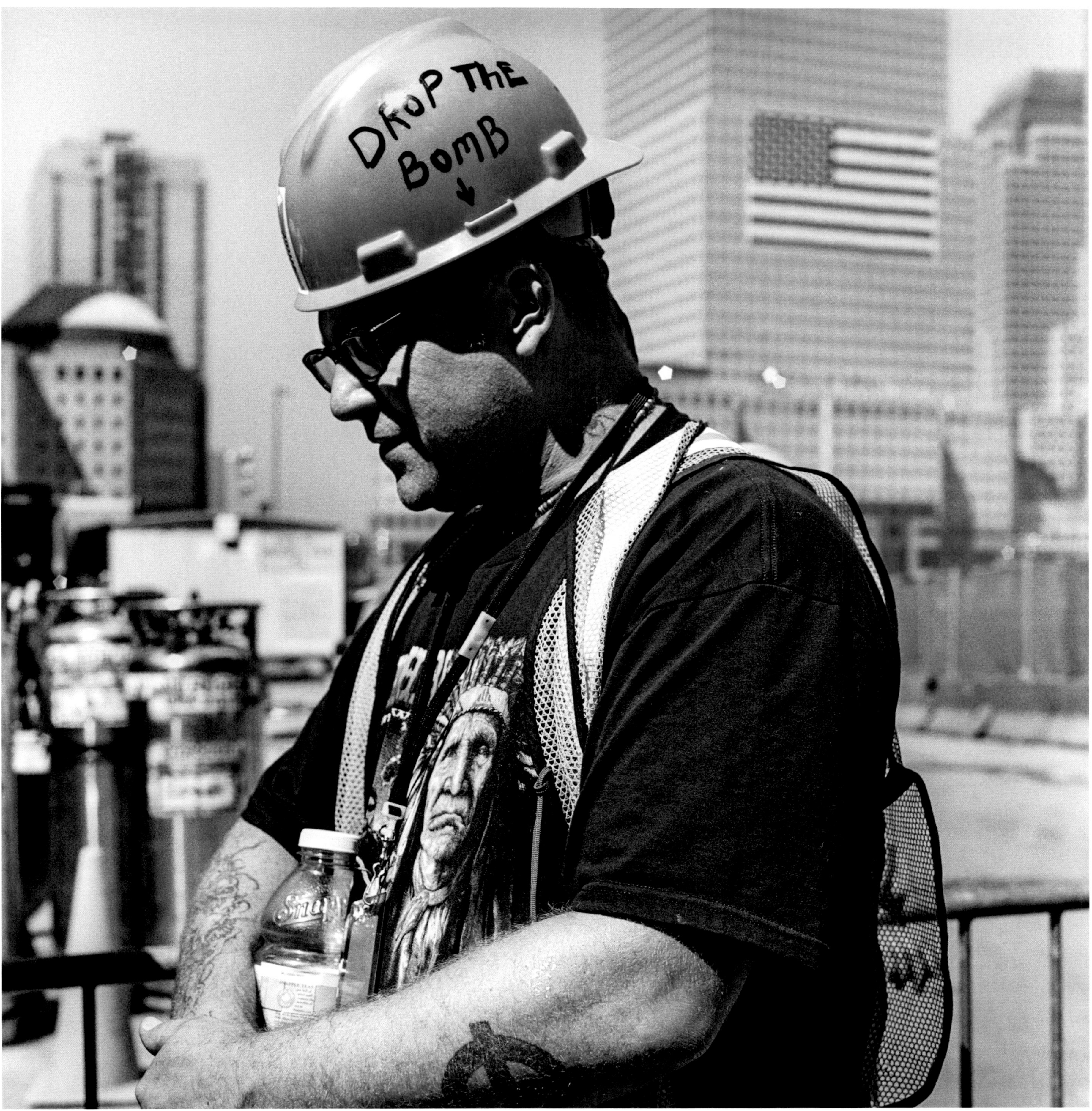
DROP THE
BomB

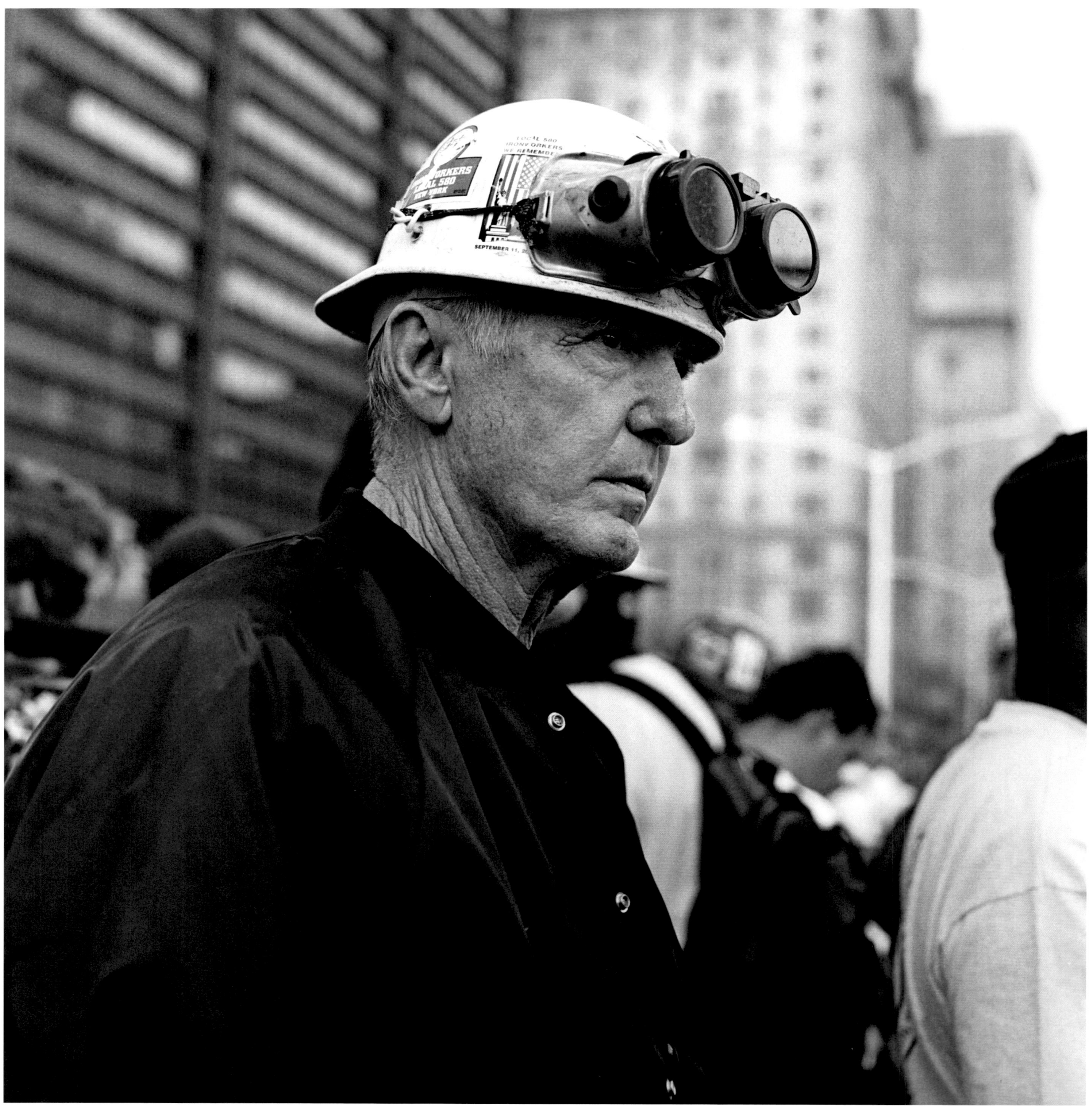
LOCAL 580
IRONWORKERS
SEPTEMBER 11,

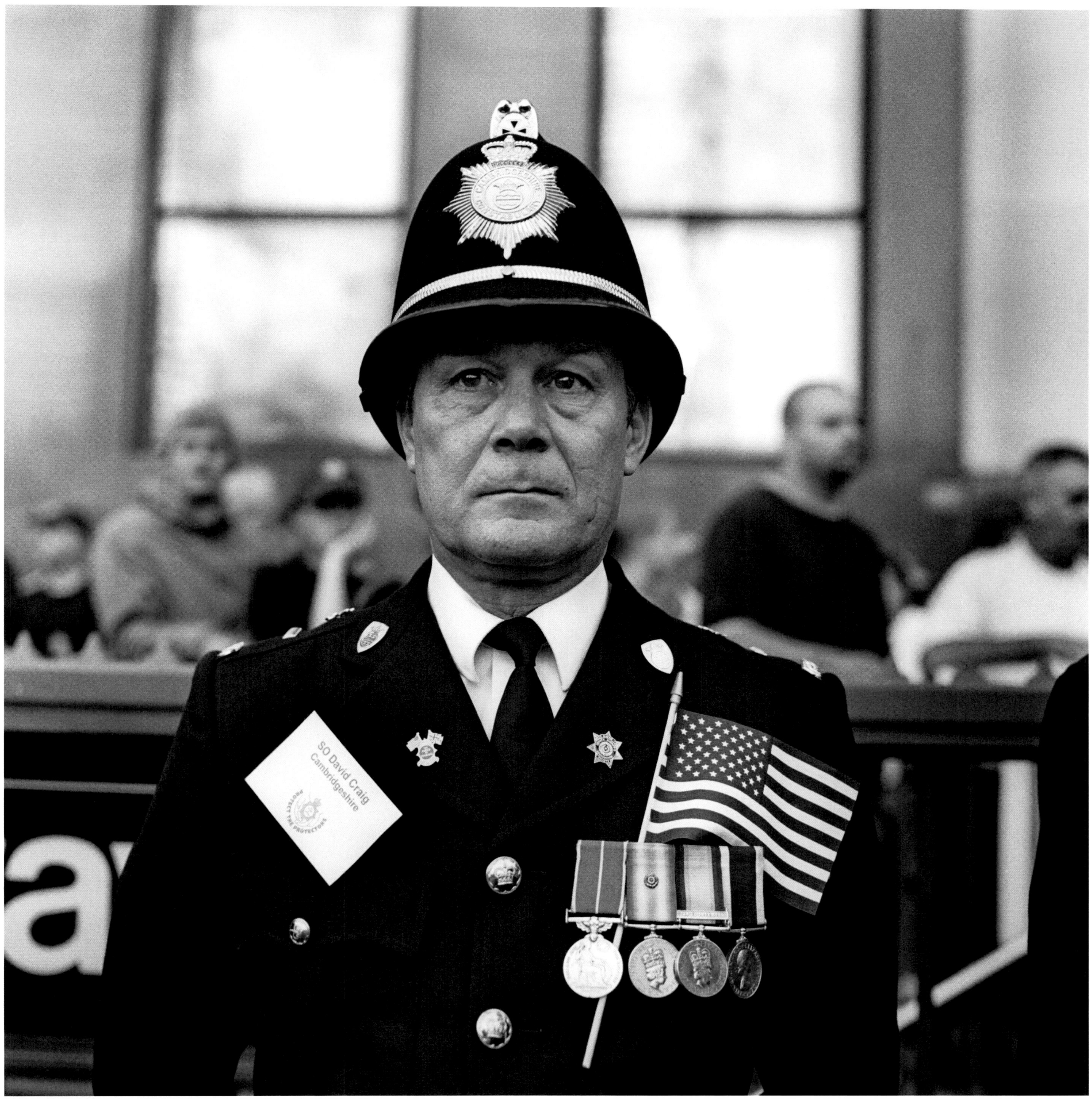
SO David Craig
Cambridgeshire
PROTECT THE PROTECTORS

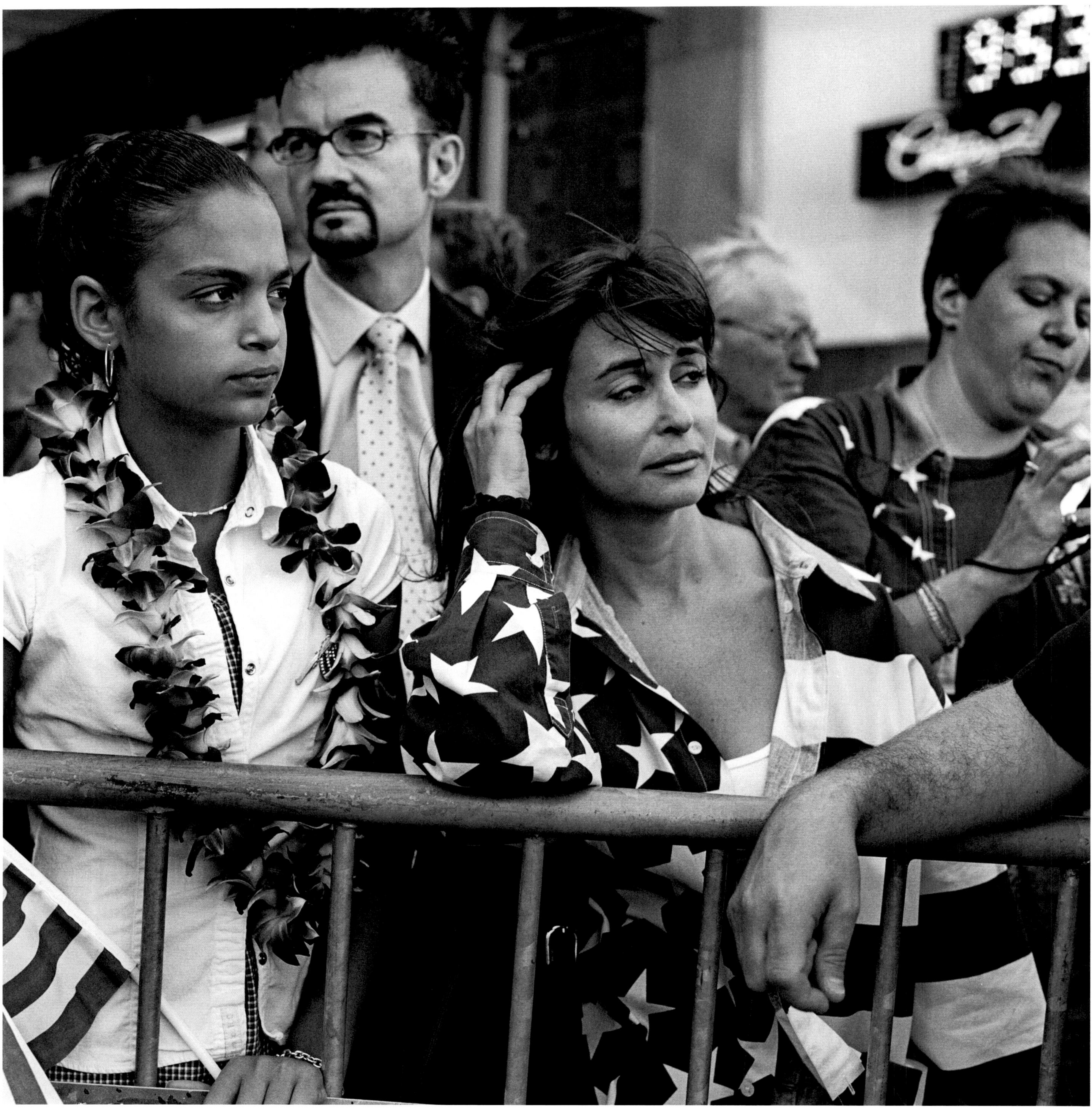

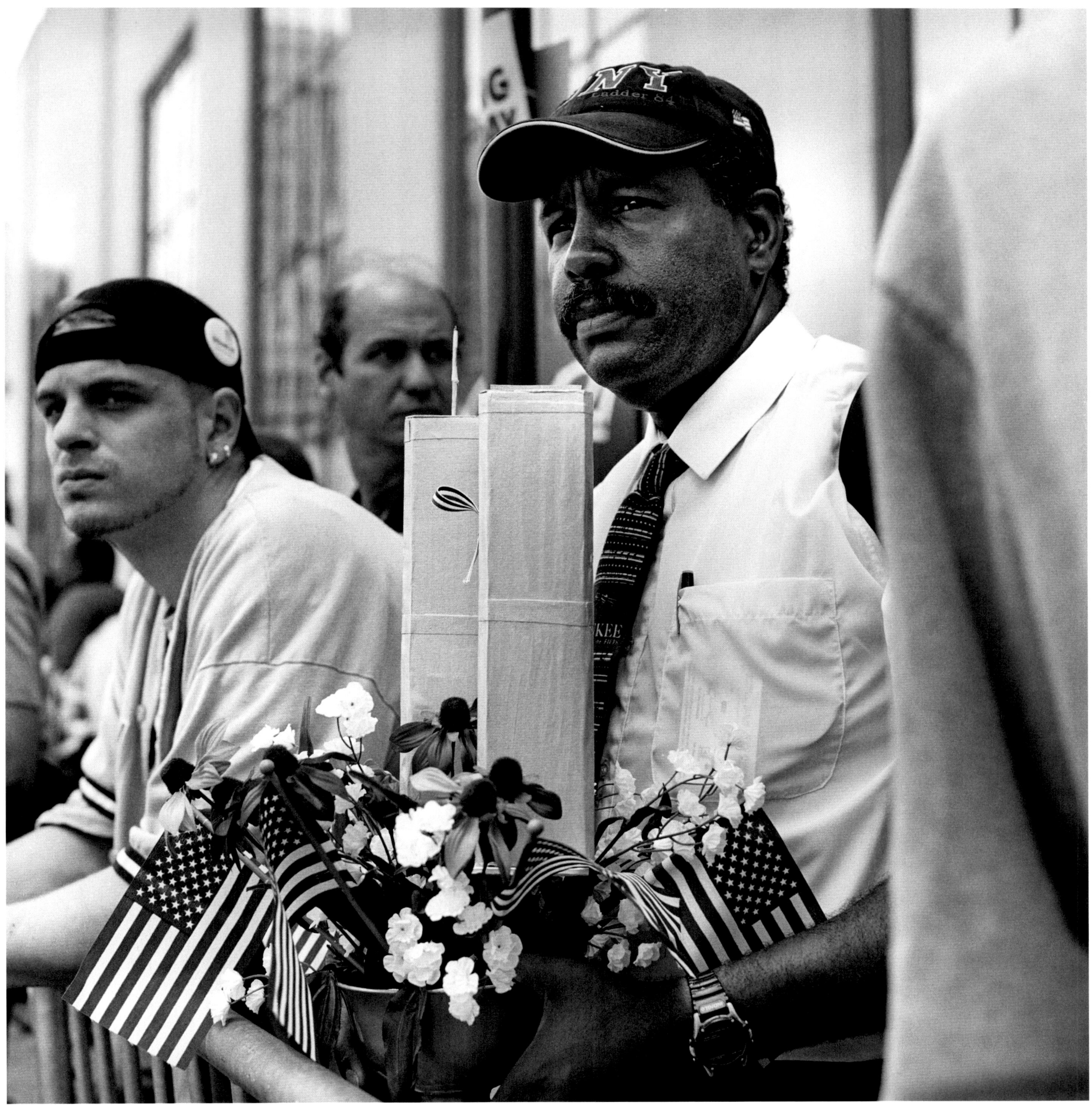
NY

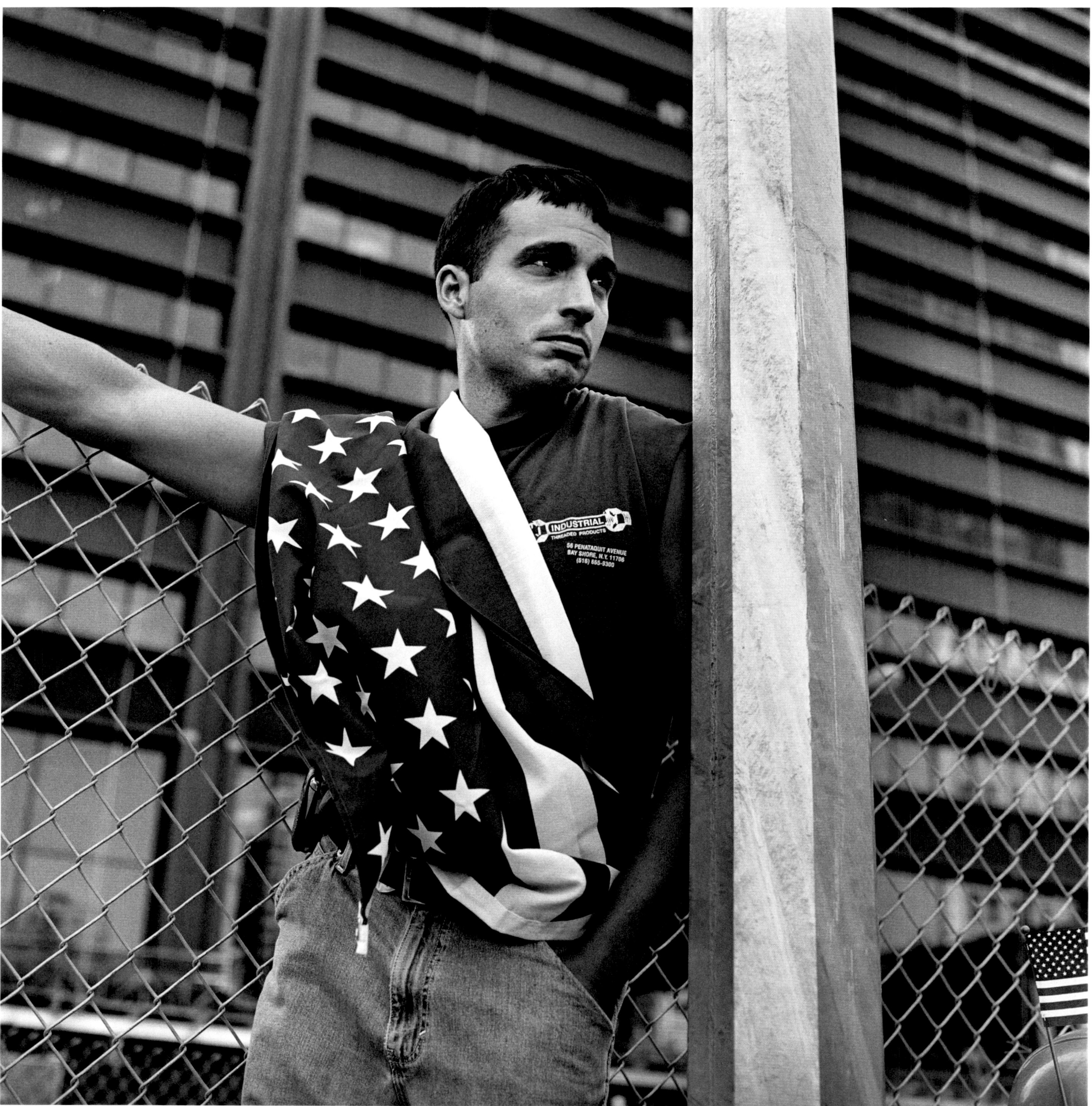
INDUSTRIAL
THREADED PRODUCTS
56 PENATAQUIT AVENUE
BAY SHORE, N.Y. 11706
(516) 665-9300

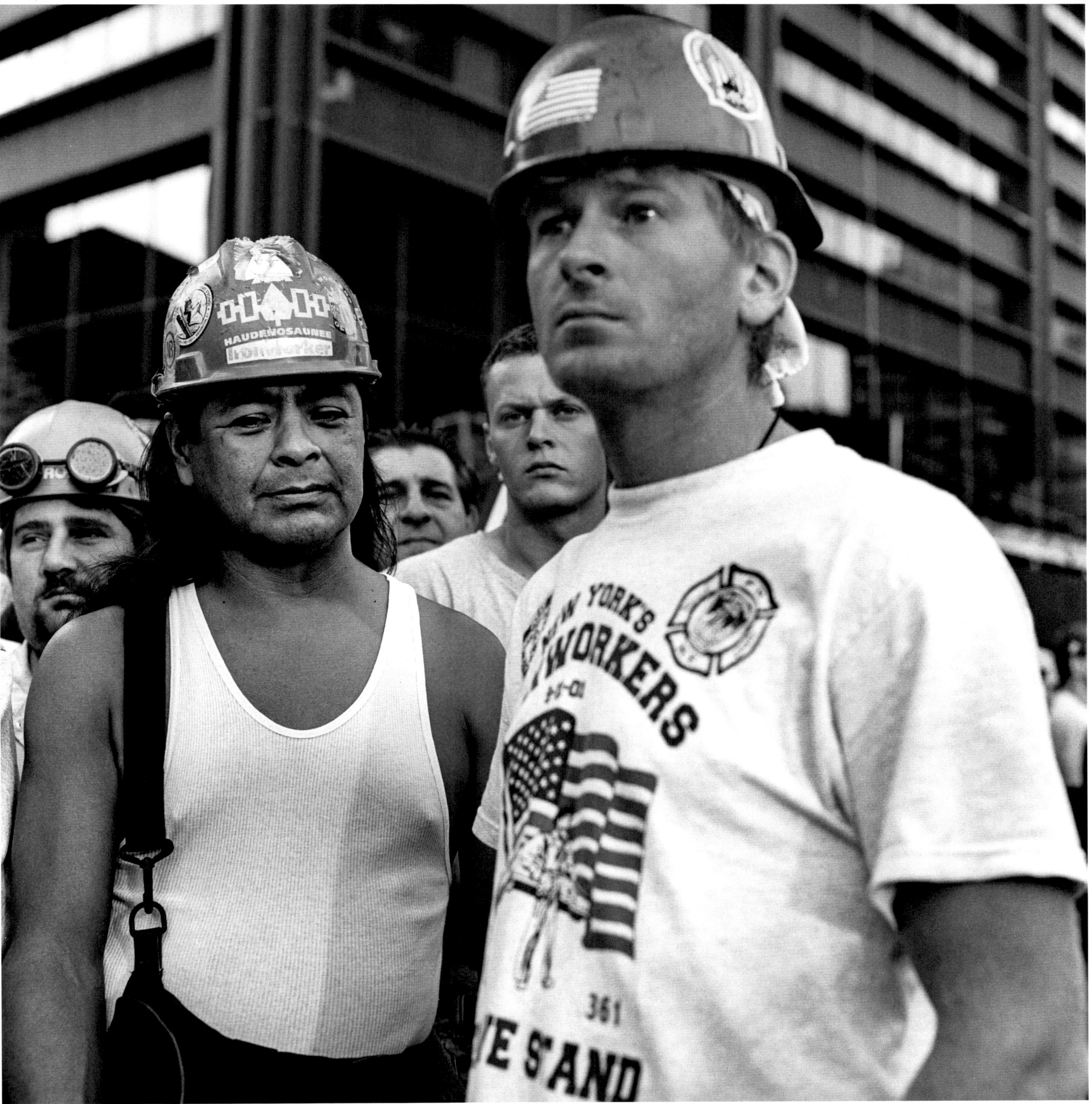
HAUDENOSAUNEE
Ironworker
YORK'S
WORKERS
361

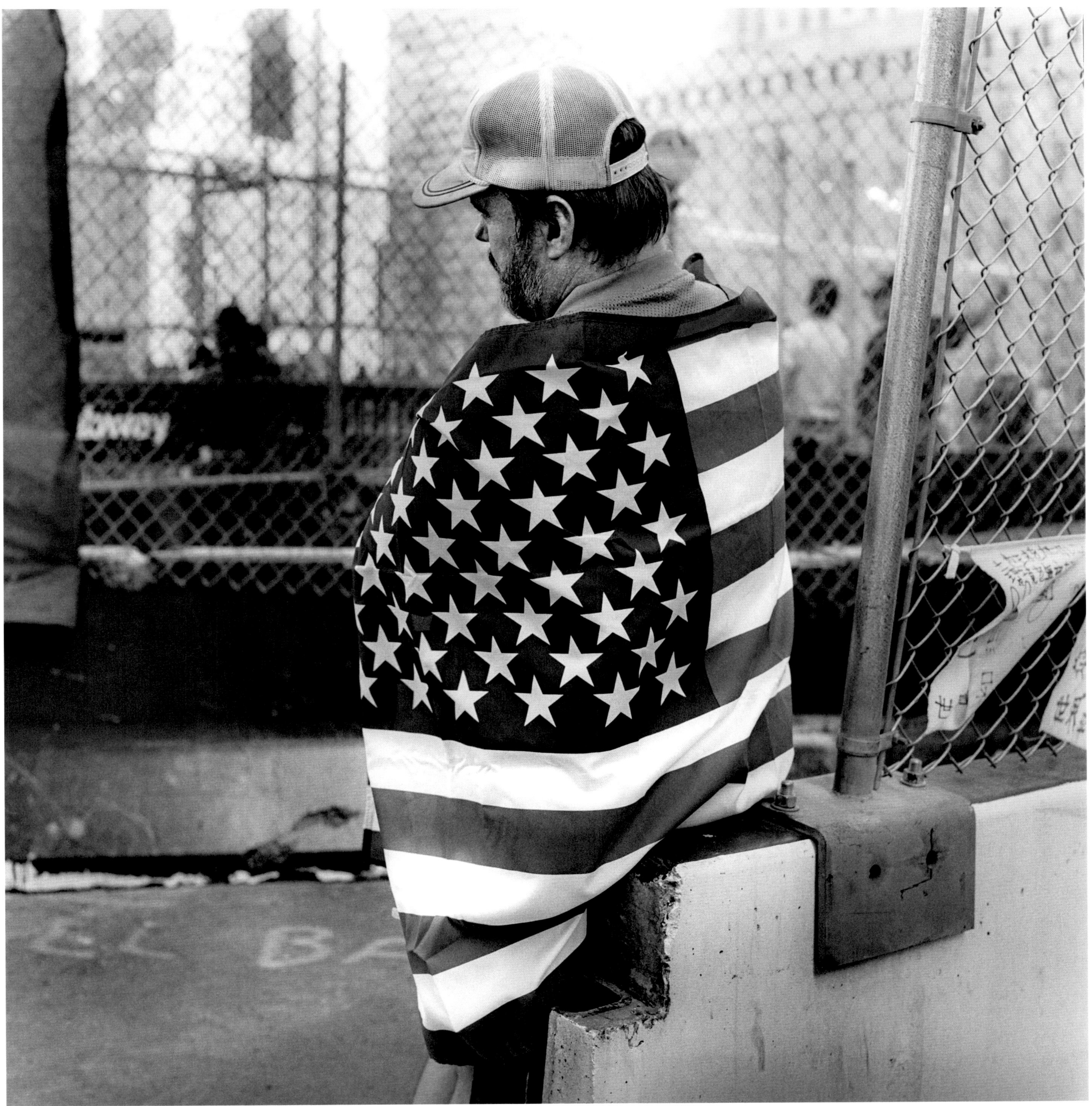

Washington, D.C., October 26, 2002

Anti-War March

Just six weeks after the solemn silence of the first anniversary of the World Trade Center attacks, Washington, D.C. erupted with loud protests against the Bush administration's overtures to war with Iraq. Like the peace march and anti-war demonstration six months earlier, busses and cars full of people came in from communities near and far to stand, march, and shout slogans of solidarity and peace against the run up to war. Unofficial estimates put the number of demonstrators at over 200,000. While the crowds and signs expressed an incredible diversity of humor, fear, compassion, and concern, there was a remarkable unity of all present in their demand for the Bush administration to retreat from its march toward war.

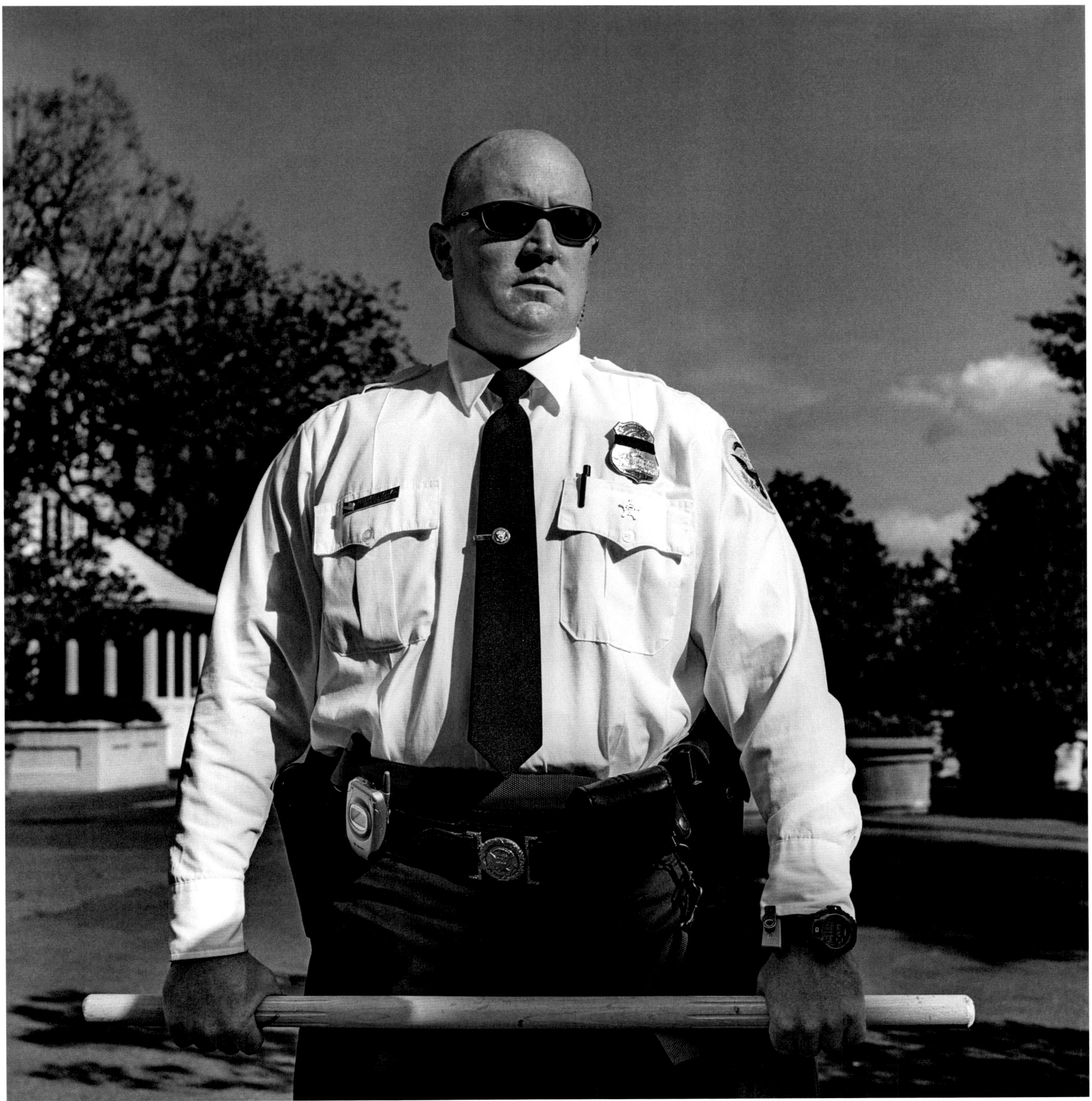

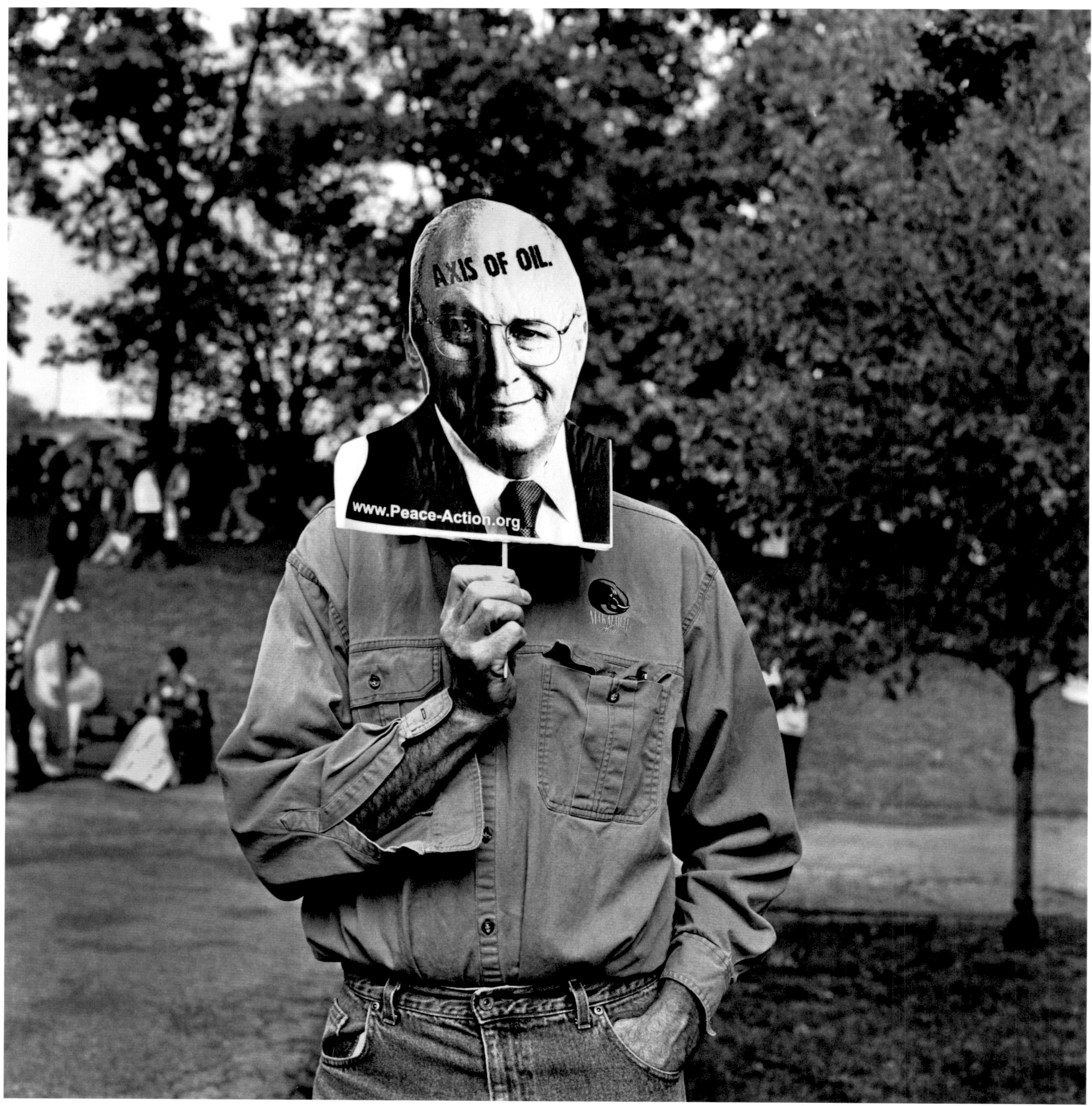
AXIS OF OIL.
www.Peace-Action.org

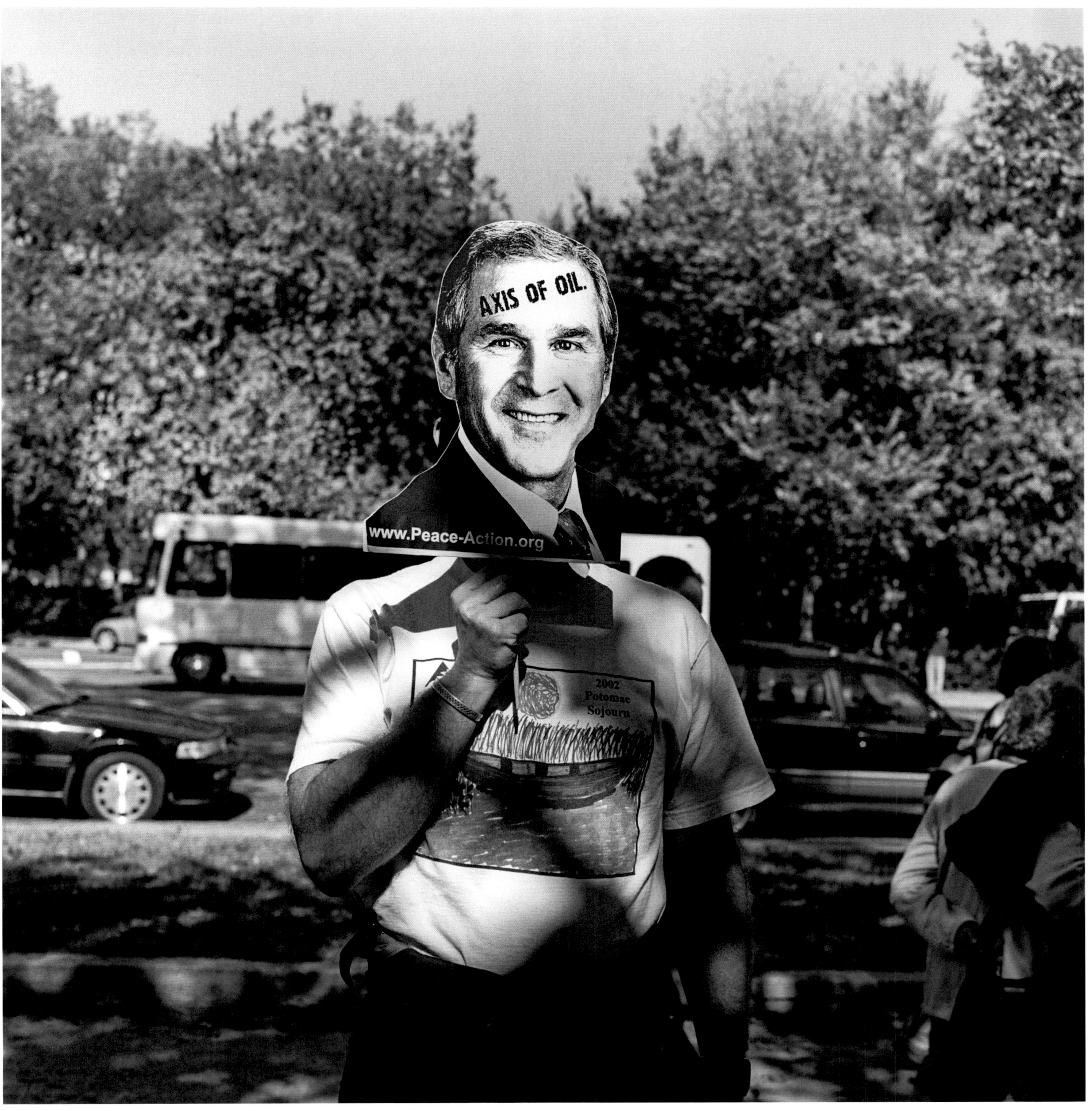
AXIS OF OIL.
www.Peace-Action.org
2002
Potomac
Sojourn

Washington, D.C., March 15, 2003

Anti-War March

There was a deep sense of urgency this Sunday afternoon in Washington, D.C., as crowds assembled in a last effort to try to interrupt the momentum of war. On February 5, Colin Powell used falsified military intelligence to mislead the public during his presentation to the Security Council and General Assembly of the United Nations about Iraq's alleged weapons of mass destruction. He said, "Every statement I make today is backed up by sources, solid sources. These are not assertions. What we're giving you are facts and conclusions based on solid intelligence."

While war hawks saw his presentation as justification for war, many saw his presentation as propaganda. Meanwhile, the fear of another terrorist attack on American soil gripped the minds of many Americans. Voices of dissent within the halls of Congress were almost entirely absent. This was the atmosphere that inspired tens of thousands to convene in Washington to rally once more for peace. The bombing of Baghdad commenced four days later.

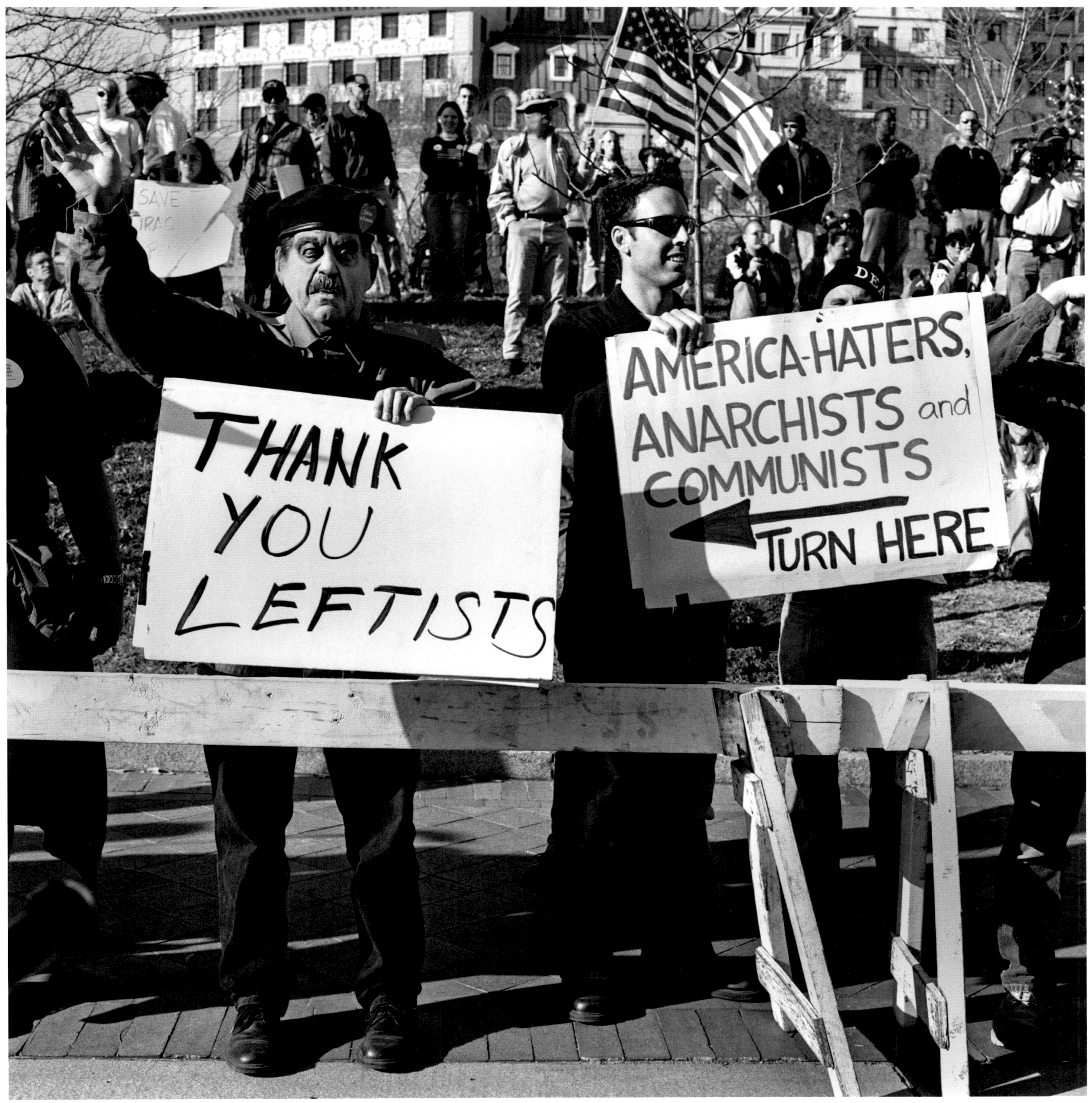
THANK YOU LEFTISTS
AMERICA-HATERS, ANARCHISTS and COMMUNISTS
TURN HERE

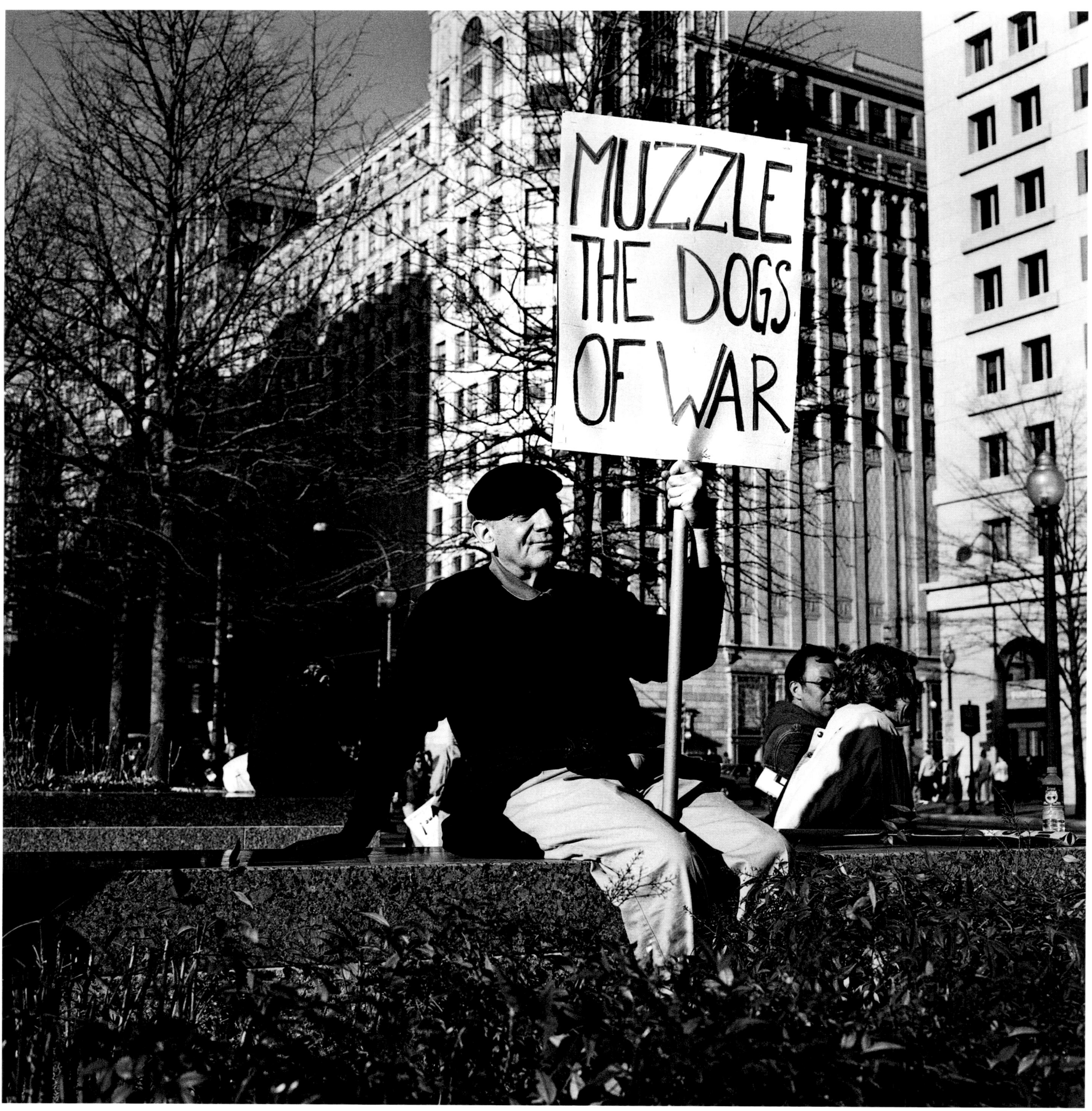
MUZZLE
THE DOGS
OF WAR

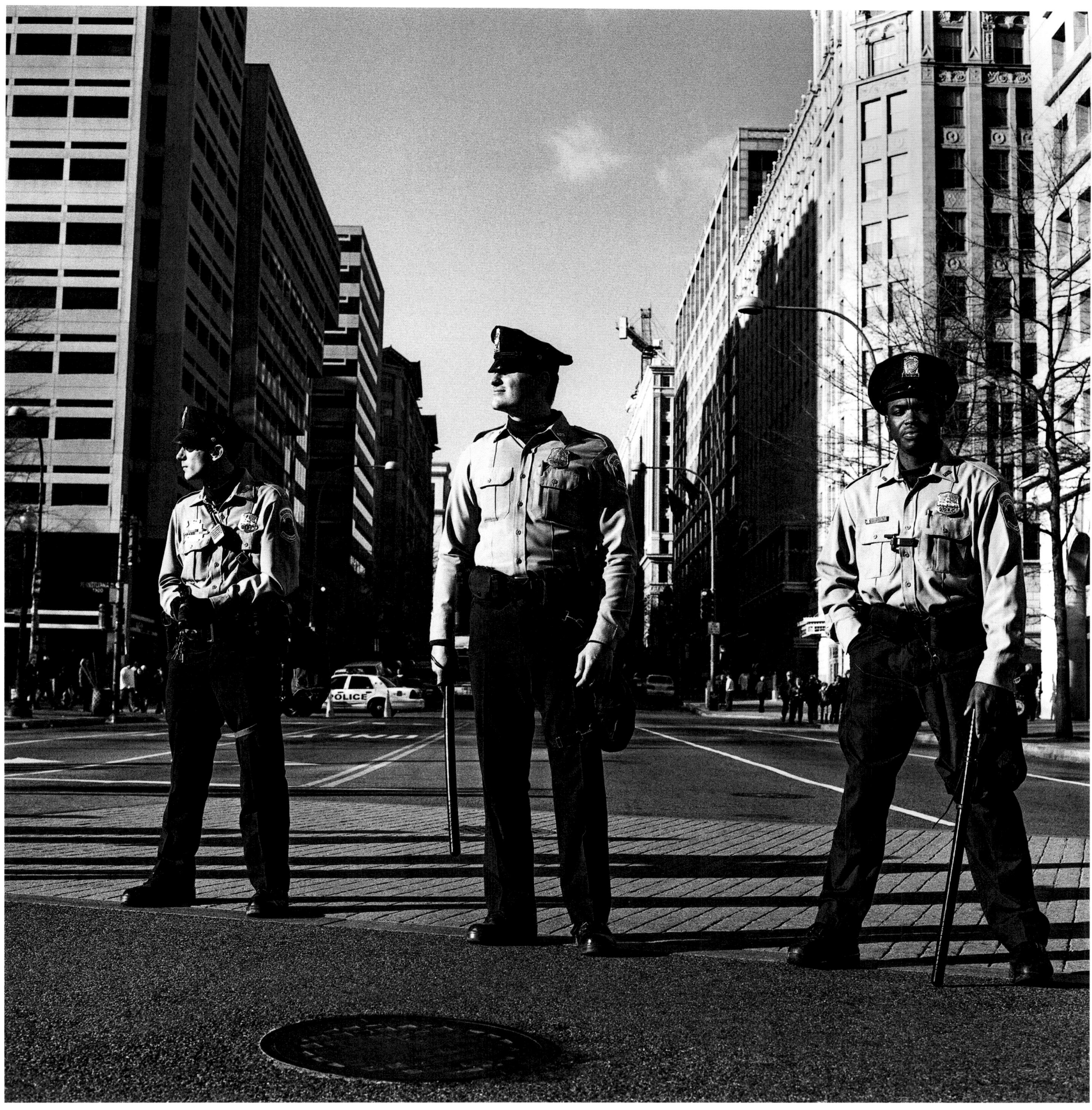
POLICE

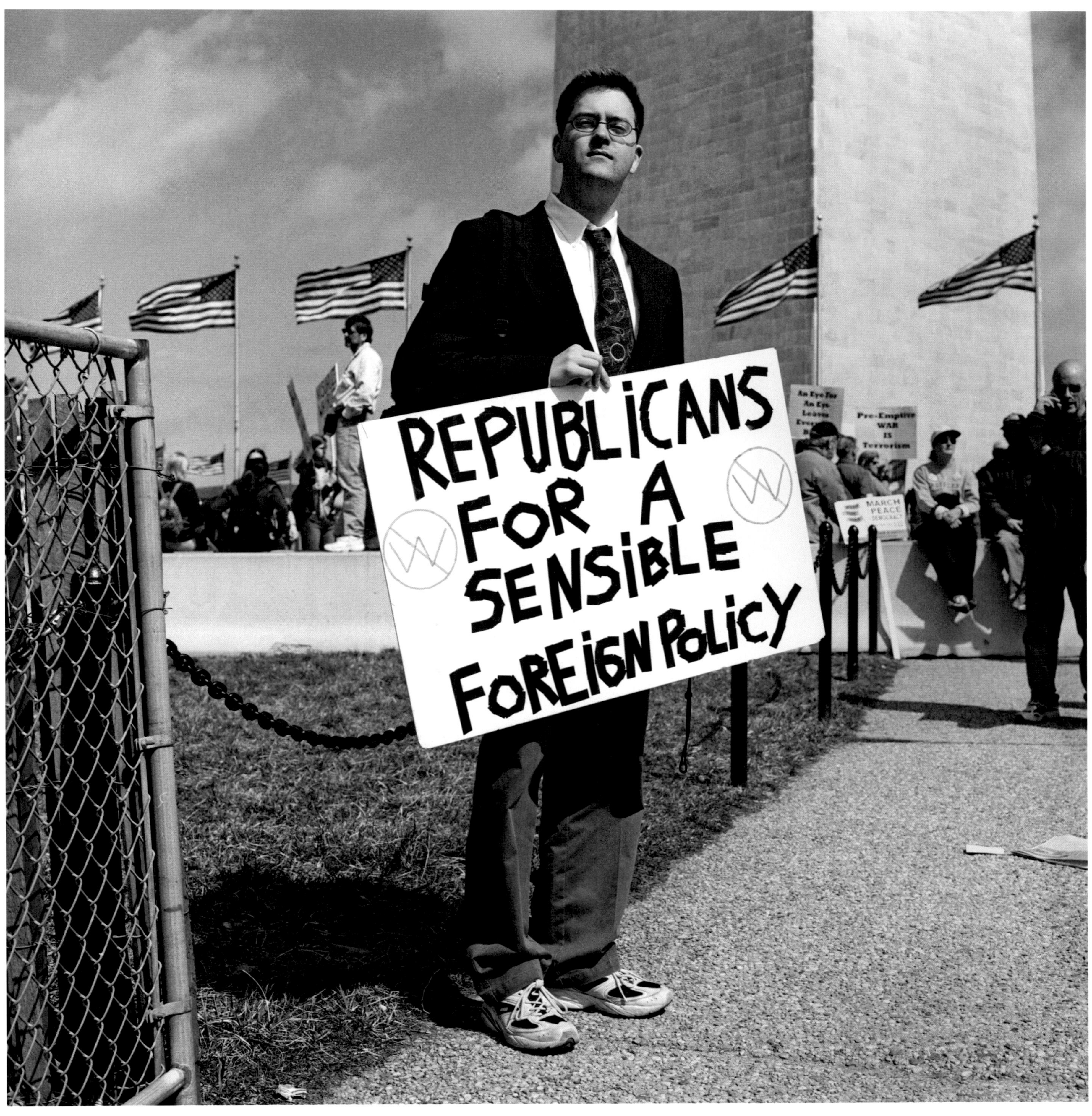
REPUBLICANS
FOR A
SENSIBLE
FOREIGN POLICY
Pre-Emptive
WAR
IS
Terrorism

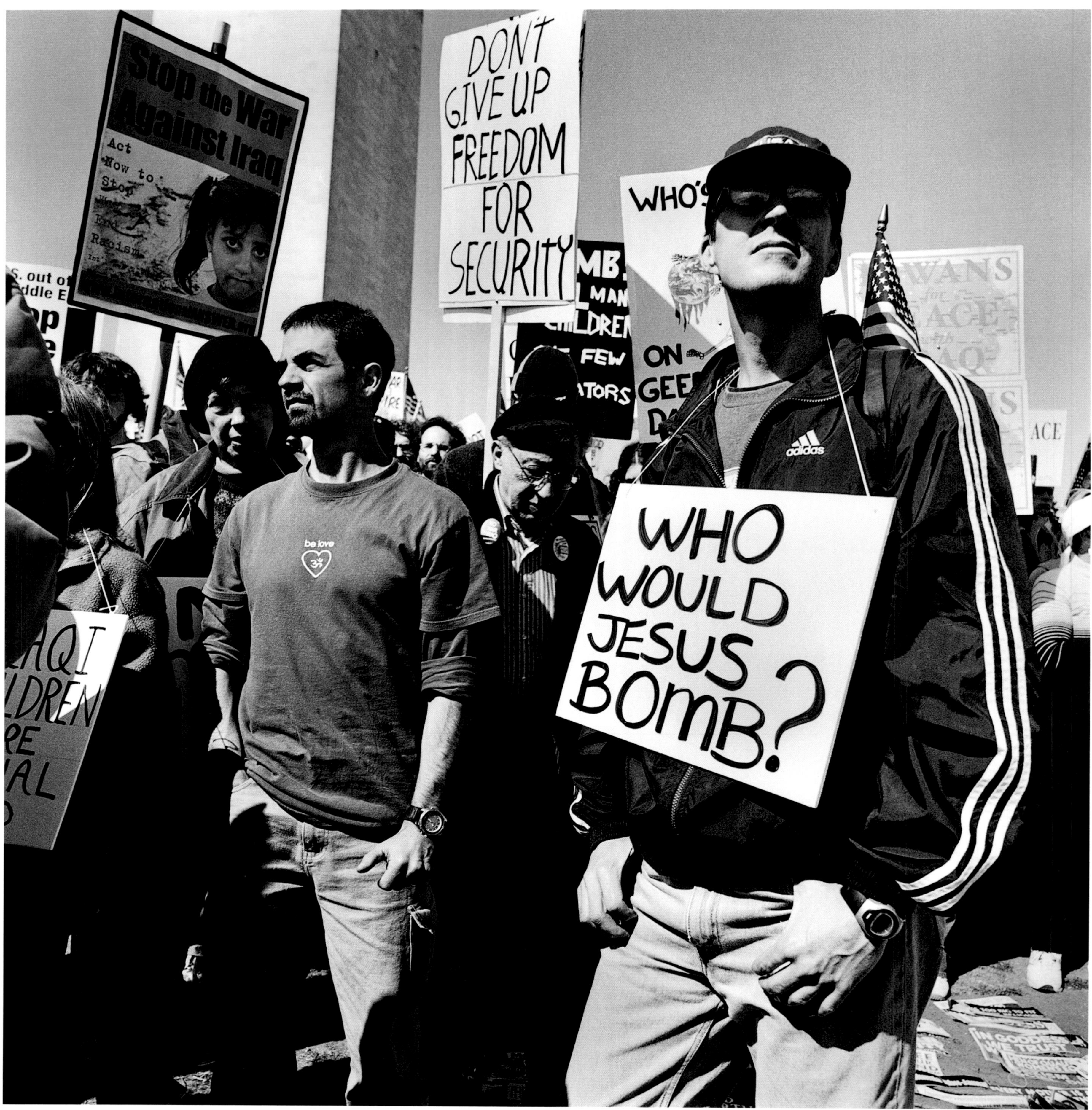
Stop the War Against Iraq
DON'T GIVE UP FREEDOM FOR SECURITY
WHO WOULD JESUS BOMB?
be love
adidas

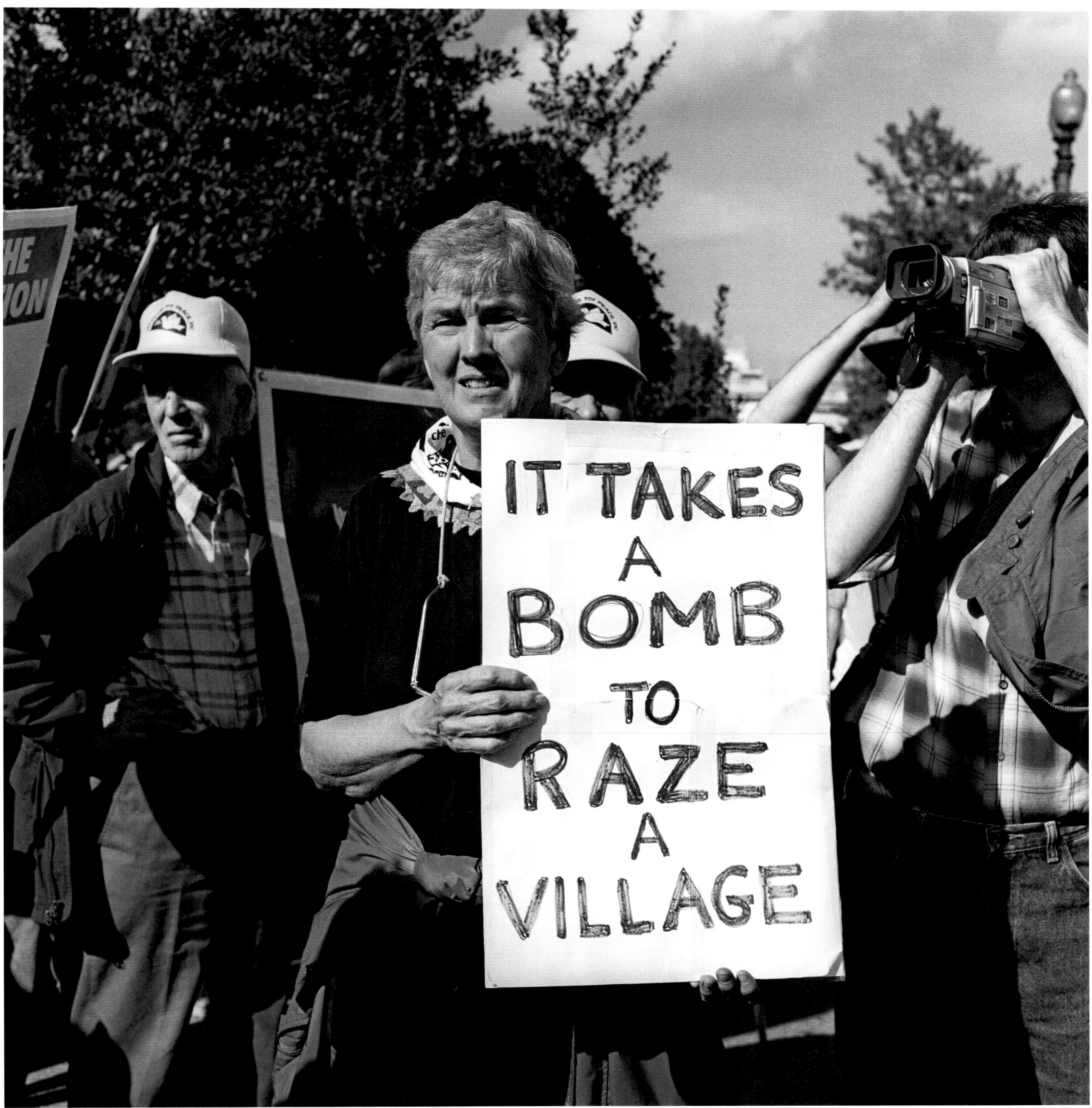
IT TAKES
A
BOMB
TO
RAZE
A
VILLAGE

Bennington, Vermont, March 20, 2003

Anti-War Civil Disobedience

The continuous bombing of Baghdad and other targets in Iraq began on March 19 and continued through March 21. The air campaign continued in the next weeks with 1,700 aerial sorties—bombings that included 504 cruise missiles—none of which were successful in killing Saddam Hussein. In response to this "shock and awe" bombing campaign, and the beginning of the Iraq War, people gathered on the morning of March 20 in downtown Bennington in an organized act of civil disobedience. Many had begun protesting before the war began, and were eager to share their stories.

"I and 11 others demonstrated at the Four Corners. We were all arrested and charged with blocking traffic although none of us did. We were advised by our lawyer to plead guilty, which we did except Rosemarie Jackowski, an Air Force veteran. We were all found guilty and did community service. Rosemarie appealed her conviction, which was overturned."

— ANDREW C. SCHOERKE, CAPTAIN USNR, RETIRED

"I just worked my way through the crowd and found a vacant spot in the middle of the Four Corners and silently stood there holding my sign. There was a lot happening around me. There was street theater. People were in costumes. Horns were blaring. I just stood in silence holding my sign. I was thinking about what was happening in Iraq. Eventually, I heard a voice behind me saying, 'You have to get out of the road.' I said, 'I'm sorry, I can't.' And the voice said, 'You have to get out of the road.' My peripheral vision told me it was an officer. I felt sorry for him. I really did. I could just tell this poor guy probably felt like he was arresting his grandmother. He was very kind, very sweet I walked with him to the police cruiser. We stood there and there's noise and chaos and police dogs and state troopers and you name it, everybody in the Sheriff's Department."

– ROSEMARIE JACKOWSKI, AIR FORCE VETERAN

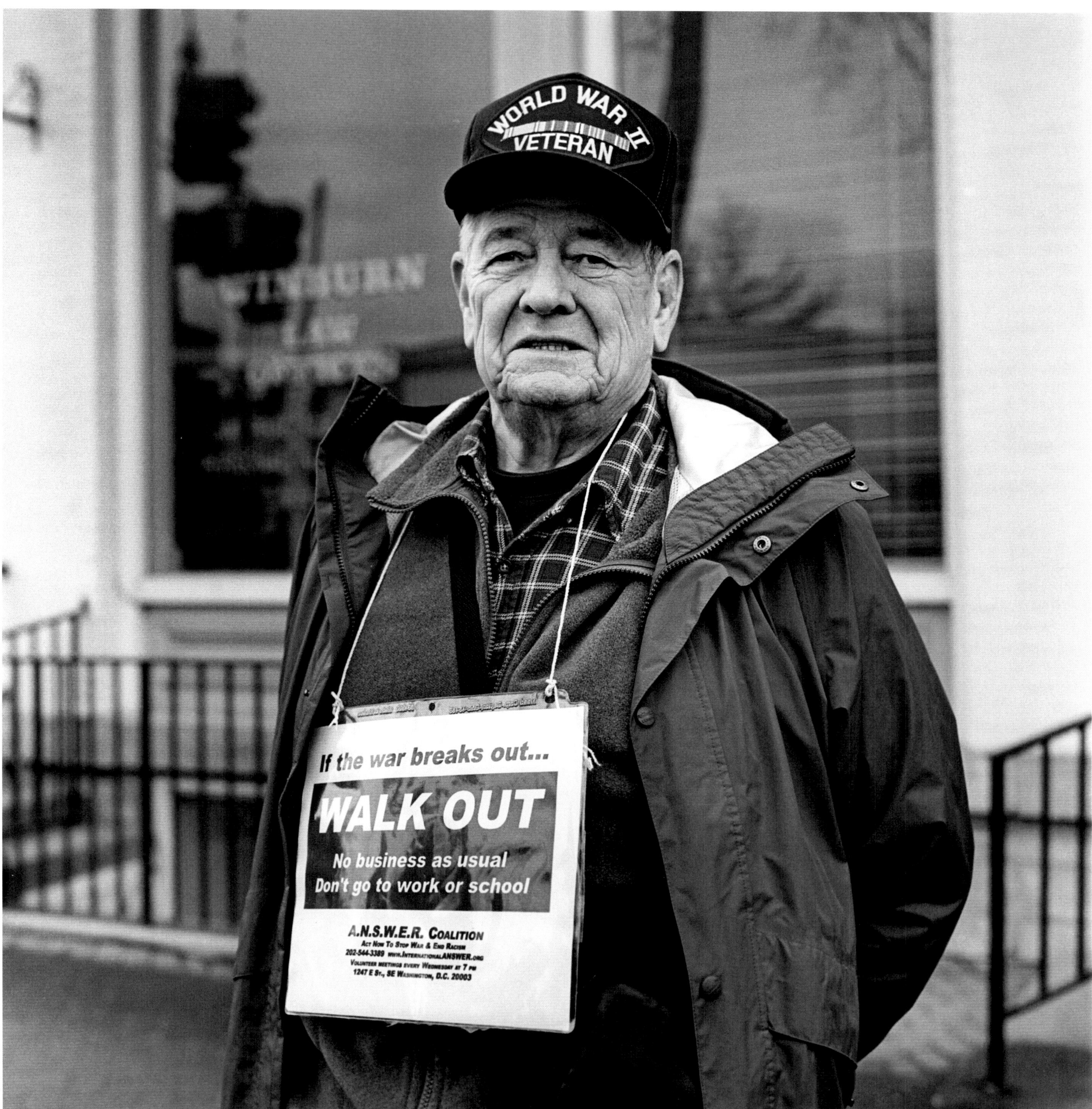
WORLD WAR II
VETERAN
If the war breaks out...
WALK OUT
No business as usual
Don't go to work or school
A.N.S.W.E.R. Coalition
Act Now To Stop War & End Racism
202-544-3389 www.InternationalANSWER.org
Volunteer meetings every Wednesday at 7 pm
1247 E St., SE Washington, D.C. 20003

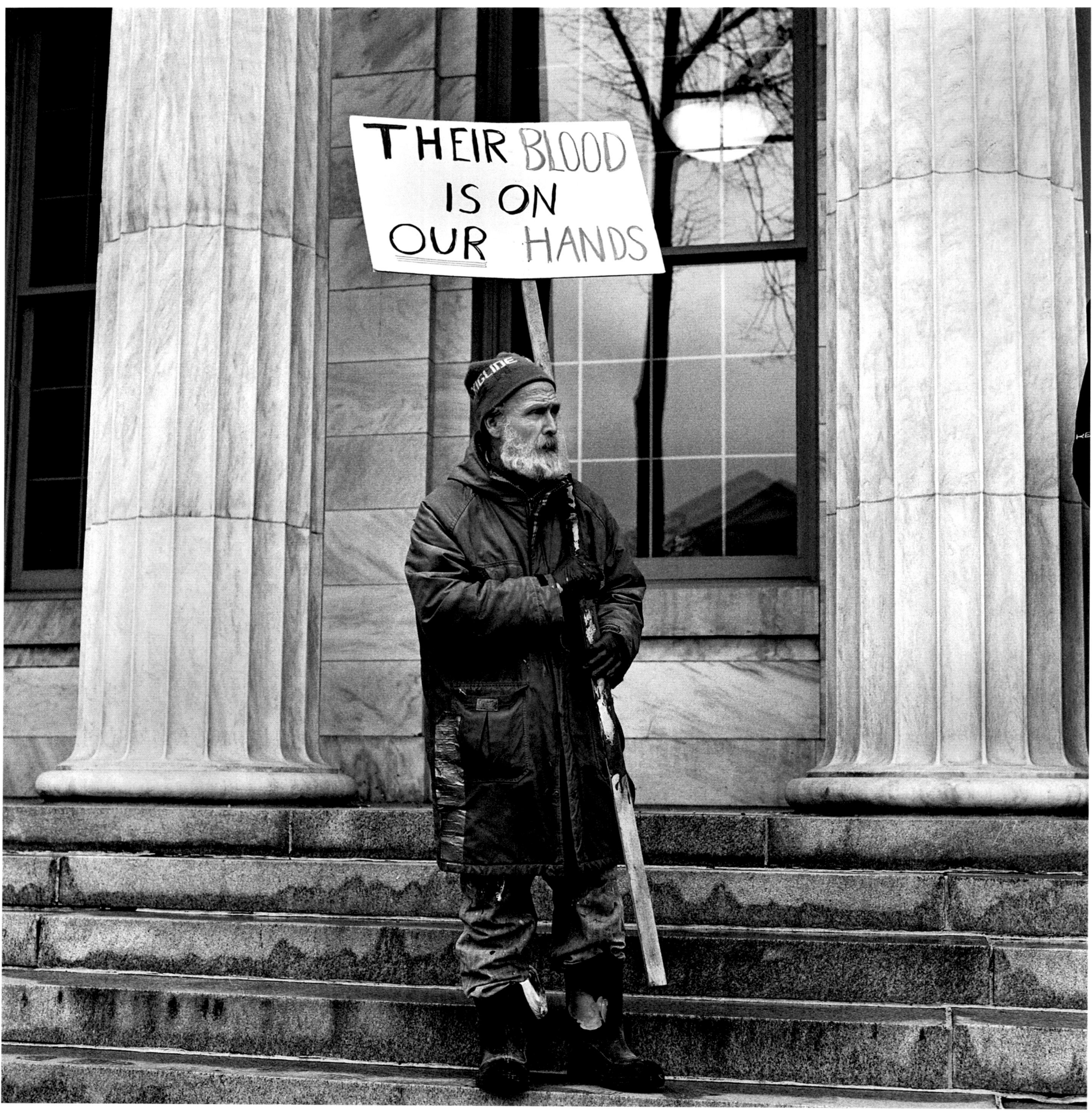
THEIR BLOOD
IS ON
OUR HANDS

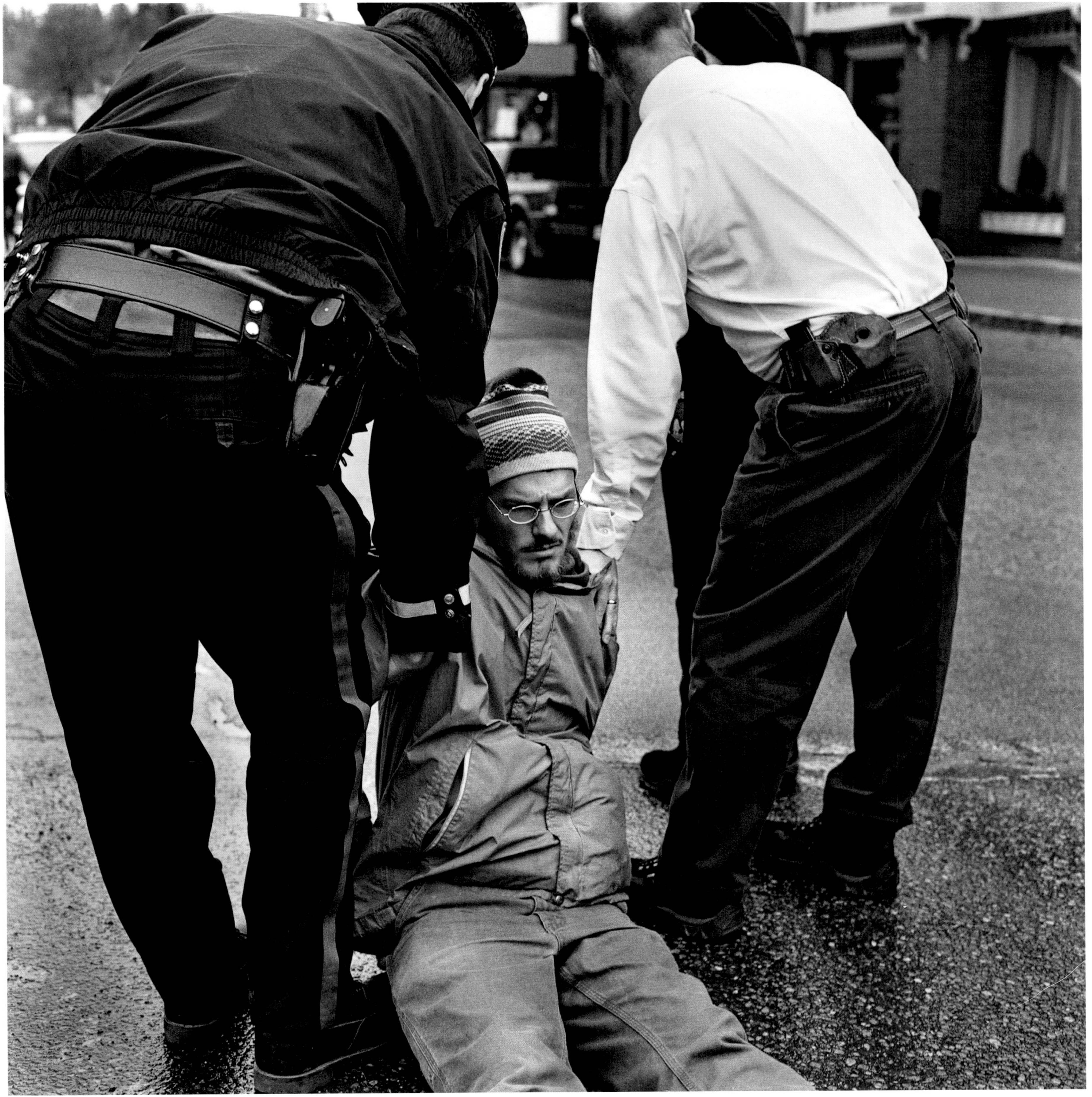

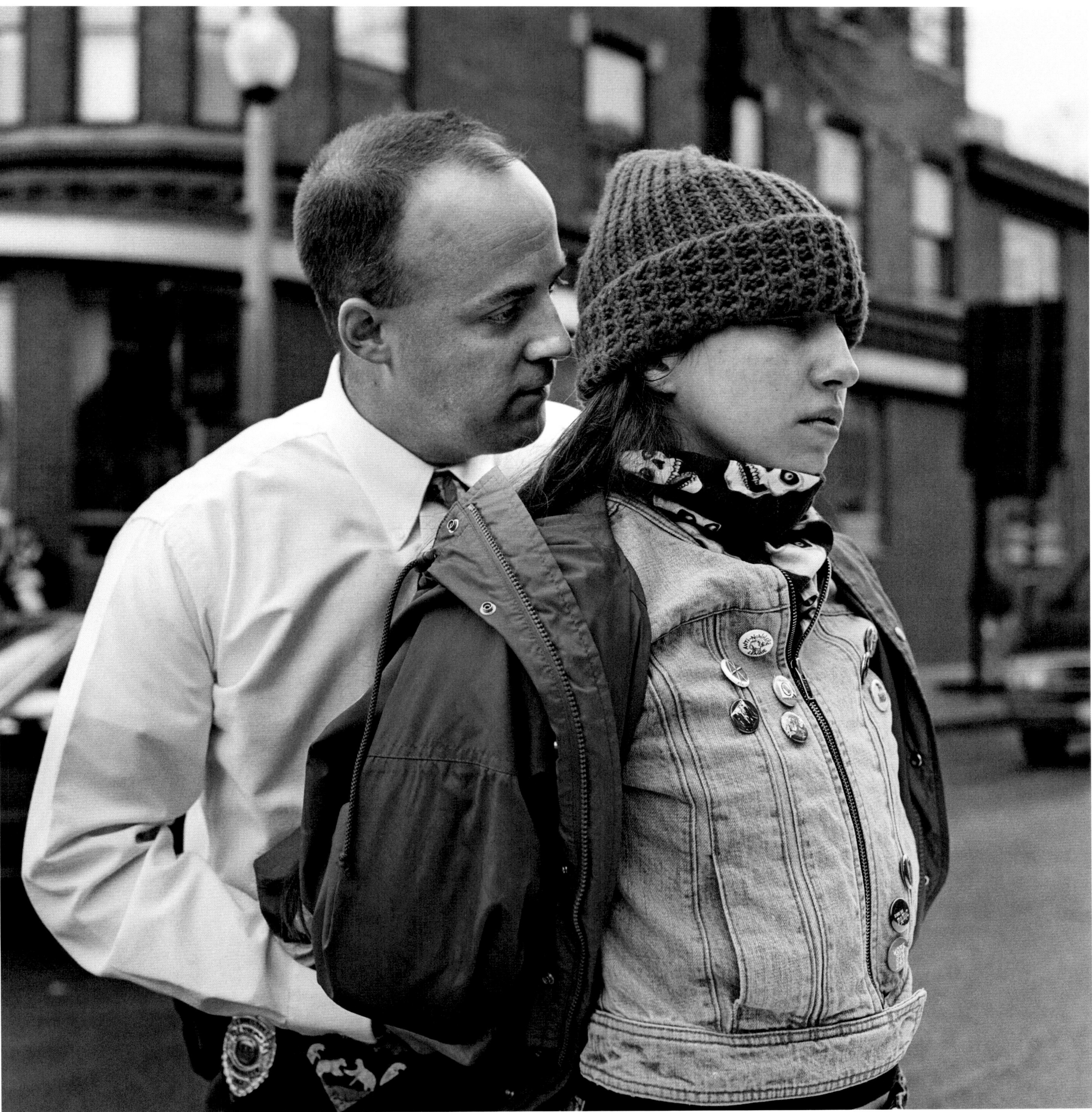

New York City, March 22, 2003

Anti-War March

Warm spring sunshine poured directly onto Broadway as crowds of demonstrators and anti-war activists—estimated at over a quarter of a million—marched from Herald Square to Waverly Place in downtown Manhattan. While the endless bombardment continued on Baghdad and numerous targets across Iraq, the mood in the streets was resolute, yet celebratory; spring was in the air, and the vast crowd marched in solidarity. As they chanted and danced down Broadway, onlookers young and old smiled and applauded, offering high fives and free bottles of water to the passersby.

By late in the day, Washington Square Park was choked with protestors. Police arrived in cruisers and on horseback, adding to the confusion and urgency of the crushing crowd. Police loudspeakers congratulated the marchers on the completion of their walk and urged them to disperse. Thousands remained in the park. Forty-seven people were arrested and the park was cleared.

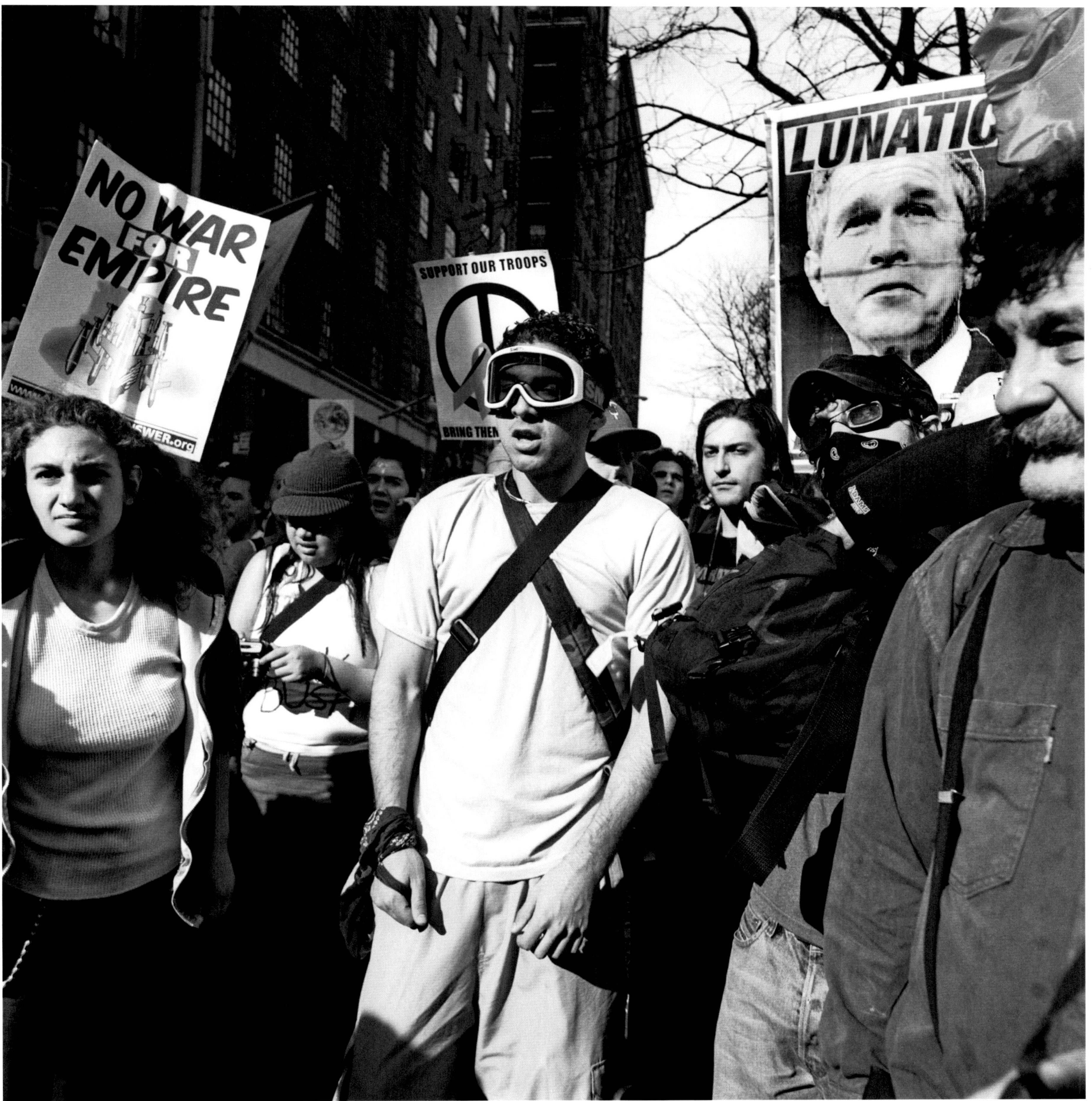
NO WAR FOR EMPIRE
SUPPORT OUR TROOPS
LUNATIC

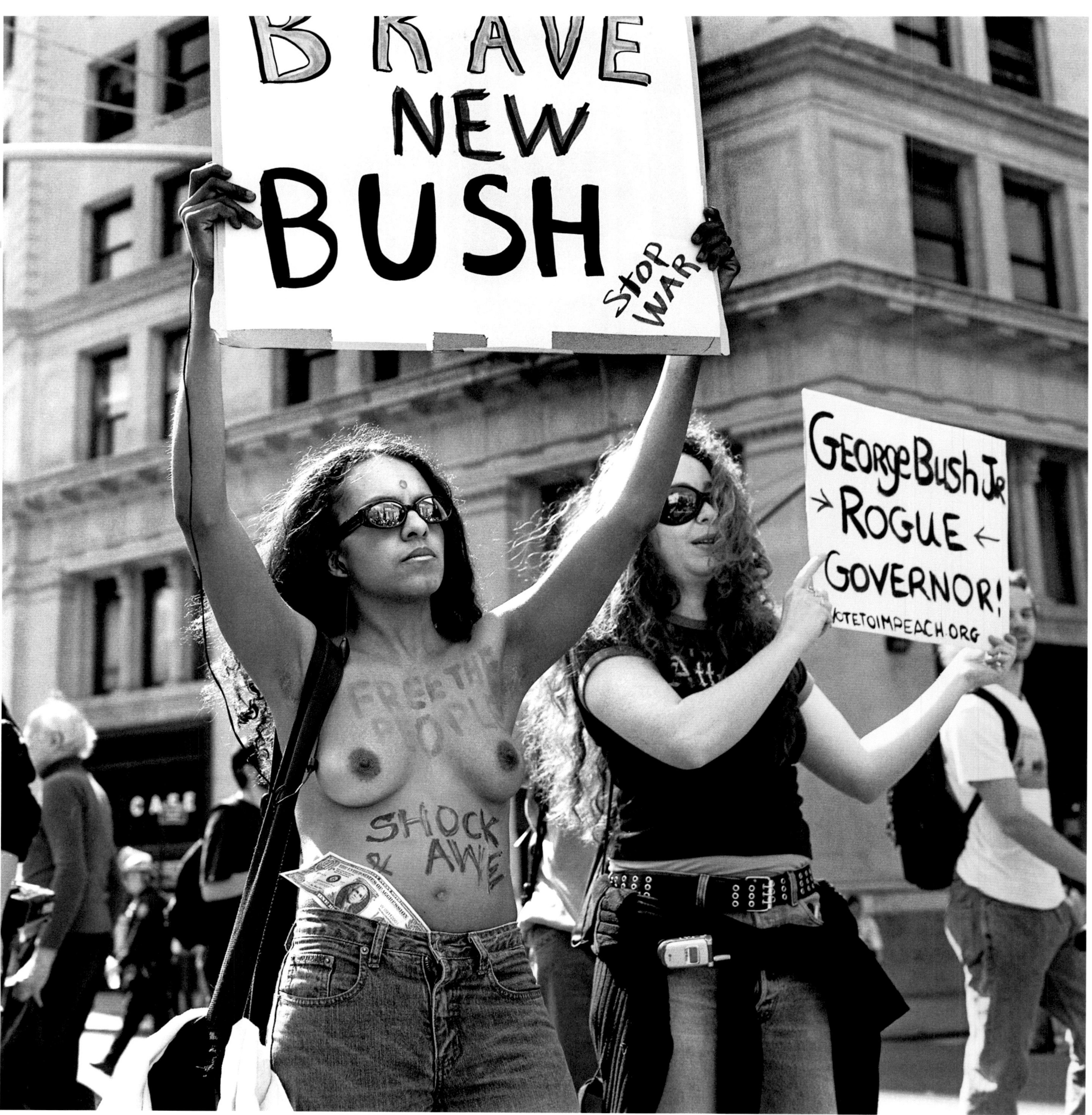
BRAVE
NEW
BUSH
STOP
WAR
George Bush Jr
→ ROGUE ←
GOVERNOR!
VOTETOIMPEACH.ORG
SHOCK
& AWE

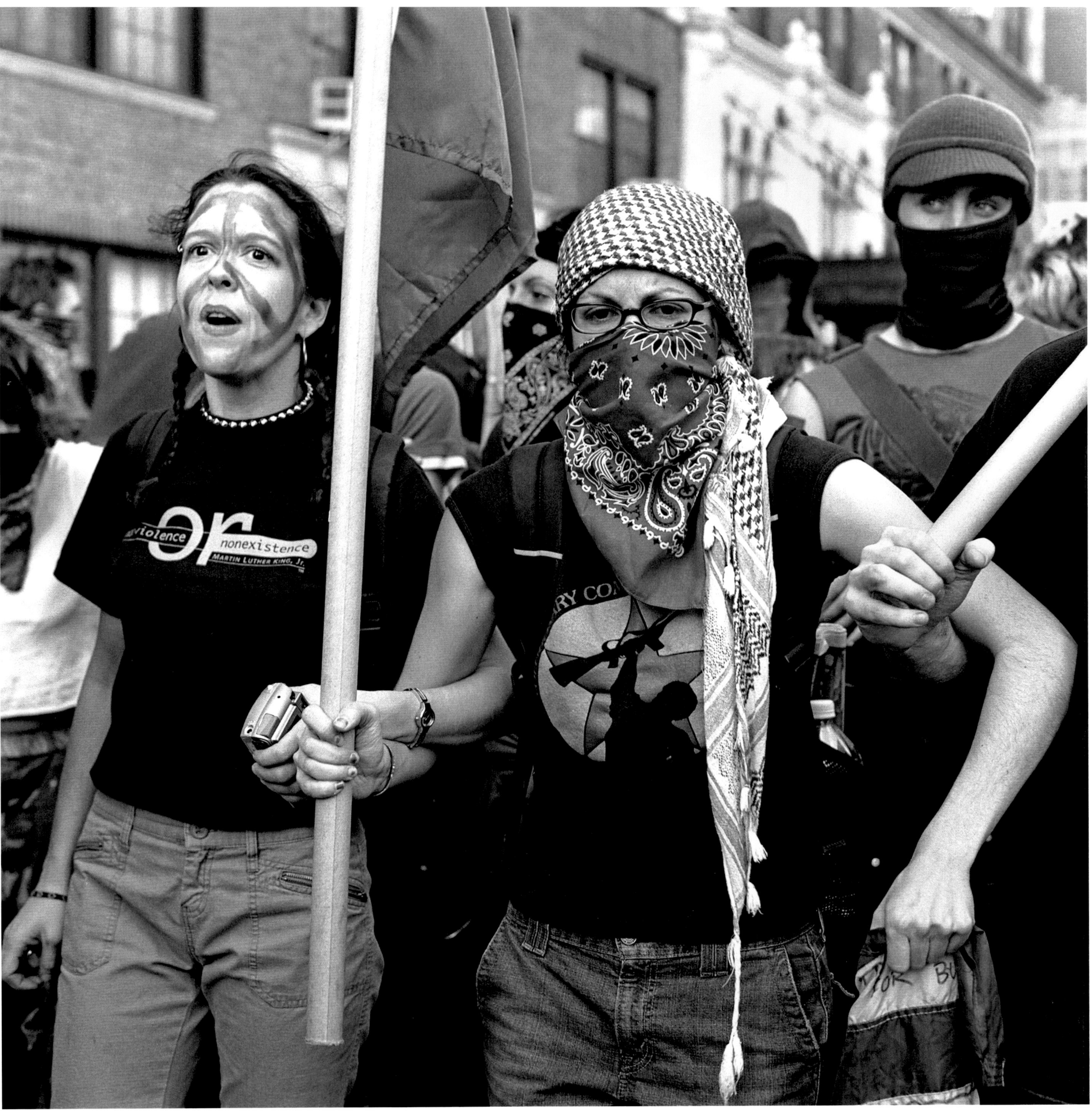
violence
or
nonexistence
MARTIN LUTHER KING, Jr.

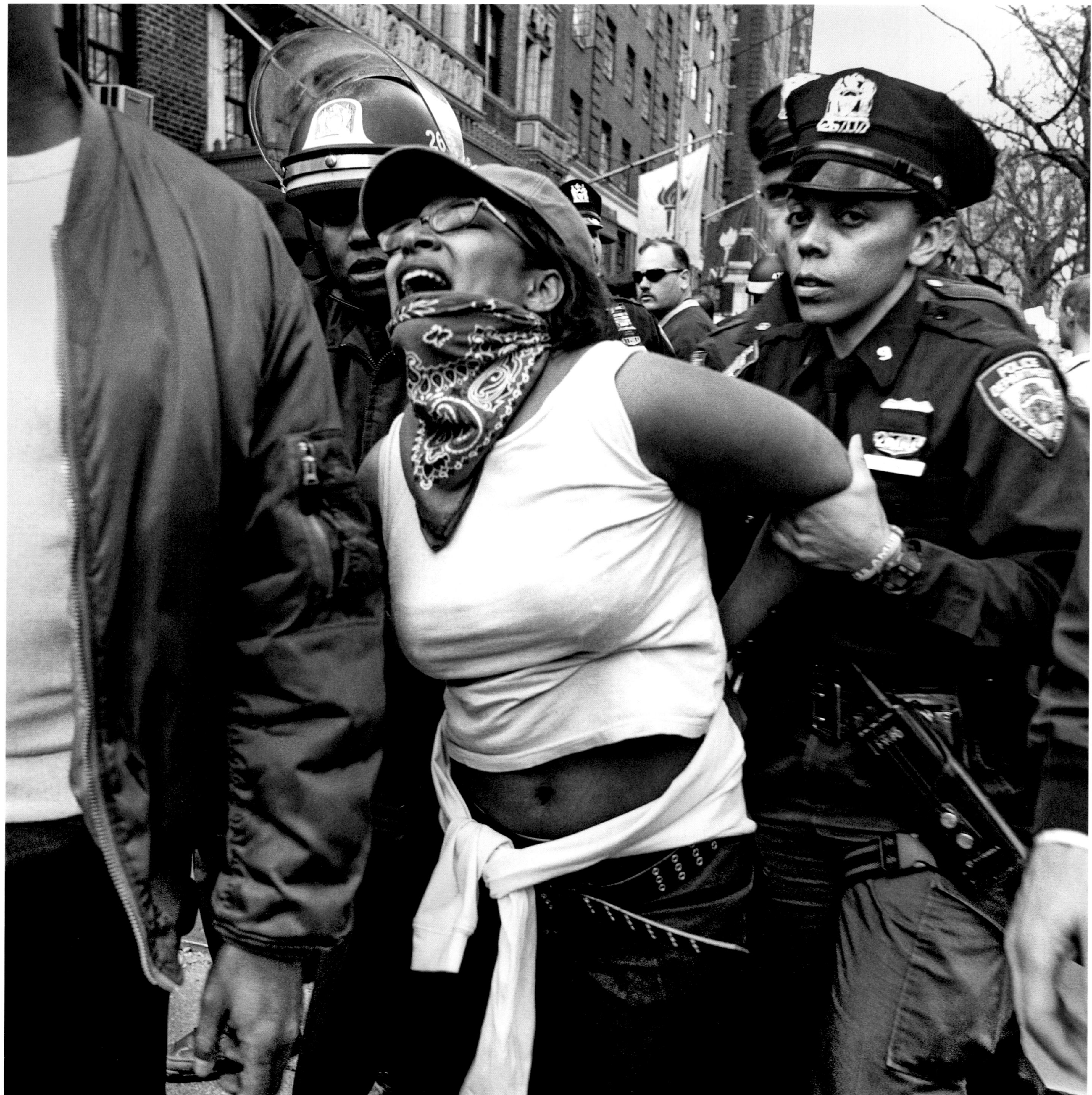
26

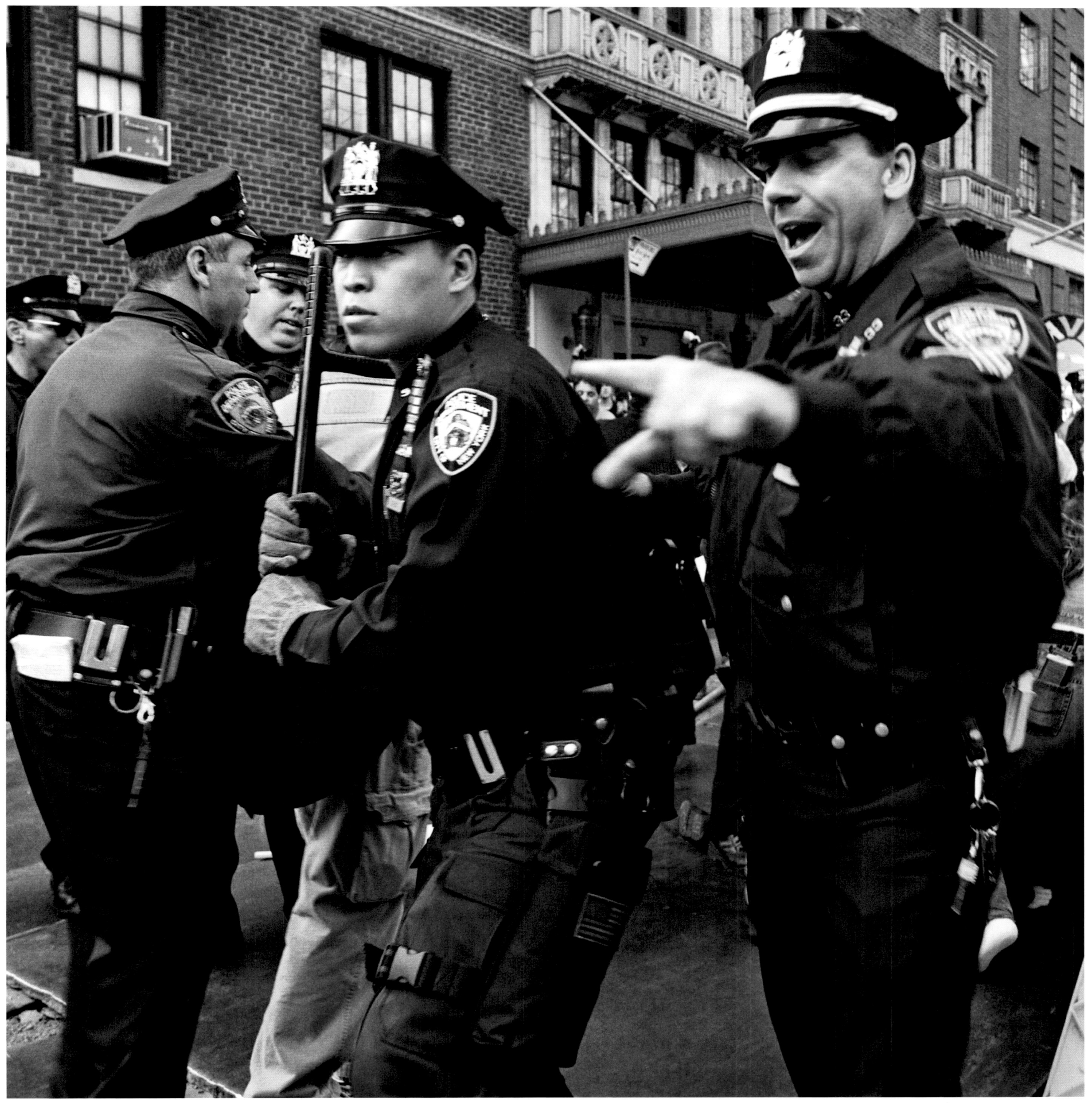

Bennington, Vermont, April 17, 2003

Funeral of CW4 Erik Anders Halvorsen

"The painful memory of a lost son or daughter lasts forever in the heart of a parent. The last moments of when you spoke with him and the memory of where you were when you said goodbye is imprinted in a parent's mind forever. These are the thoughts that come to mind as I recall the moment I was notified of the death of my son, CW4 Erik A. Halvorsen, who was killed in a helicopter crash in Karbala Gap, Iraq, April 2, 2003.

So let us never forget the courage and dedication of our military men and women today who travel to foreign shores and face foreign adversaries and who have offered to give, and have given, their lives in the hope that there will be a better tomorrow for those they left behind."

— DOROTHY HALVORSEN, GOLD STAR MOTHER

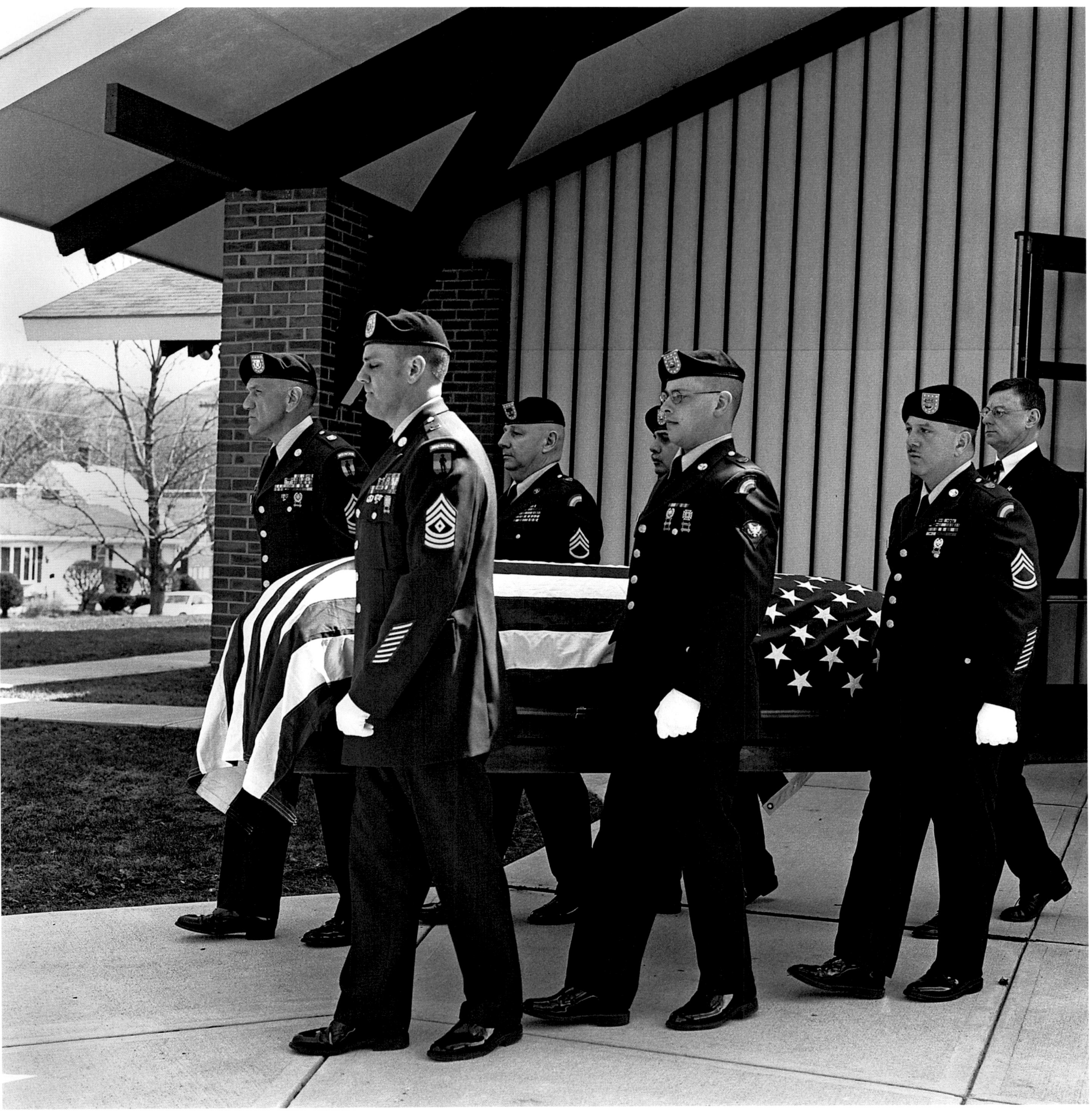

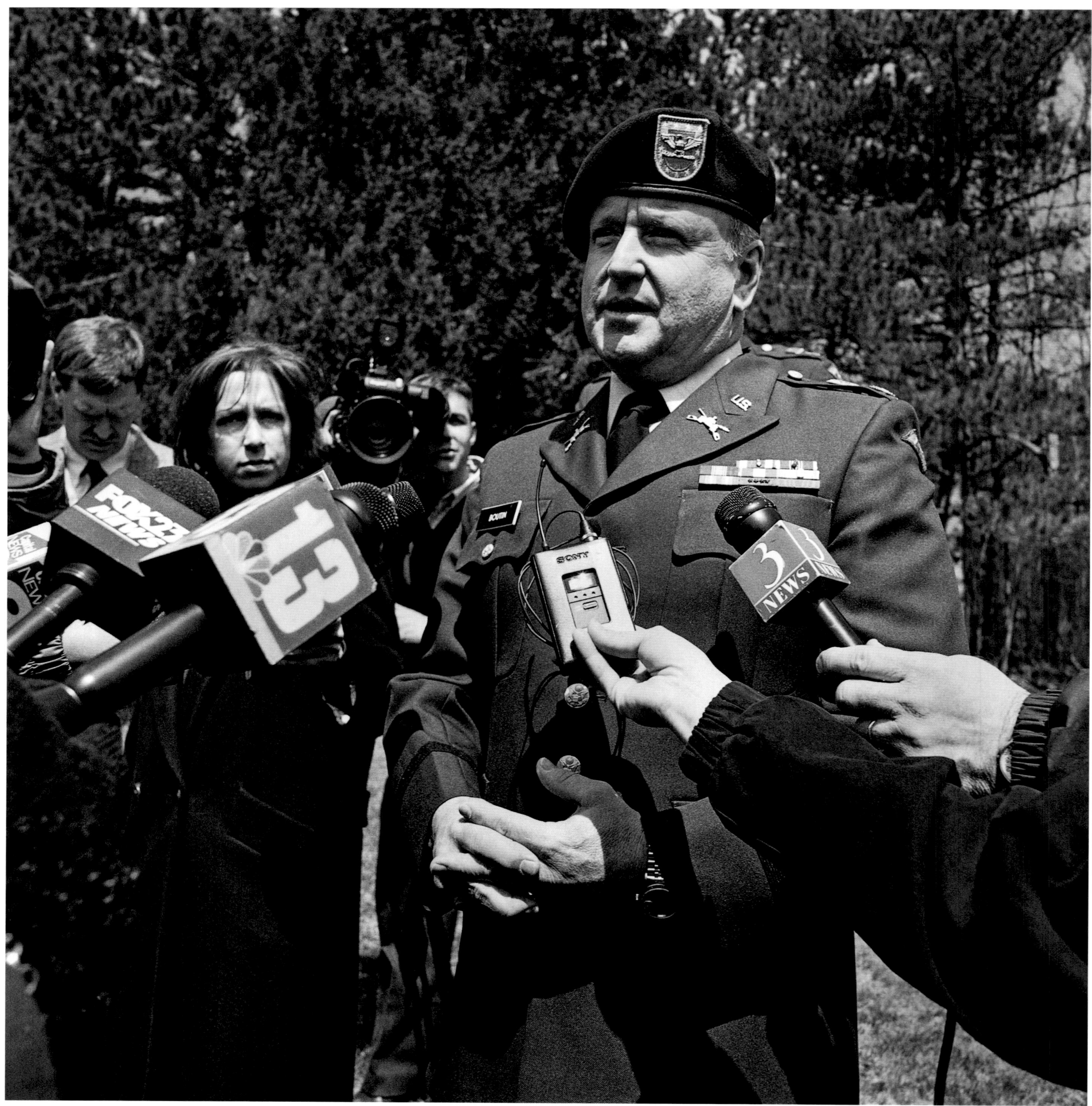
13
SONY
3 NEWS

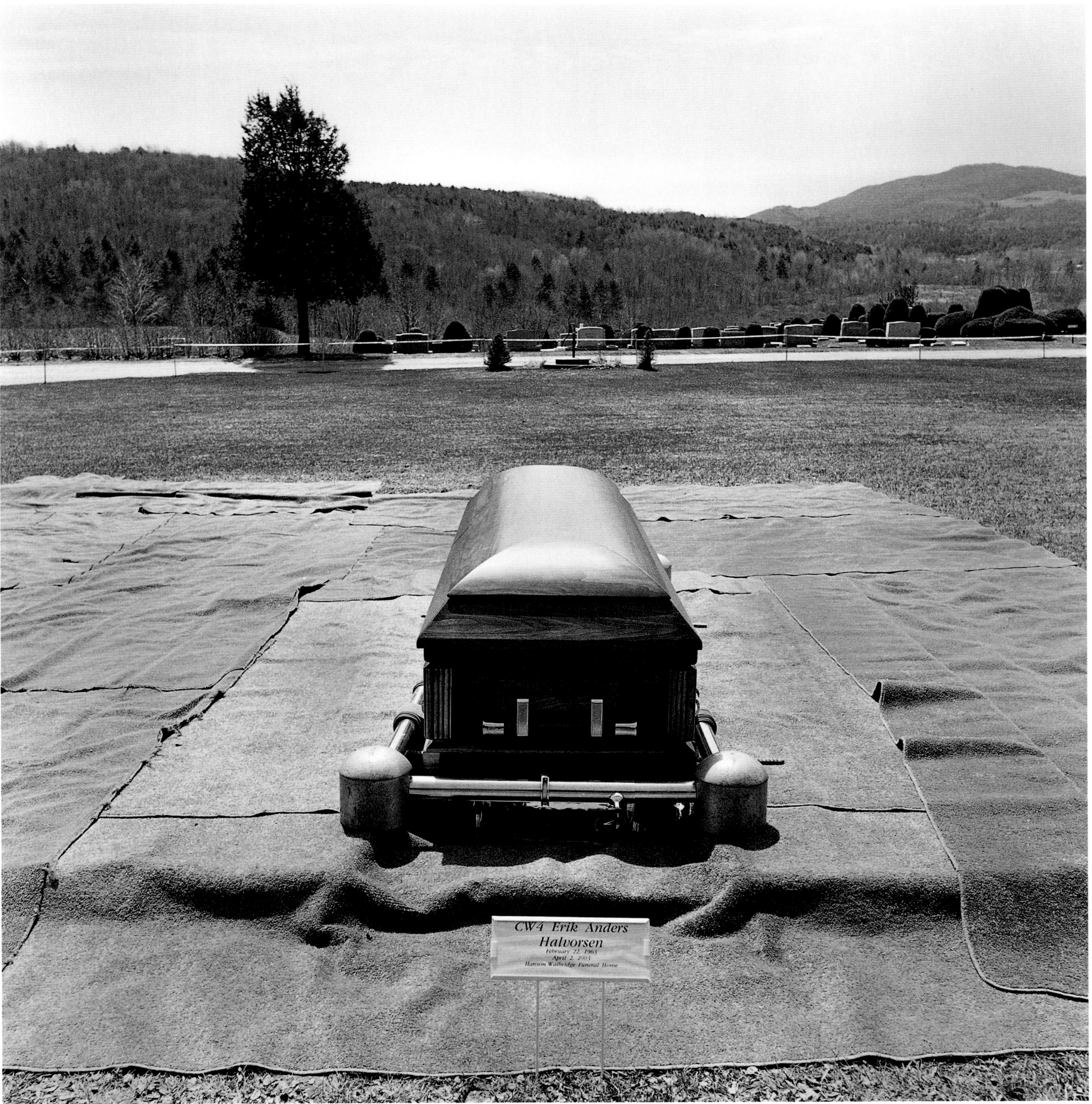
CW4 Erik Anders
Halvorsen
February 22, 1963
April 2, 2003
Hanson Walbridge Funeral Home

New York City, September 11, 2003

September 11 Anniversary Ceremony

Two years after the attacks at the World Trade Center the public expression of grief was palpable and visceral. Fastened to the heavy mesh wire barricade around the site were photographs of those who died in the attacks, personalized with flowers and notes from their families. Fire fighters, police, and construction workers gathered at the site, many with flags in hand. T-shirts, emblazoned with American flags, and slogans ("We Will not Forget" and "Remember 9/11") were visible in the gathered crowd. Friends and family members of those lost in the 2001 attacks held bouquets of flowers to lay at the site. A lone father in his wheelchair slowly moved himself forward as he balanced in his lap a framed portrait of his son.

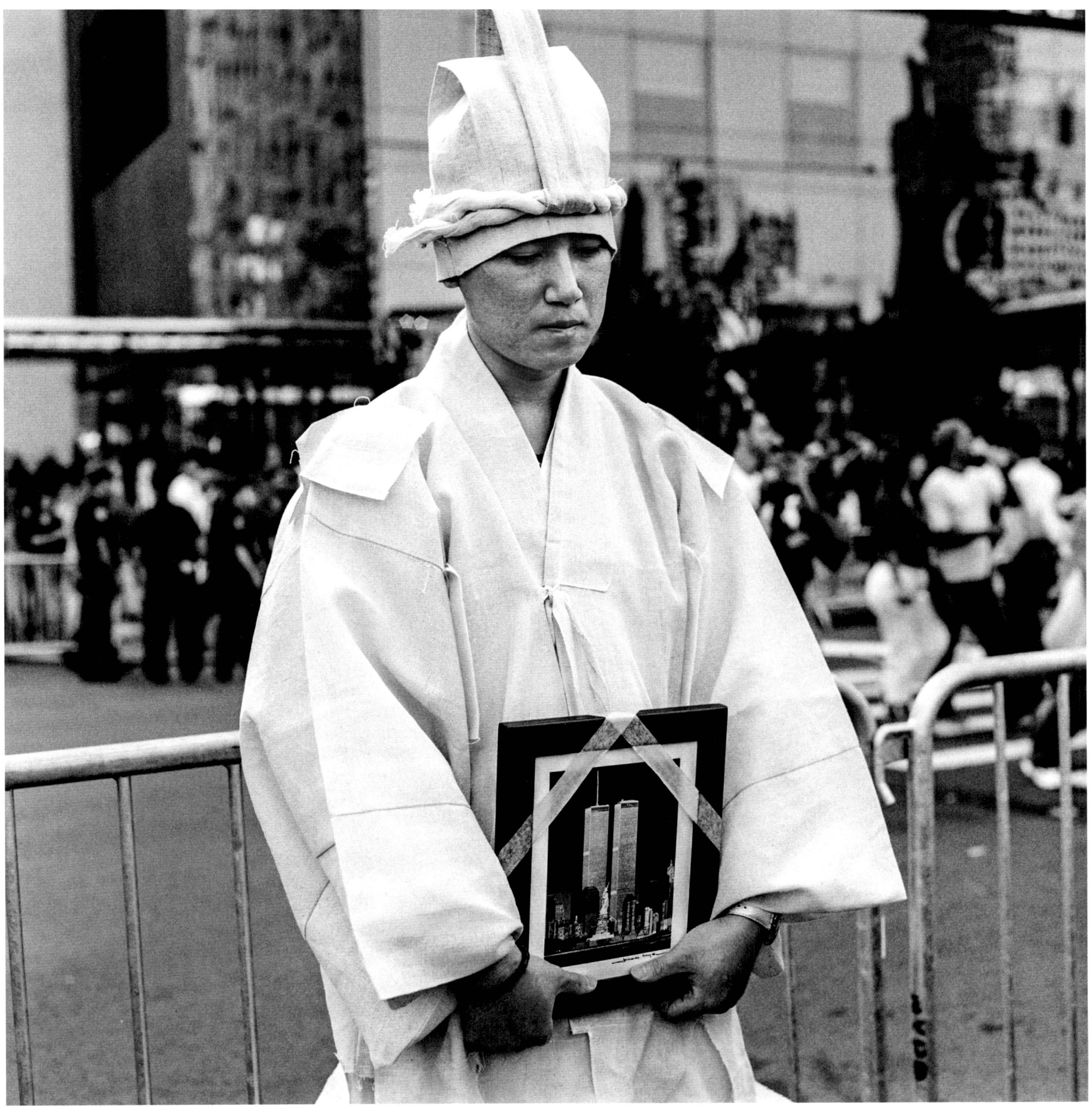

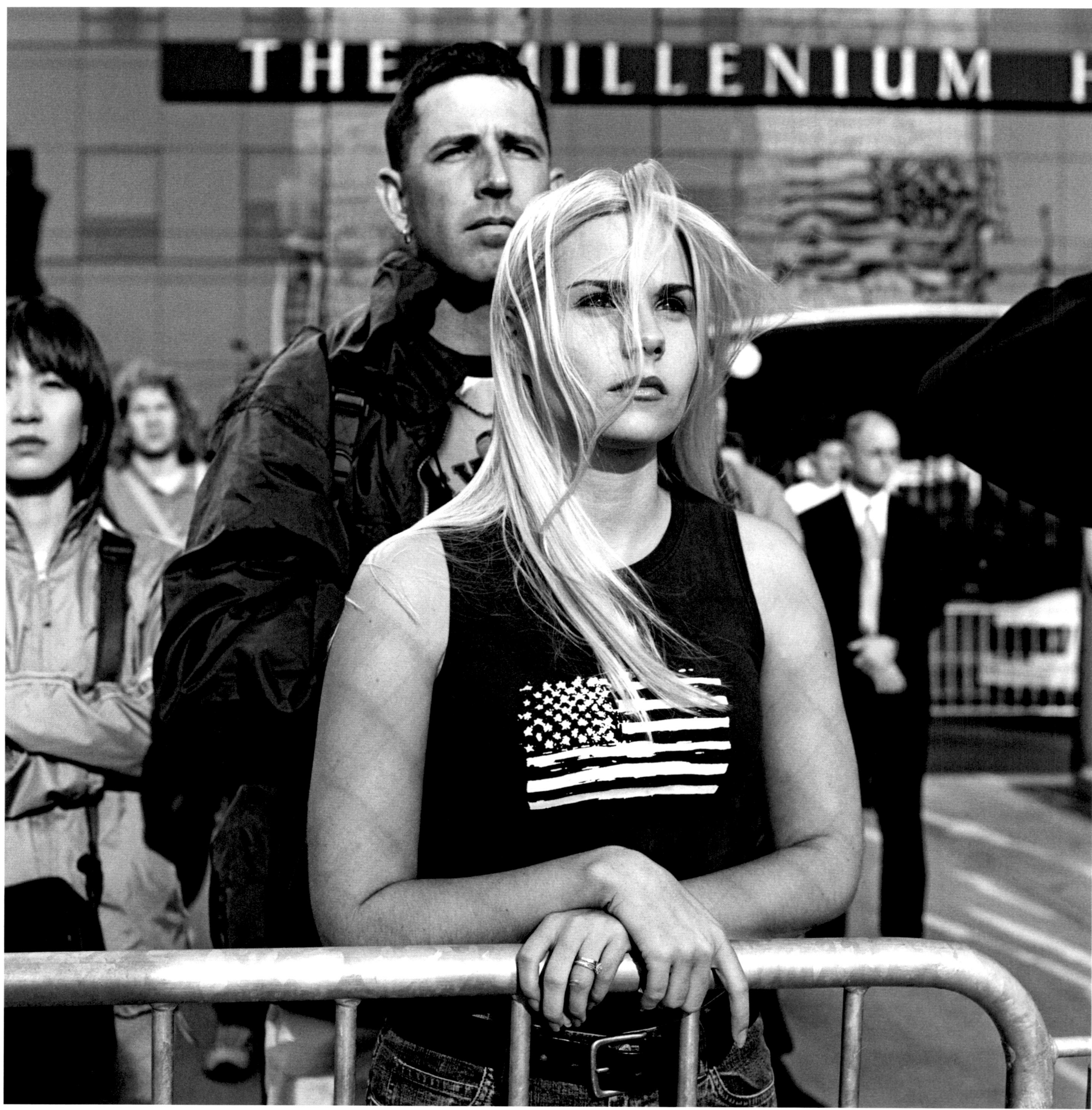
THE MILLENIUM

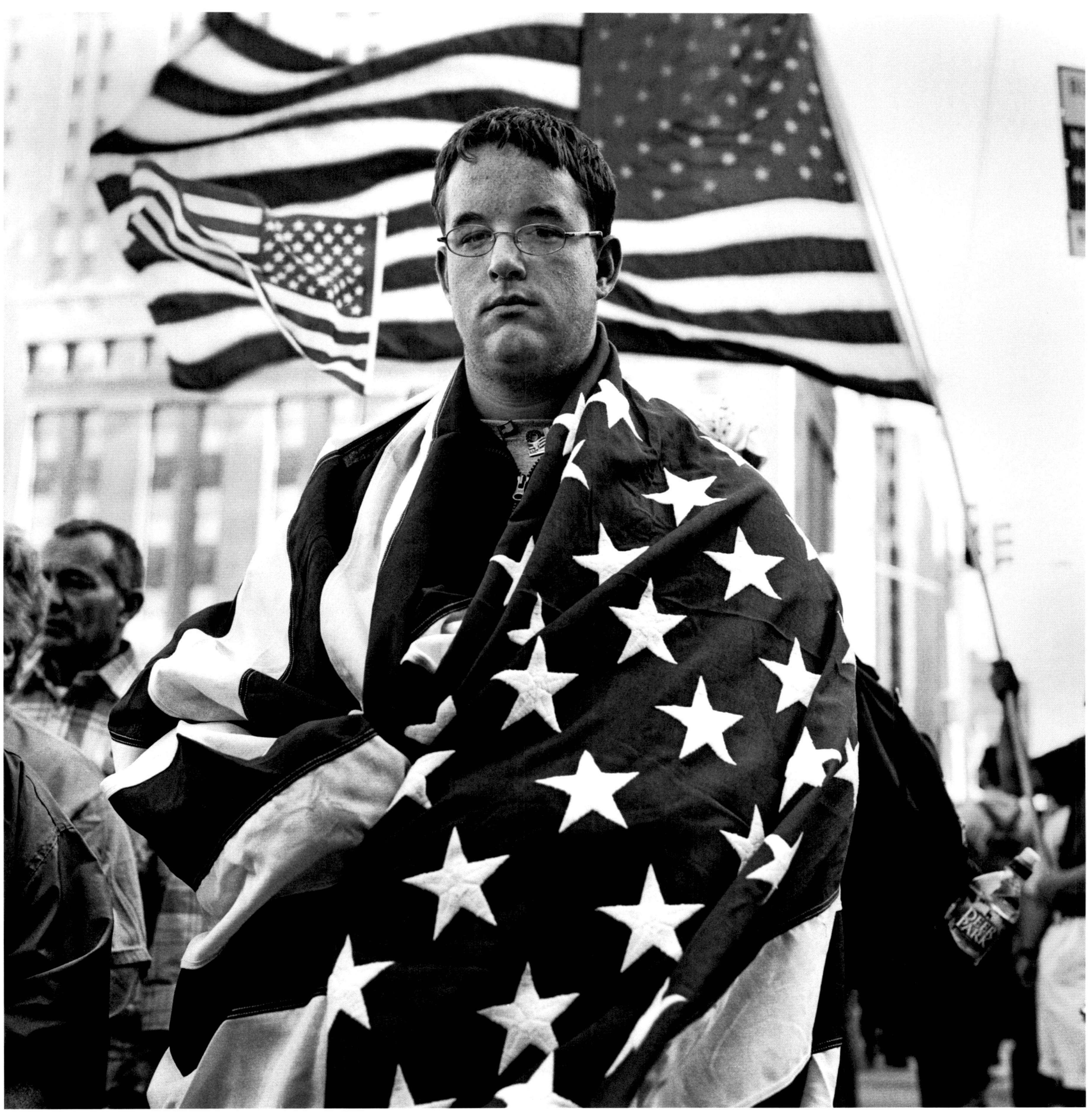
DEER PARK

Bennington, Vermont, July 3, 2004

Parade for CPL Ricky Greene

On the Saturday of the July 4th weekend, Ricky Greene was given a welcome home hero's parade down the Main Street of Bennington. Ricky, a member of an elite special ops force, the Army's 75th Ranger division, was severely injured early in the Iraq War. "I was manning a machine gun on a Humvee and I was hit by the gun turret of a M1 Abrams tank while we were traveling at speed of excess of 60 miles an hour," CPL Ricky Greene told me. In the heat of battle, a U.S. Army tank turret swiveled and struck him in the face. "I don't remember all the details because of traumatic brain injury," he continued, "but this is the true story as far as what I've been told. My whole face is reconstructed with 13 titanium plates and 70 or so screws."

For his service, Ricky Greene received a Bronze Star Medal with Valour, Purple Heart, Global War on Terrorism Service Medal, Ranger Tab and Scroll, and Parachutist Badge.

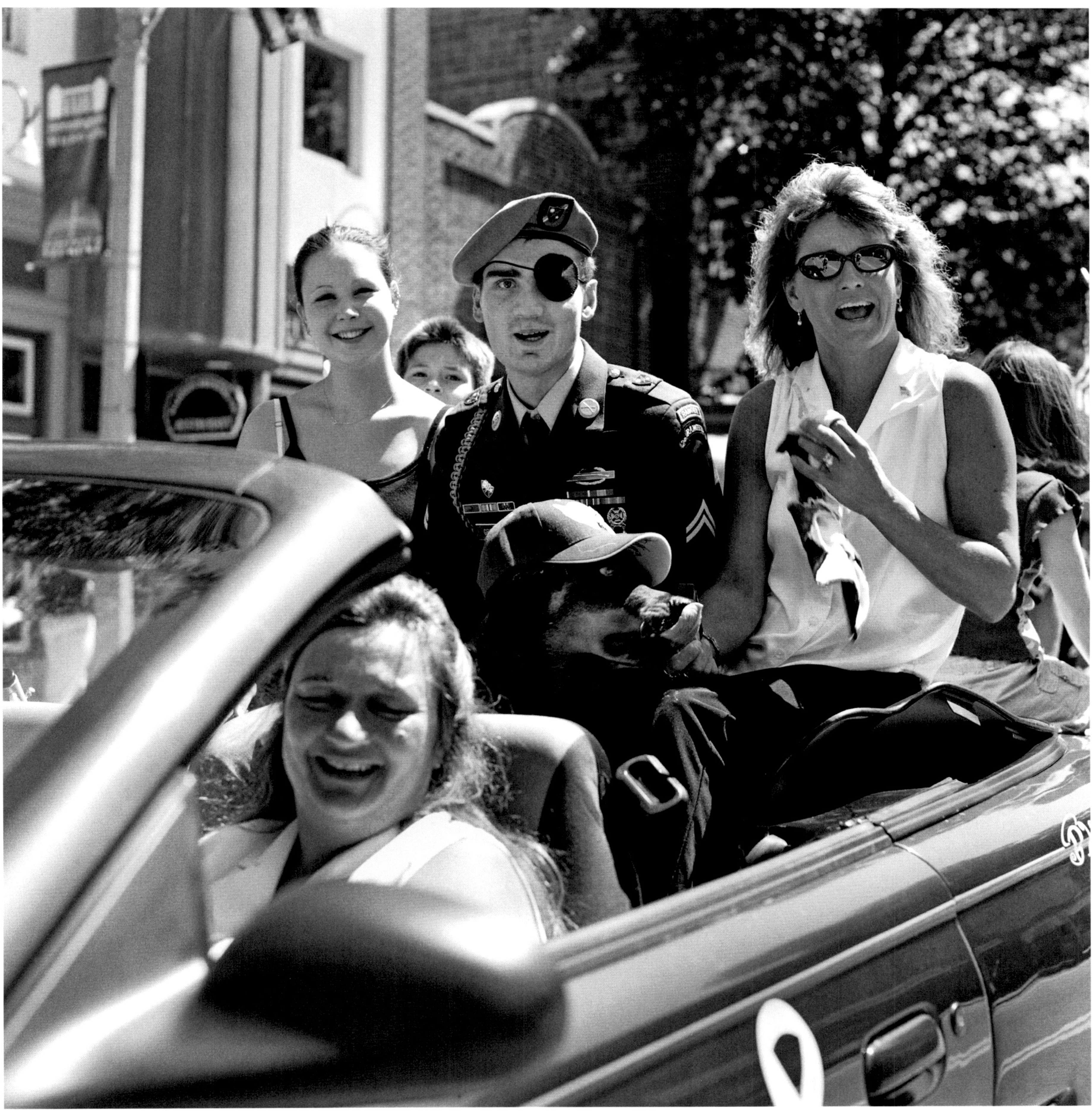

New York City, August 29, 2004

Republican National Convention

Humid summer heat engulfed New York City. While many lucky residents were out of town on the Long Island beaches, or at least in the air conditioning of their apartments, hundreds of thousands of demonstrators poured into the city for the Republican National Convention at Madison Square Garden. With numbers exceeding 800,000 protestors, this was one of the largest mass marches in recent American history. Members of the street theater troupe Billionaires for Bush, as well as members of the radical Bread and Puppet Theater of Vermont, brought vibrant performances to the march, while One Thousand Coffins' procession of cardboard caskets draped with American flags somberly commemorated the lives—one for each coffin—of the over 1,000 American servicemen and women killed to date in action in the Iraq War.

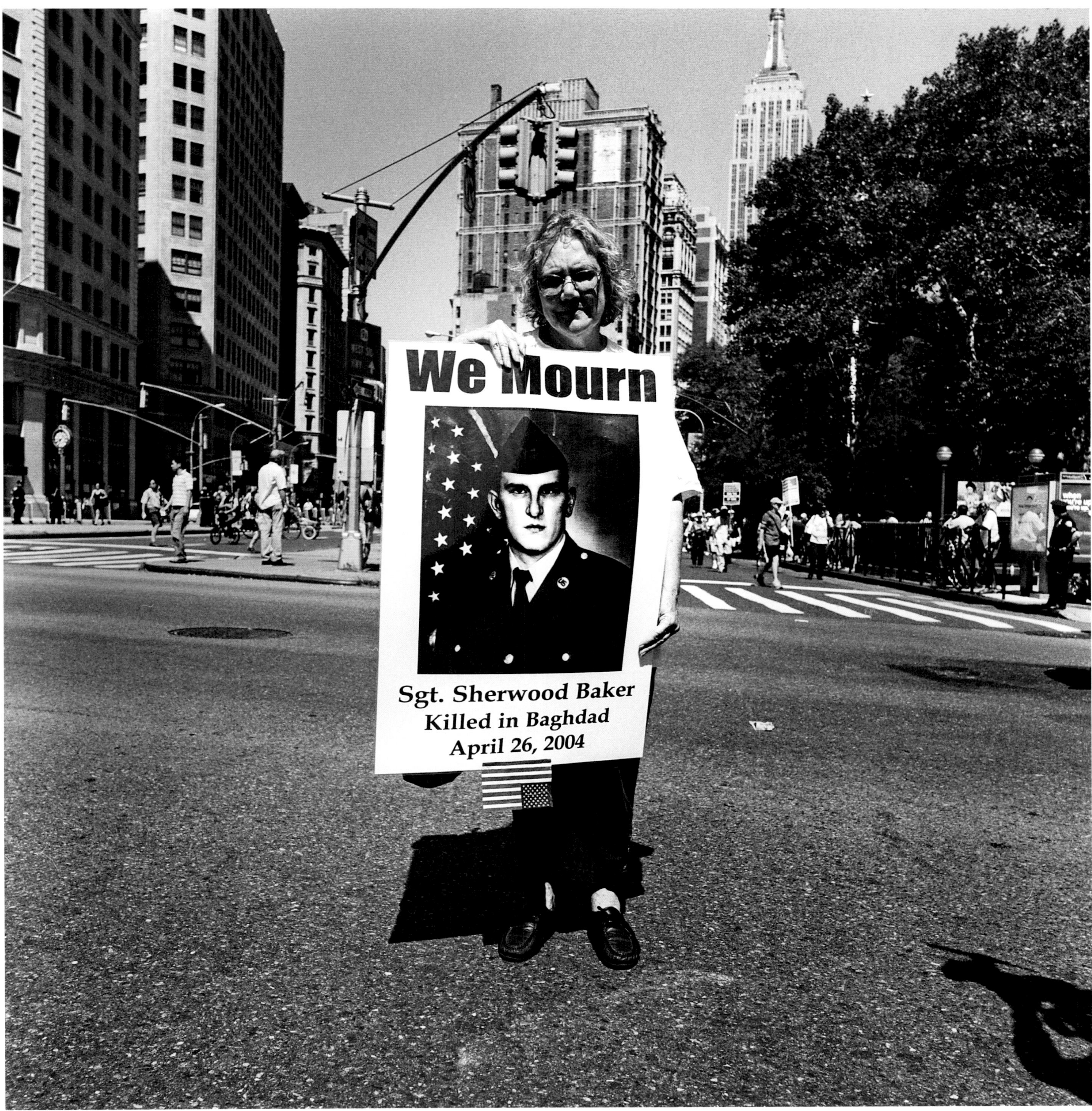
We Mourn
Sgt. Sherwood Baker
Killed in Baghdad
April 26, 2004

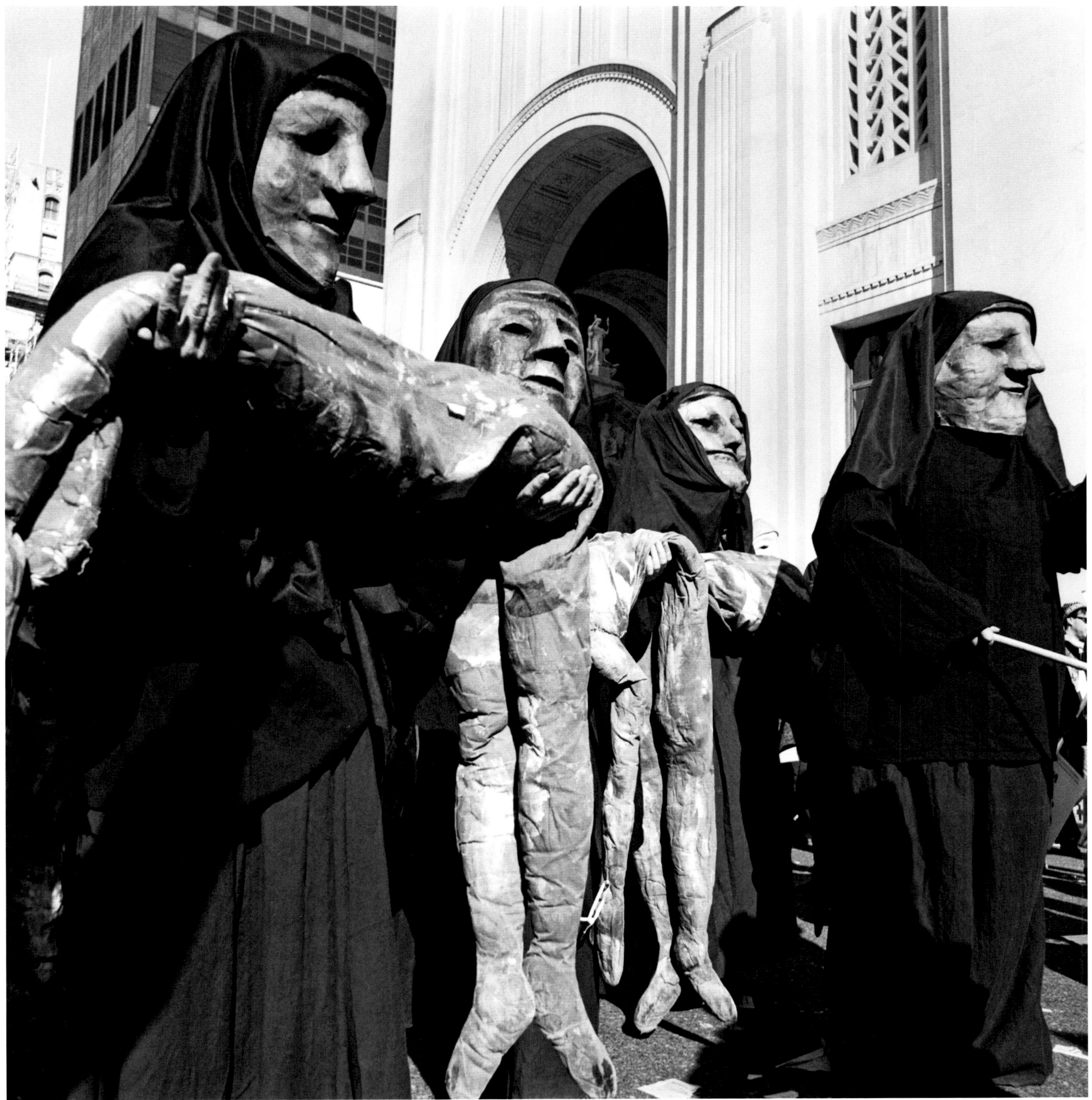

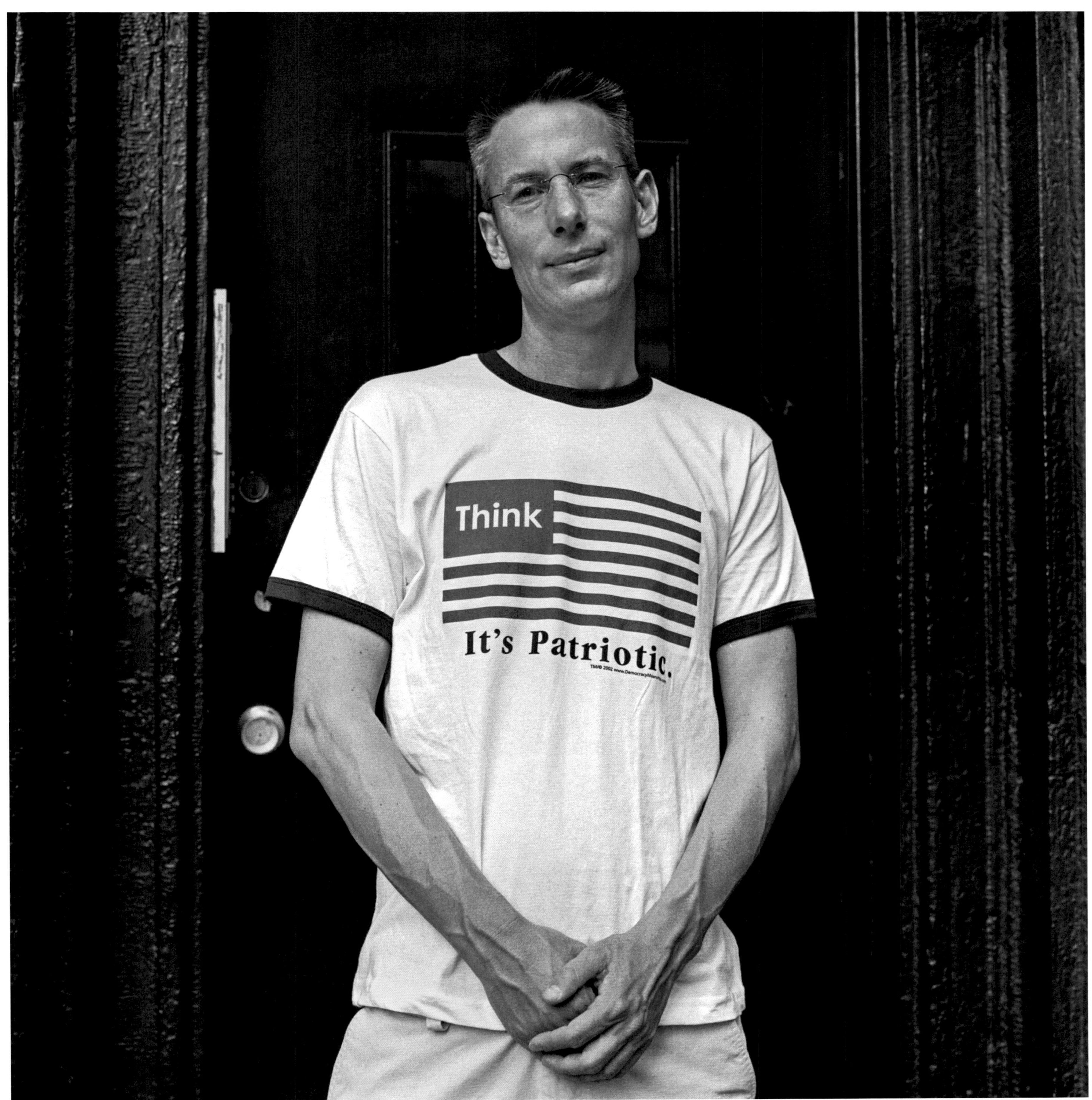
Think
It's Patriotic.

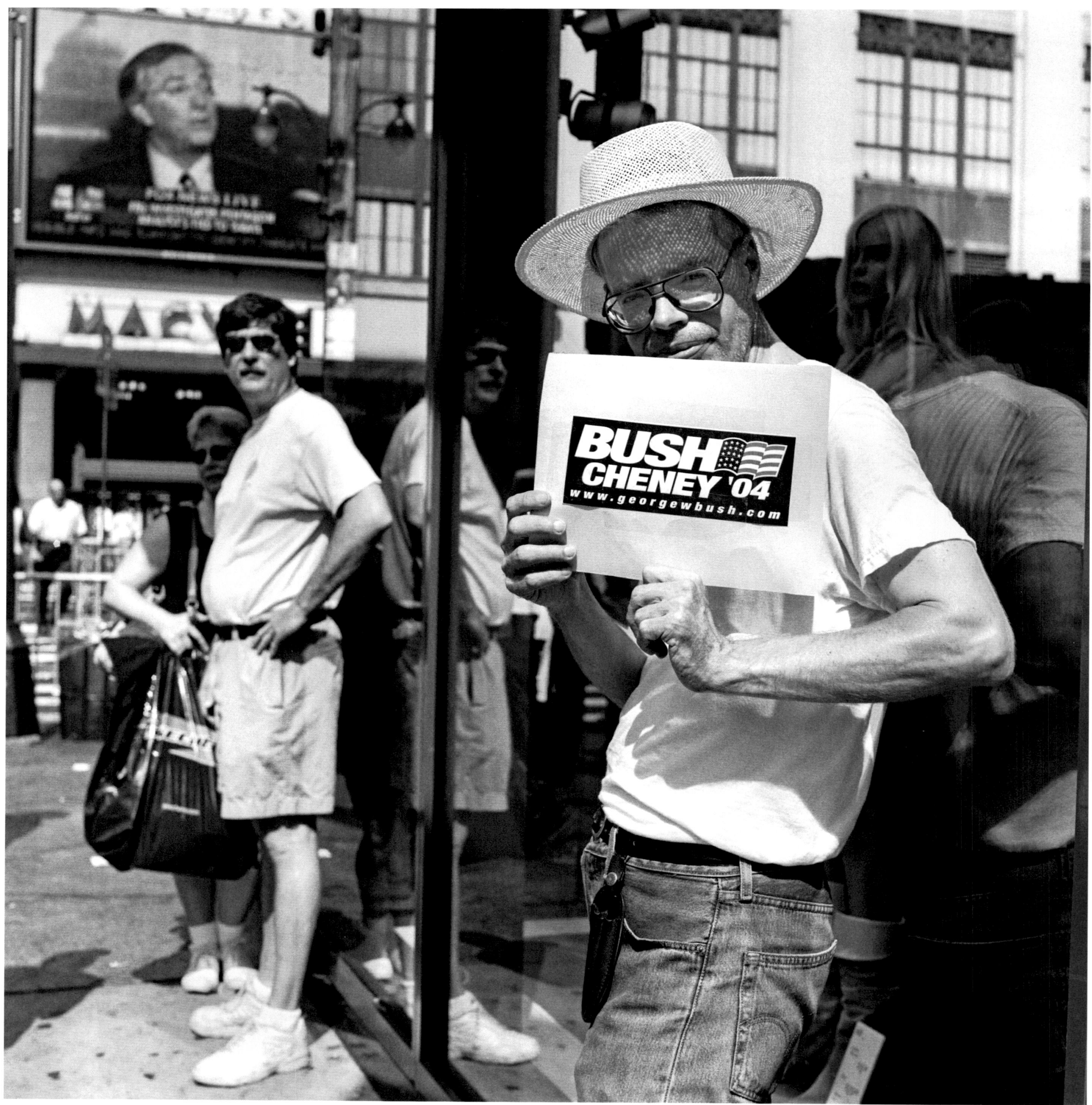
BUSH
CHENEY '04
www.georgewbush.com

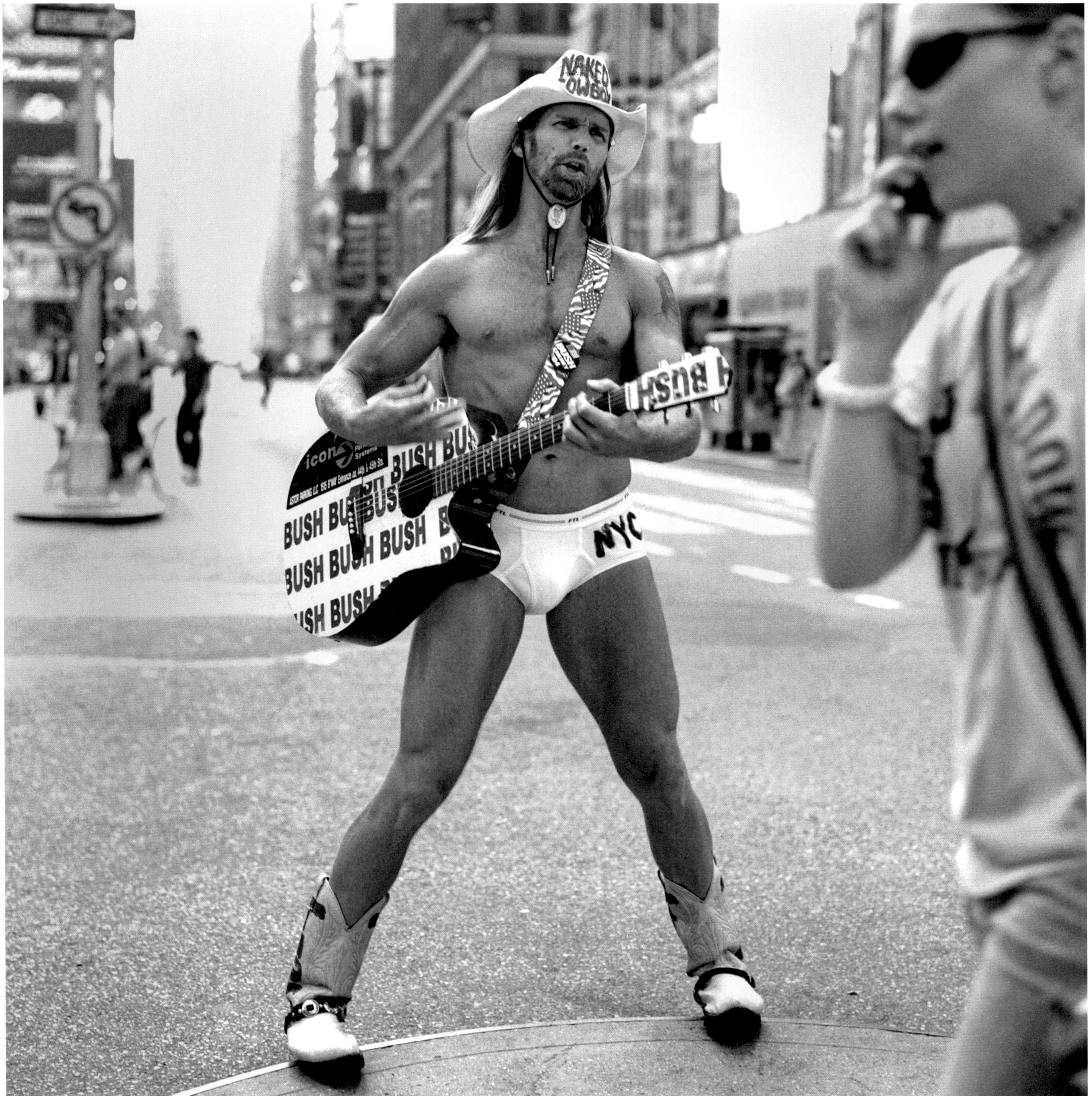
NAKED
icon
BUSH BUSH
BUSH BUSH BUSH
BUSH BUSH
BUSH
NYC

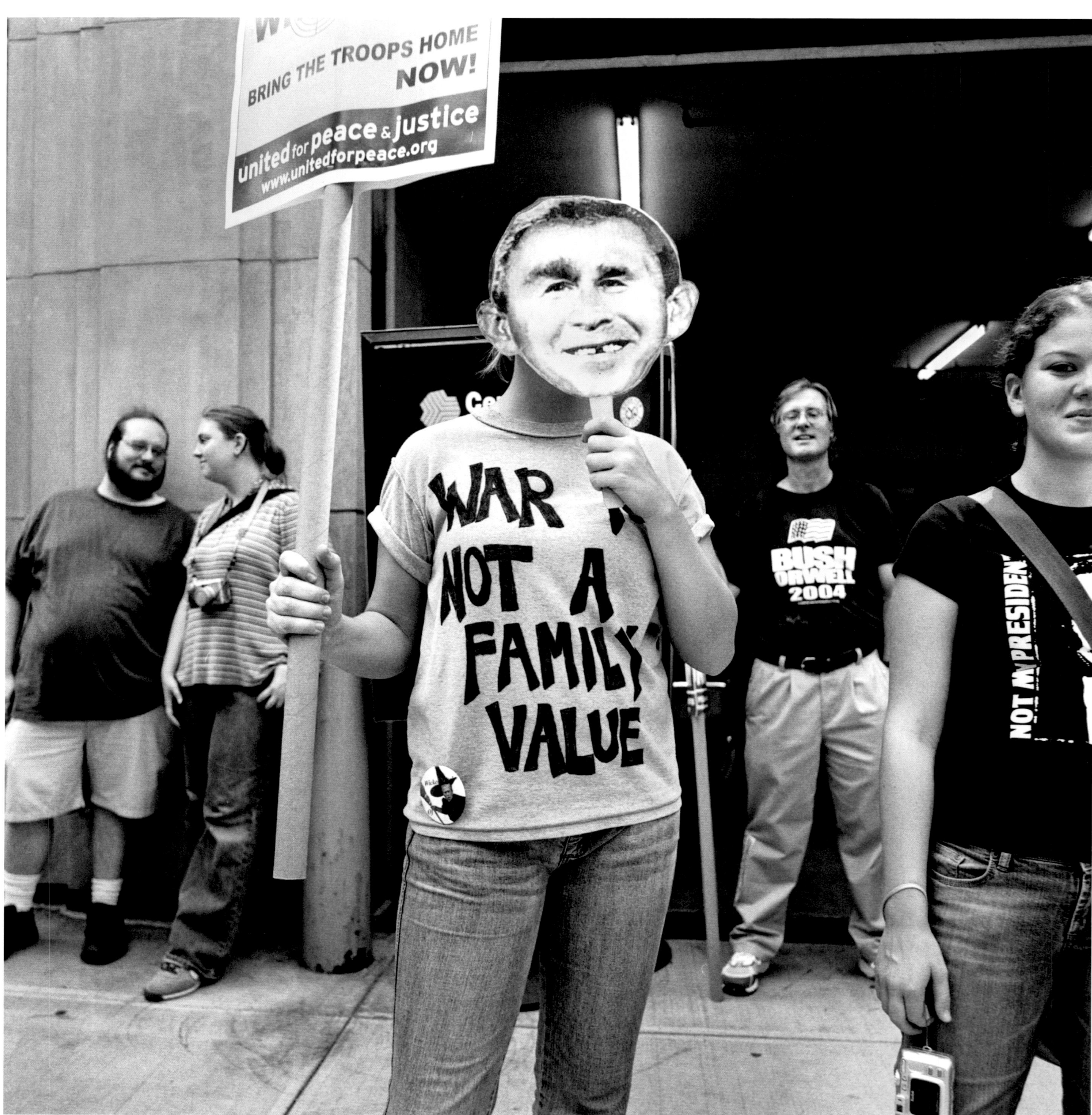
BRING THE TROOPS HOME
NOW!
united for peace & justice
www.unitedforpeace.org
WAR
NOT A
FAMILY
VALUE
BUSH
ORWELL
2004
NOT MY PRESIDEN

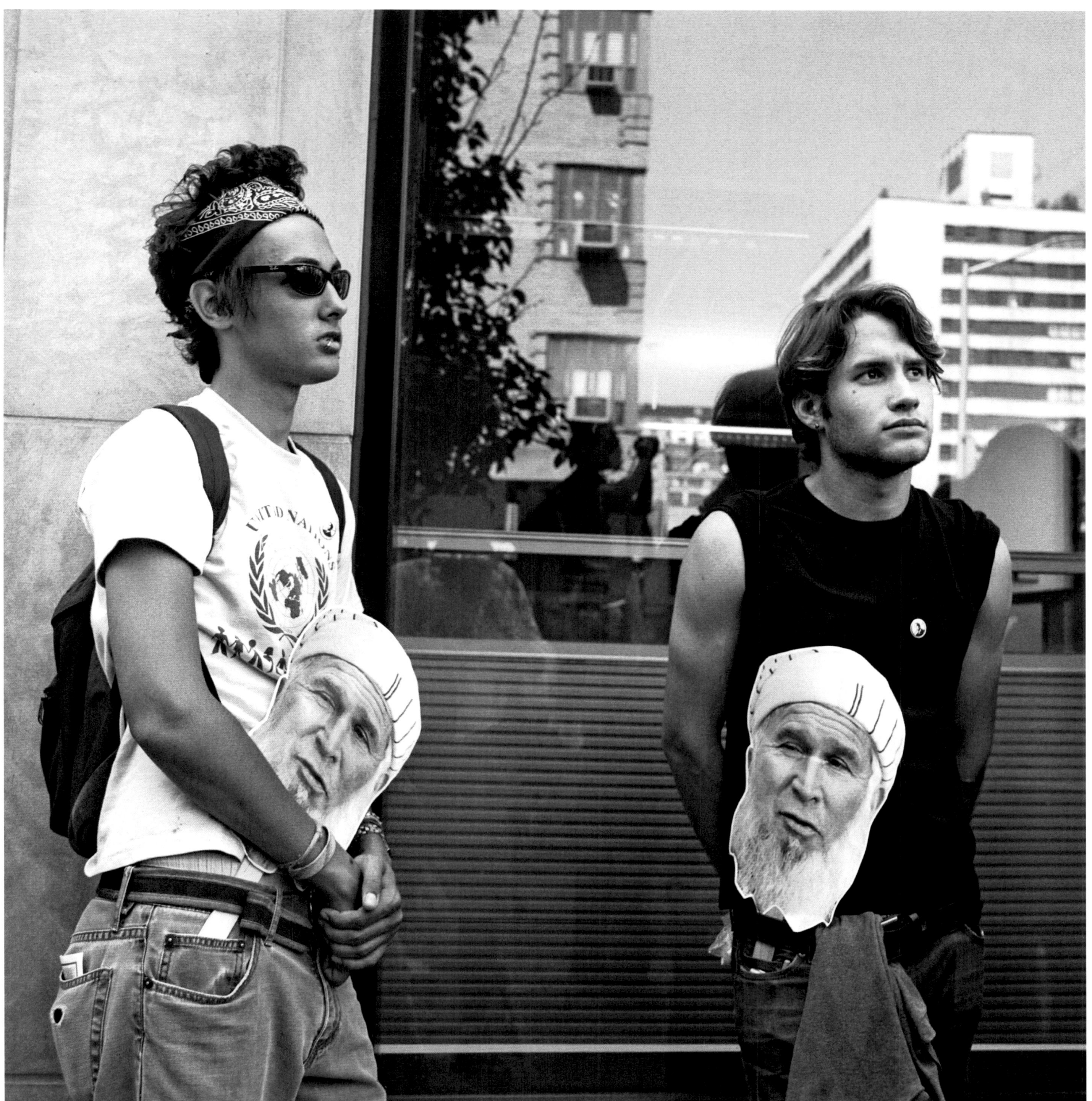

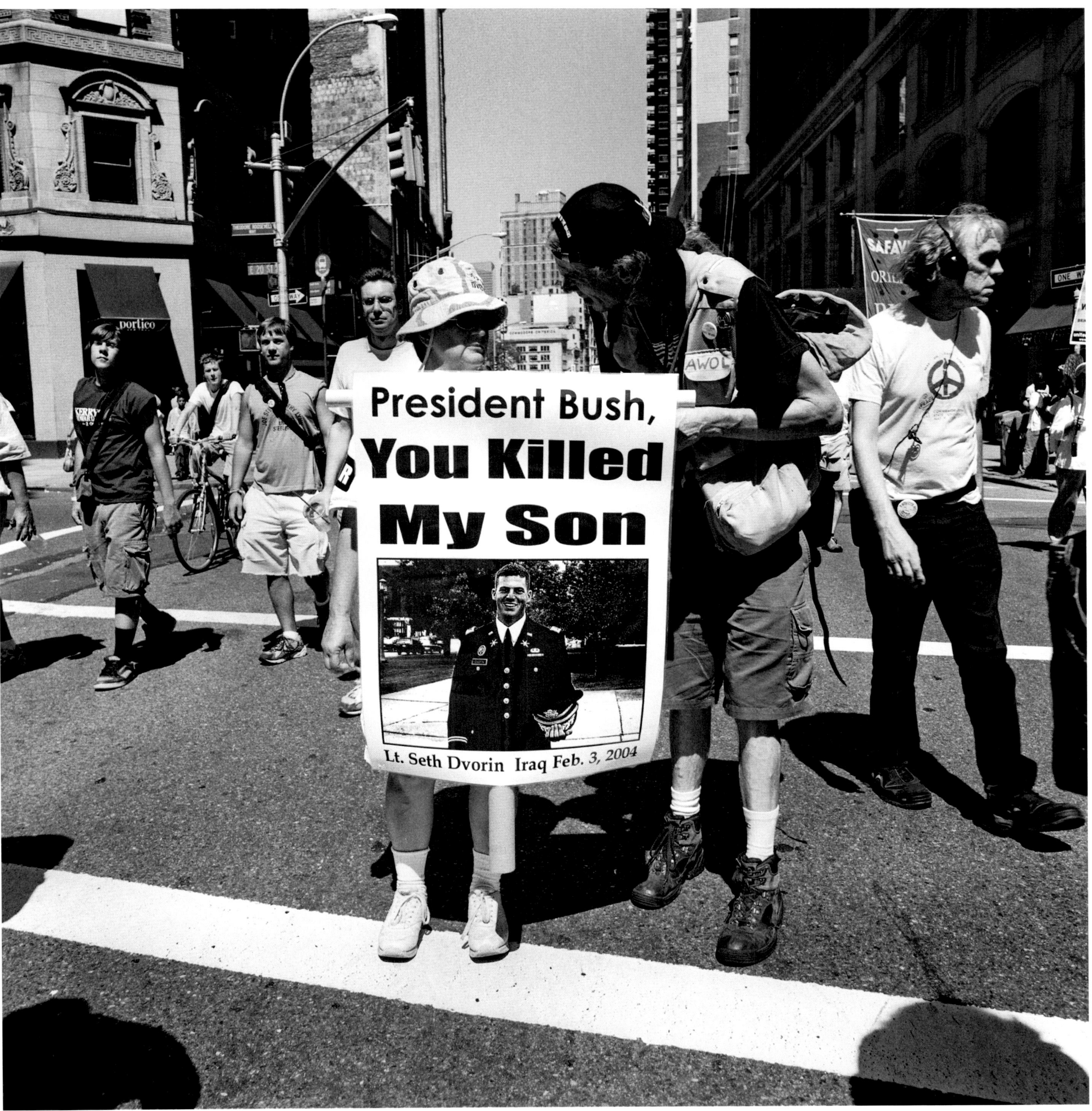
President Bush,
You Killed
My Son
Lt. Seth Dvorin Iraq Feb. 3, 2004
portico
AWOL

Bennington, Vermont, November 19, 2004
Vermont National Guard Deployment

Men and women of the Vermont National Guard gathered in the evening in the Bennington Armory with their families, sweethearts, children, parents, and grandparents as they made final adjustments, packing their duffle bags and preparing for their nine-month deployment to Iraq and Kuwait. There was a mix of eager anticipation and excitement along with sadness and worry as families awaited the moment of separation that night. The National Guard service members boarded buses and left Bennington in darkness, the streets quiet except for the sporadic sound of supporters' car horns and the cheers as the busses passed.

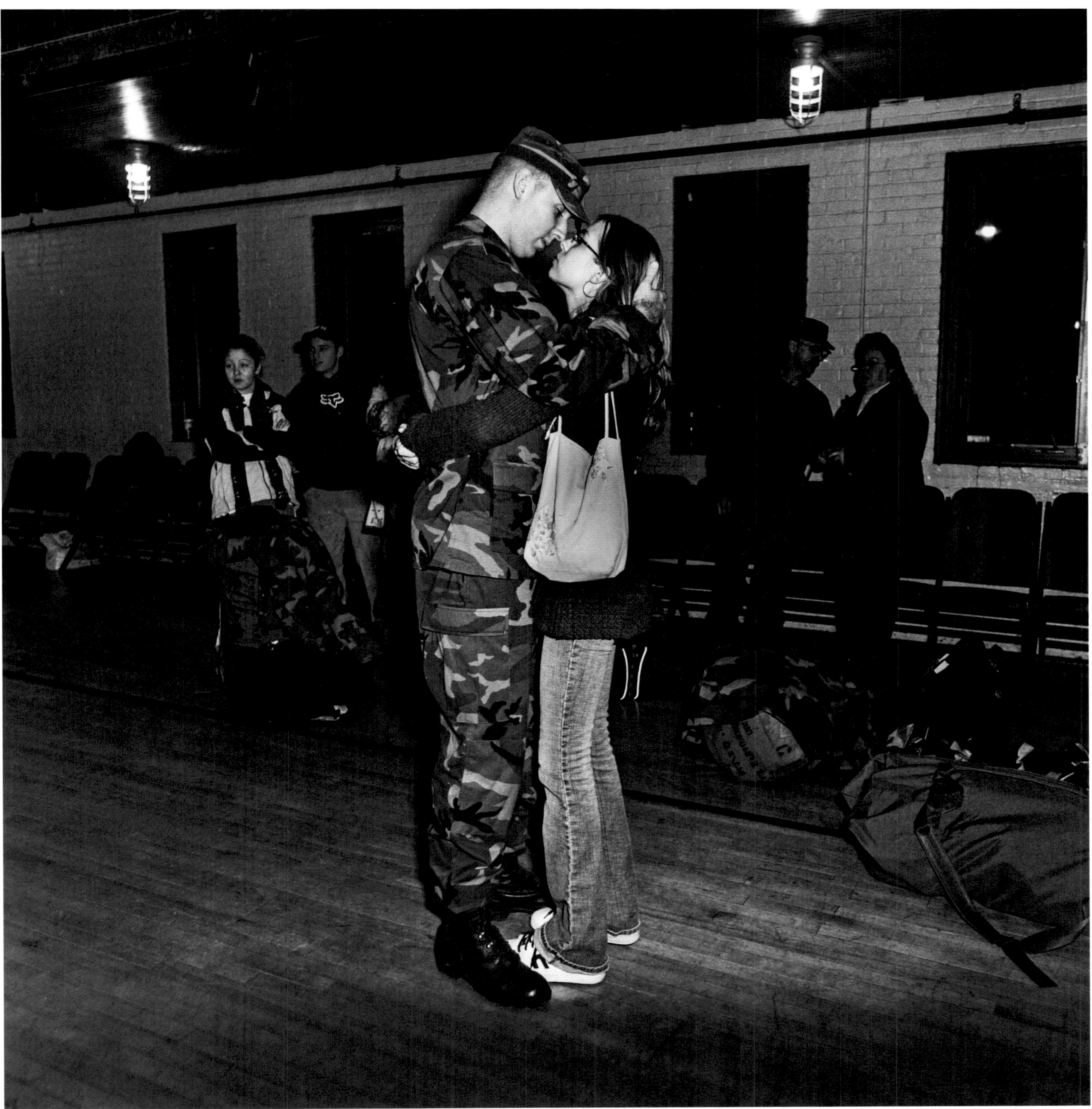

Washington, D.C., January 20, 2005

Inauguration of George W. Bush

Security seemed heightened on this inauguration day. Phalanxes of heavily armored police lined the streets and kept protesters cordoned off into small groups. Privileged guests were screened and scanned and allowed into the secured viewing areas while all others were kept at a great distance from the event. Many spectators were denied access to the viewing areas through efforts by demonstrators to clog the security operations. Reports say that 13,000 police, soldiers, and snipers guarded the parade route. A one-hundred-block area of downtown Washington, D.C. was closed to traffic, while the skies were patrolled by helicopters and fighter aircraft. Despite such a heavy security presence there were fewer than a dozen arrests.

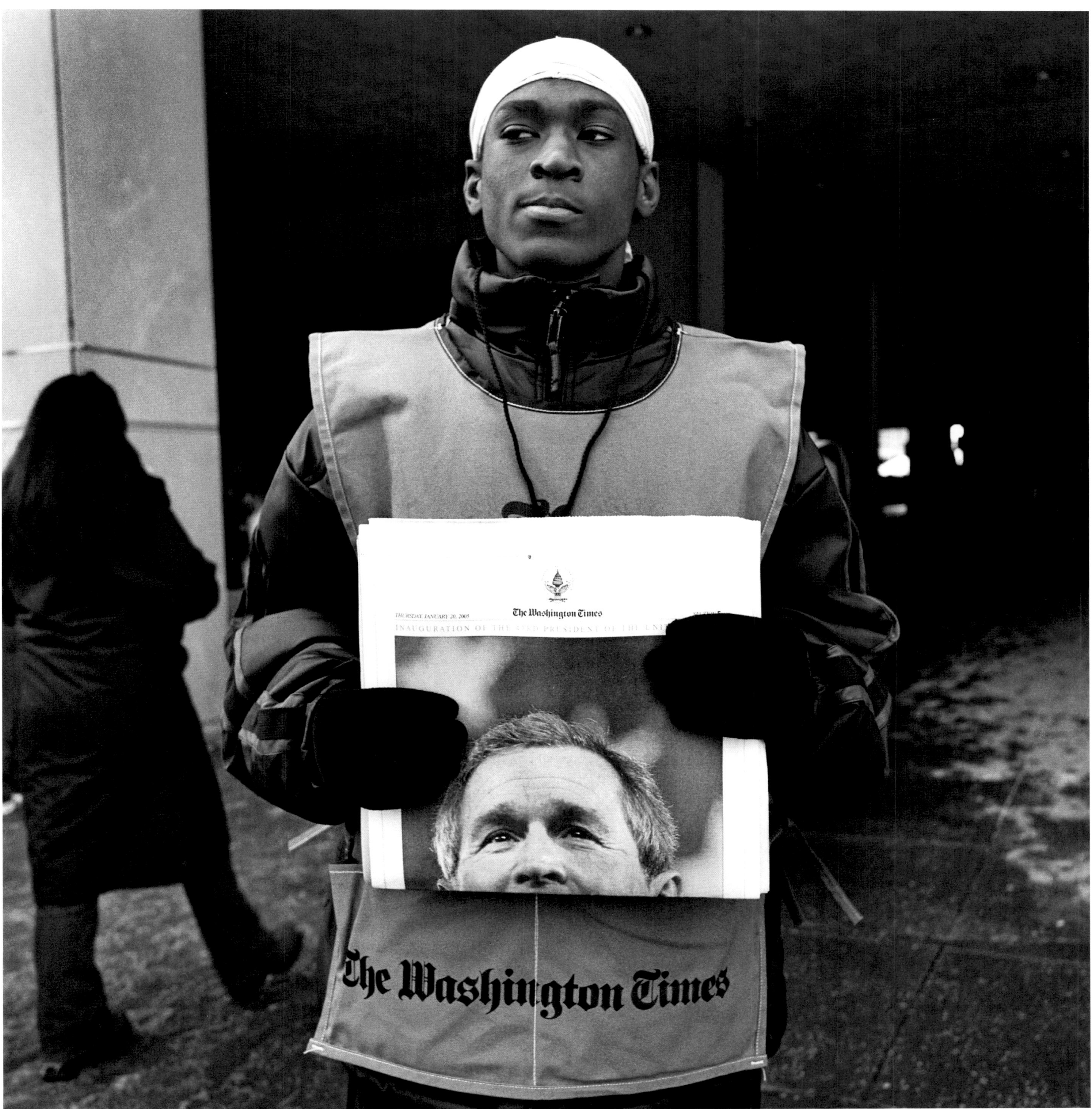
The Washington Times
THURSDAY, JANUARY 20, 2005
The Washington Times

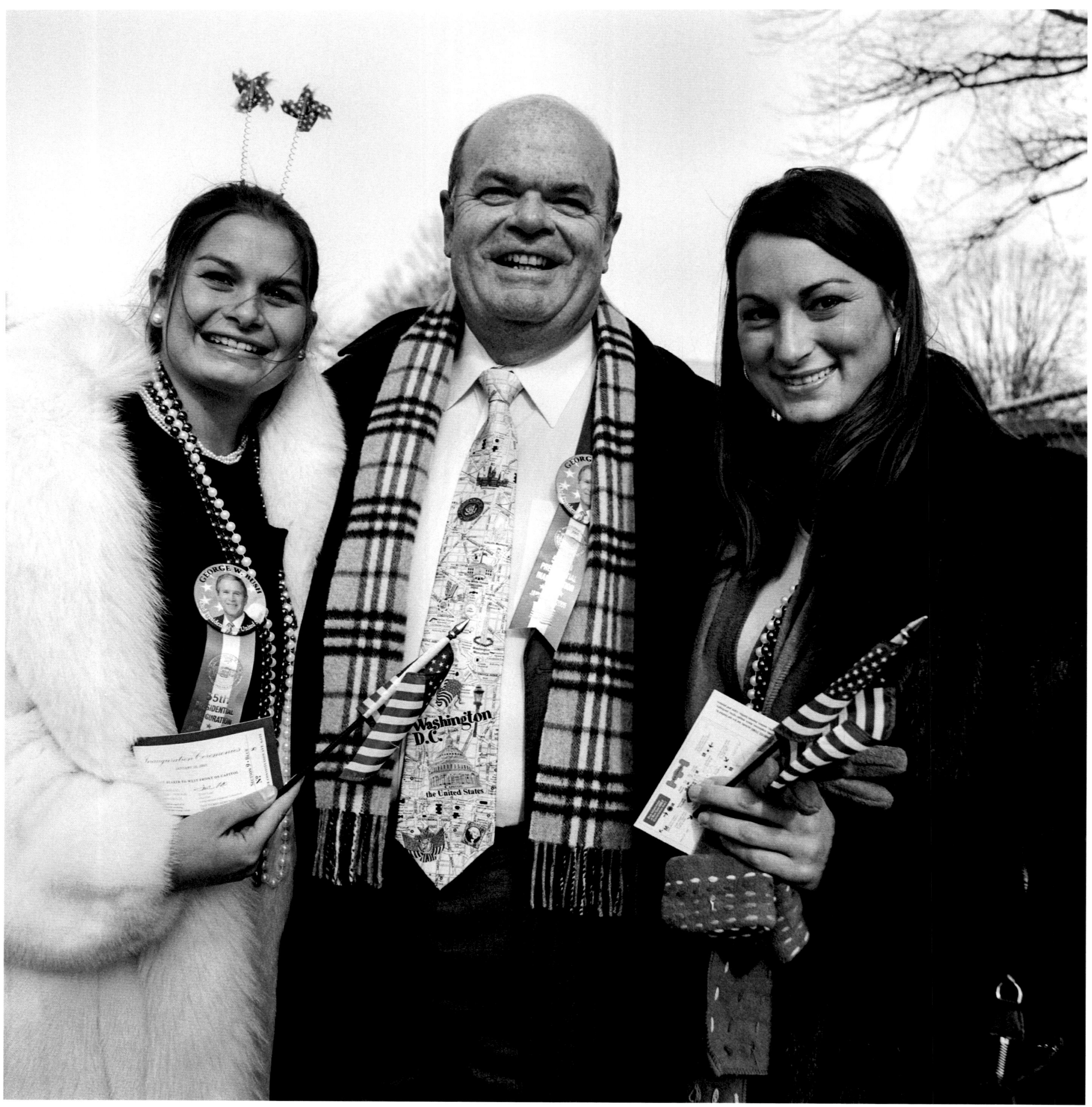
GEORGE W. BUSH
Washington
D.C.
the United States

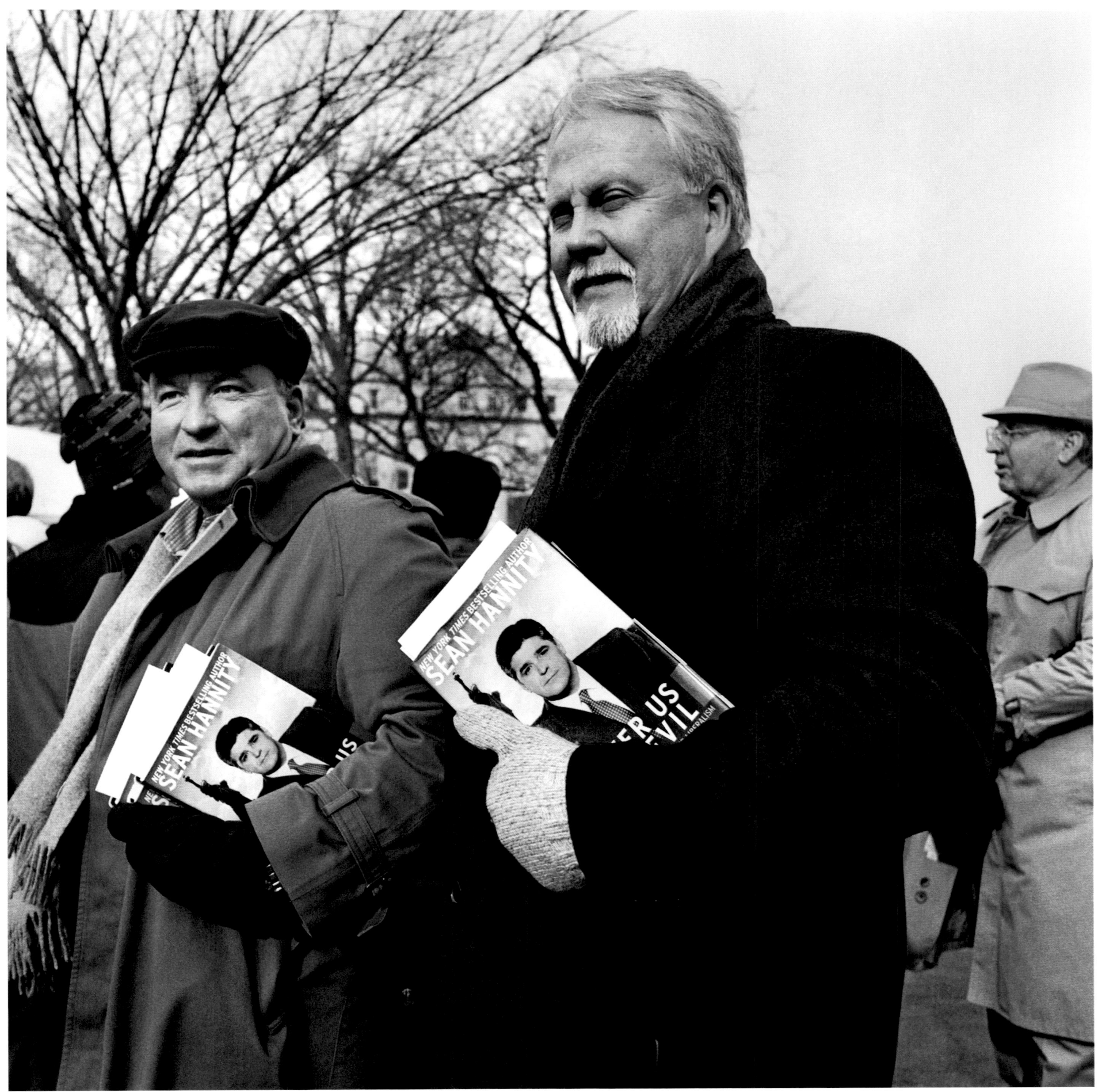
NEW YORK TIMES BESTSELLING AUTHOR
SEAN HANNITY
NEW YORK TIMES BESTSELLING AUTHOR
SEAN HANNITY

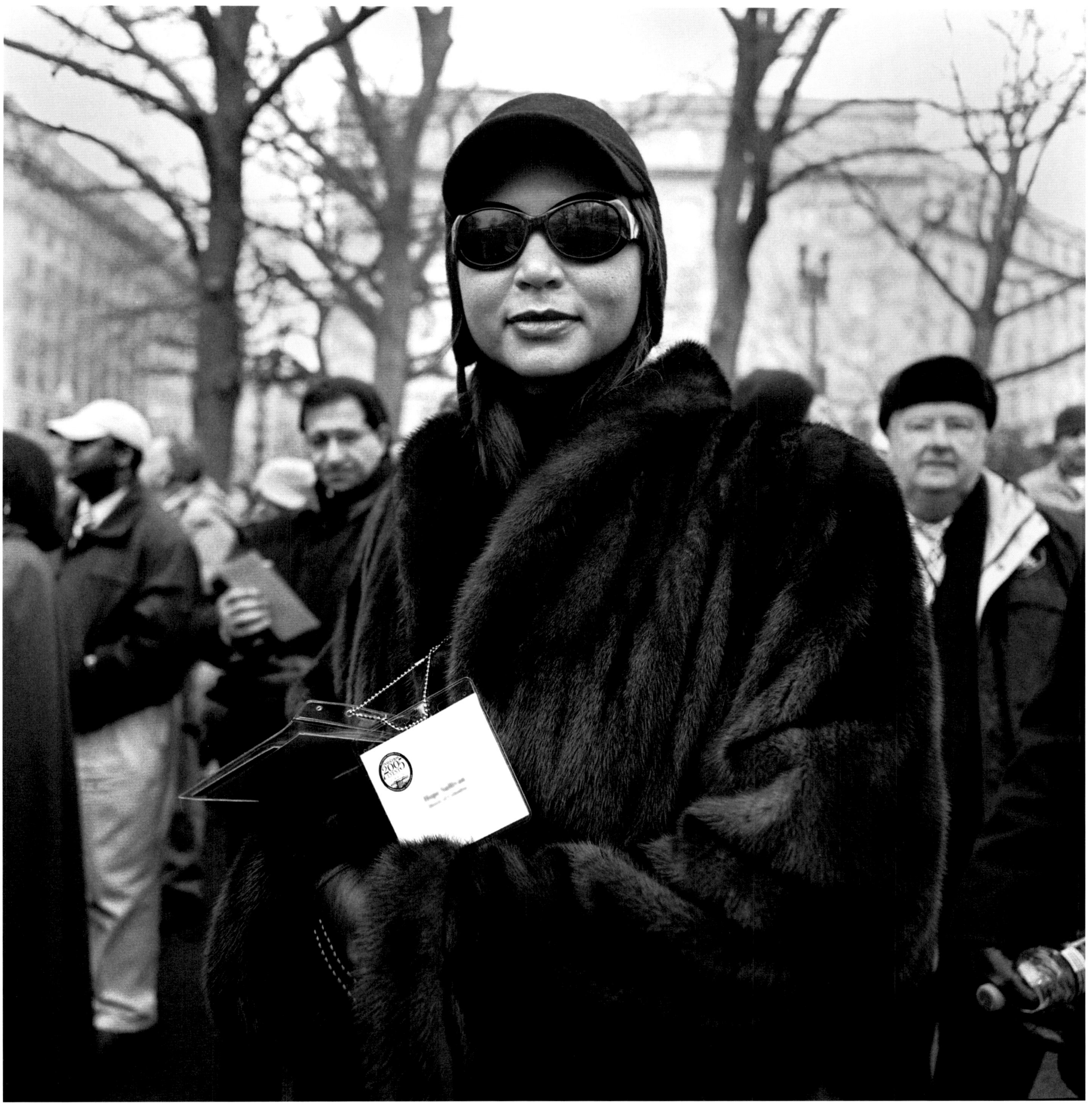

Washington, D.C., September 24, 2005

Anti-War March

Police estimates put the number of demonstrators at 150,000, while organizers of the massive march claimed that 300,000 supporters had come to Washington. Well represented were the peace and anti-war groups Veterans for Peace, Military Families Speak Out, United for Peace and Justice, and the ANSWER Coalition (Act Now to Stop War and End Racism). Many mothers and fathers marched with poster-sized portraits of sons and daughters killed in action in the Iraq War, bringing a wrenching specificity to the grave losses of the war.

"I marched and protested as a retired Navy captain because on October 12, 1956, I swore 'to protect, preserve, and defend the Constitution of the United States from all enemies both foreign and domestic,'" Andrew C. Schoerke, a Vermont veteran said. "Bush's unprovoked attack on Iraq was a direct violation of Article VI of the Constitution which states that 'all treaties made or which shall be made…shall be the supreme law of the land.' The attack, invasion, and occupation of Iraq were a clear violation. I was arrested along with nearly 400 other activists on the sidewalk outside the White House. As I was being handcuffed the arresting officer said to me, under his breath, 'If I wasn't doing this, I would be with you.'"

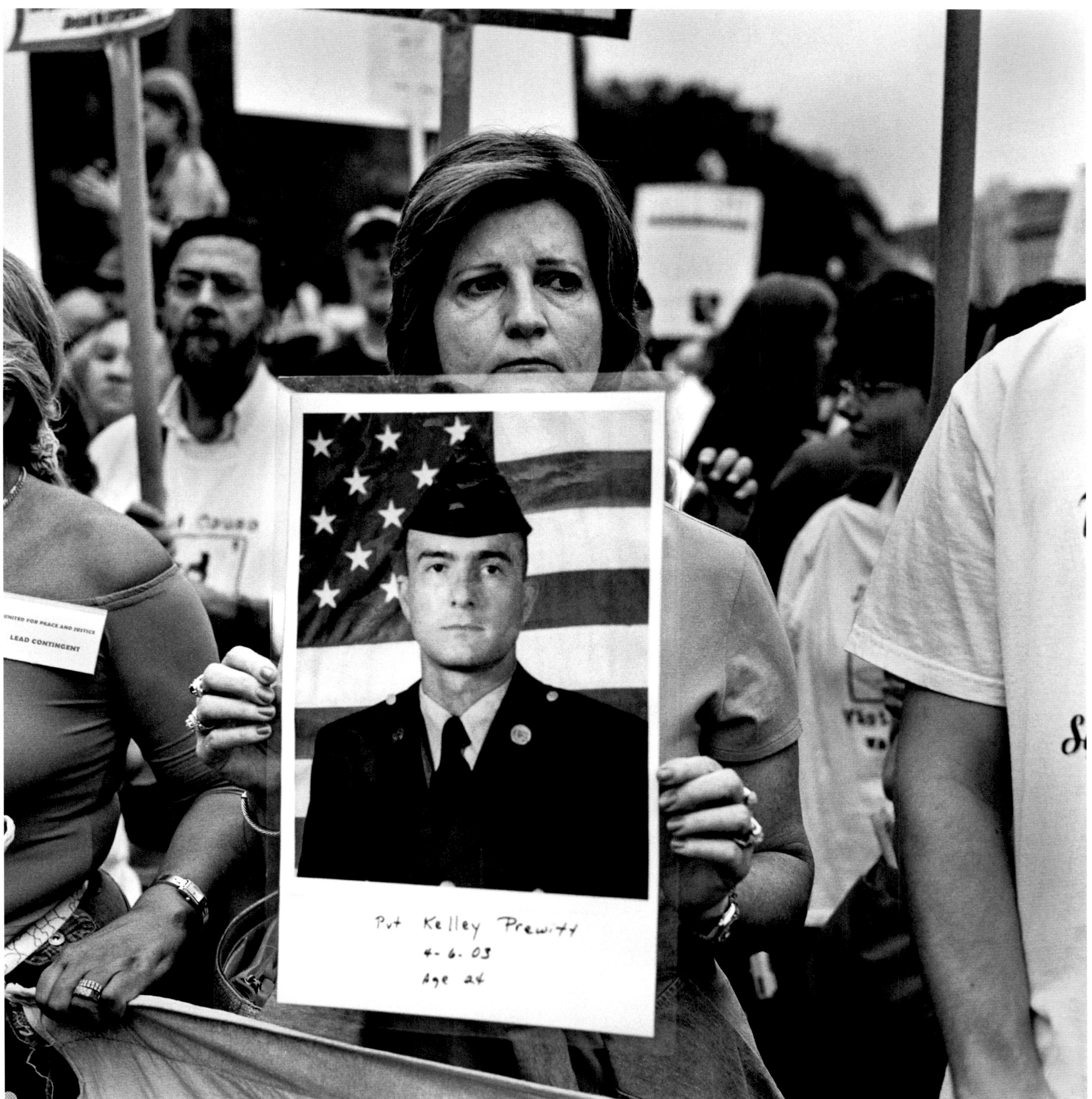
UNITED FOR PEACE AND JUSTICE
LEAD CONTINGENT
Pvt Kelley Prewitt
4-6-03
Age 24

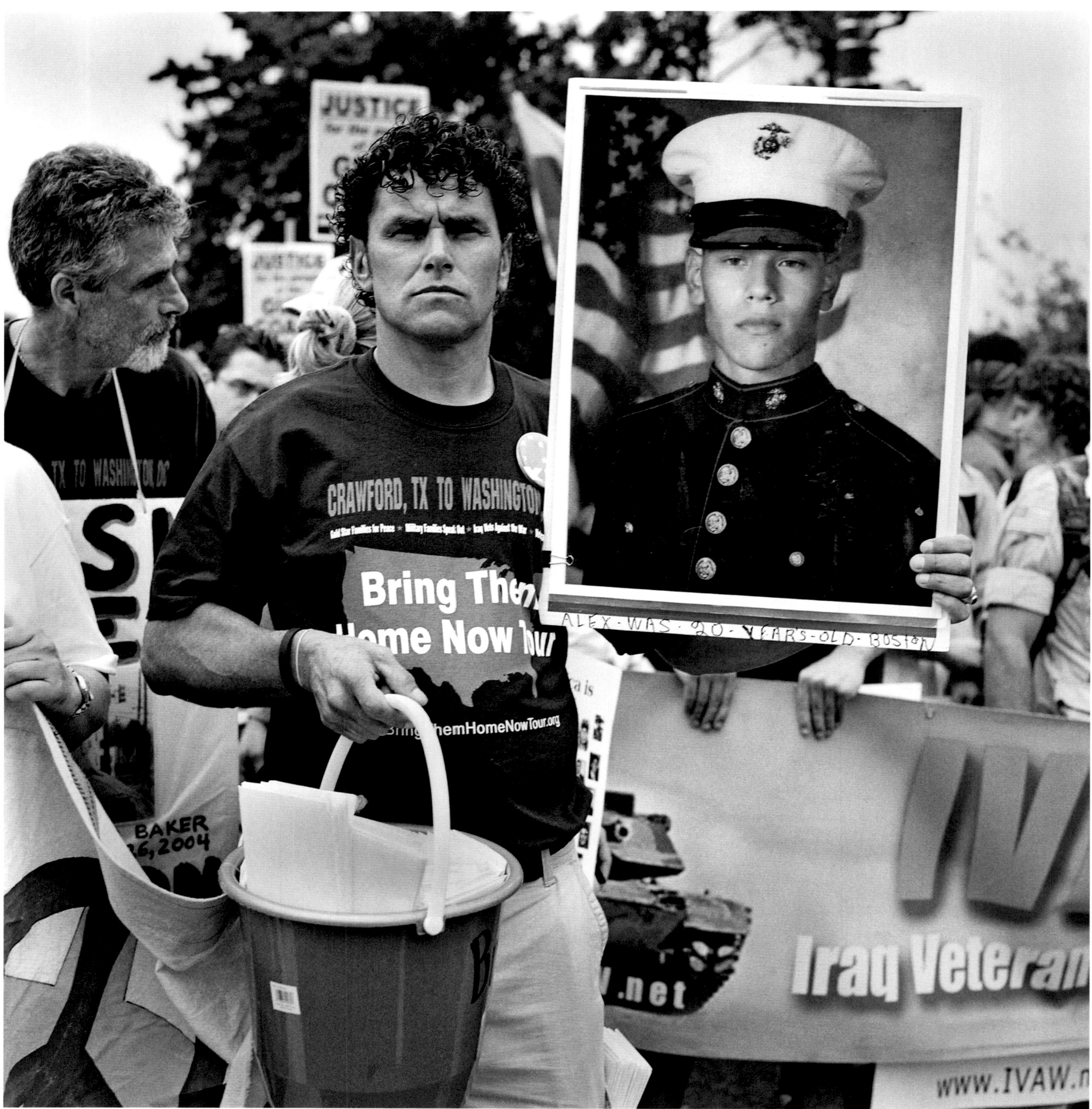
JUSTICE
CRAWFORD, TX TO WASHINGTO
Bring The
ome Now Tou
ALEX · WAS · 20 · YEARS · OLD · BOSTON
BAKER
26, 2004
Iraq Veteran
www.IVAW.n

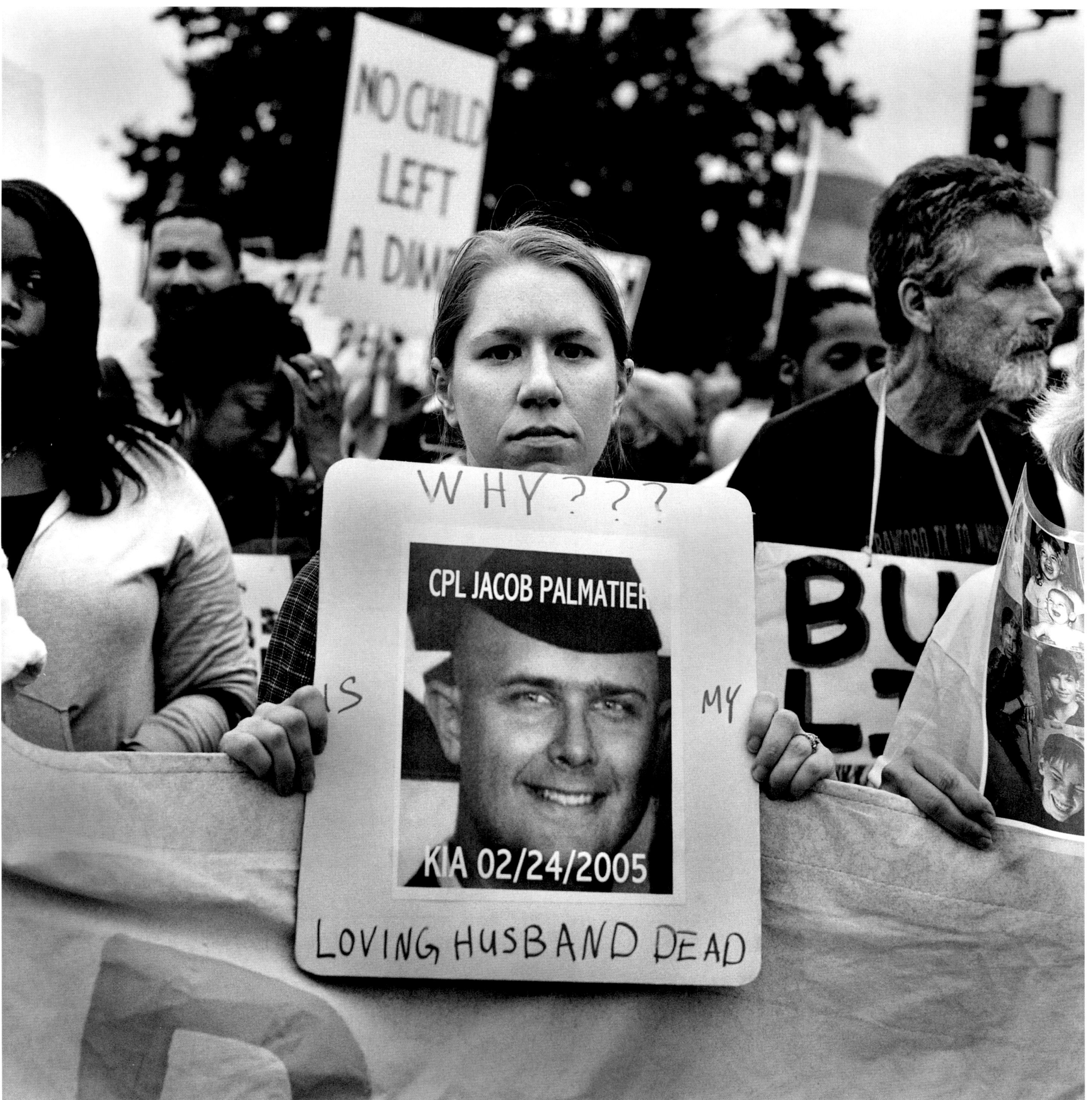
NO CHILD
LEFT
A DIM
WHY???
CPL JACOB PALMATIER
IS
MY
KIA 02/24/2005
LOVING HUSBAND DEAD

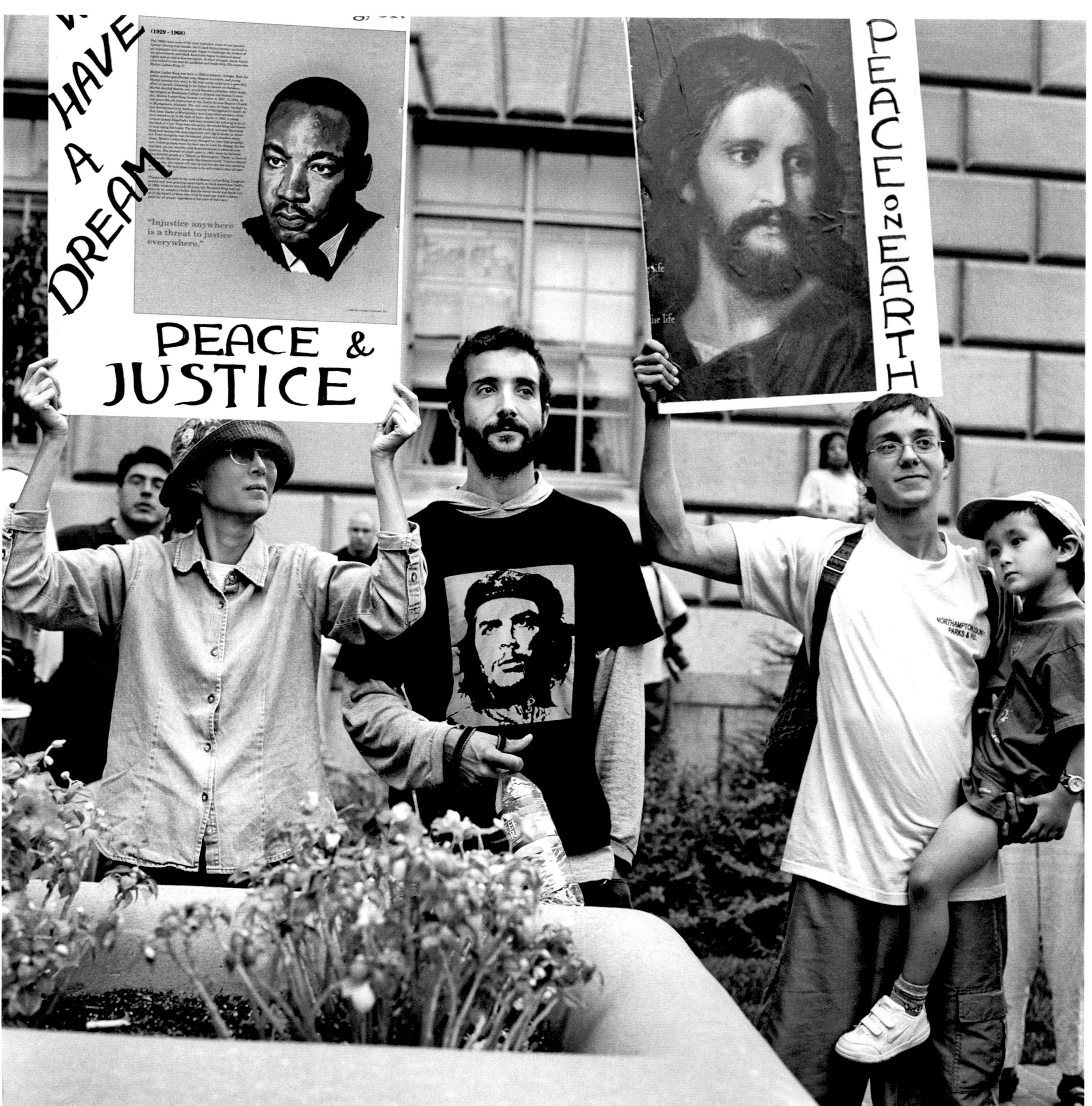
HAVE
A
DREAM
(1929 - 1968)
"Injustice anywhere is a threat to justice everywhere."
PEACE &
JUSTICE
PEACE ON EARTH

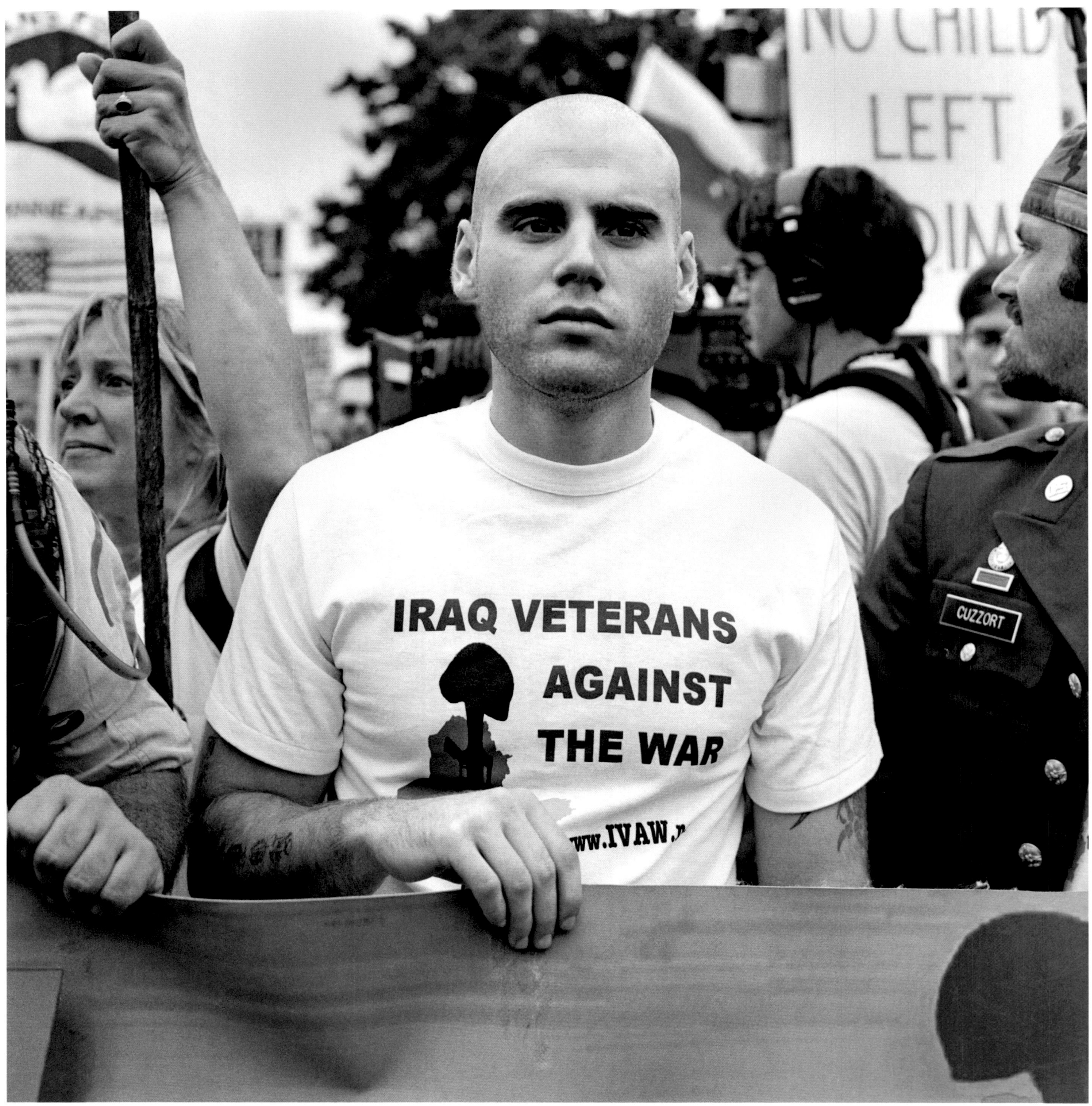
NO CHILD
LEFT
IRAQ VETERANS
AGAINST
THE WAR
CUZZORT

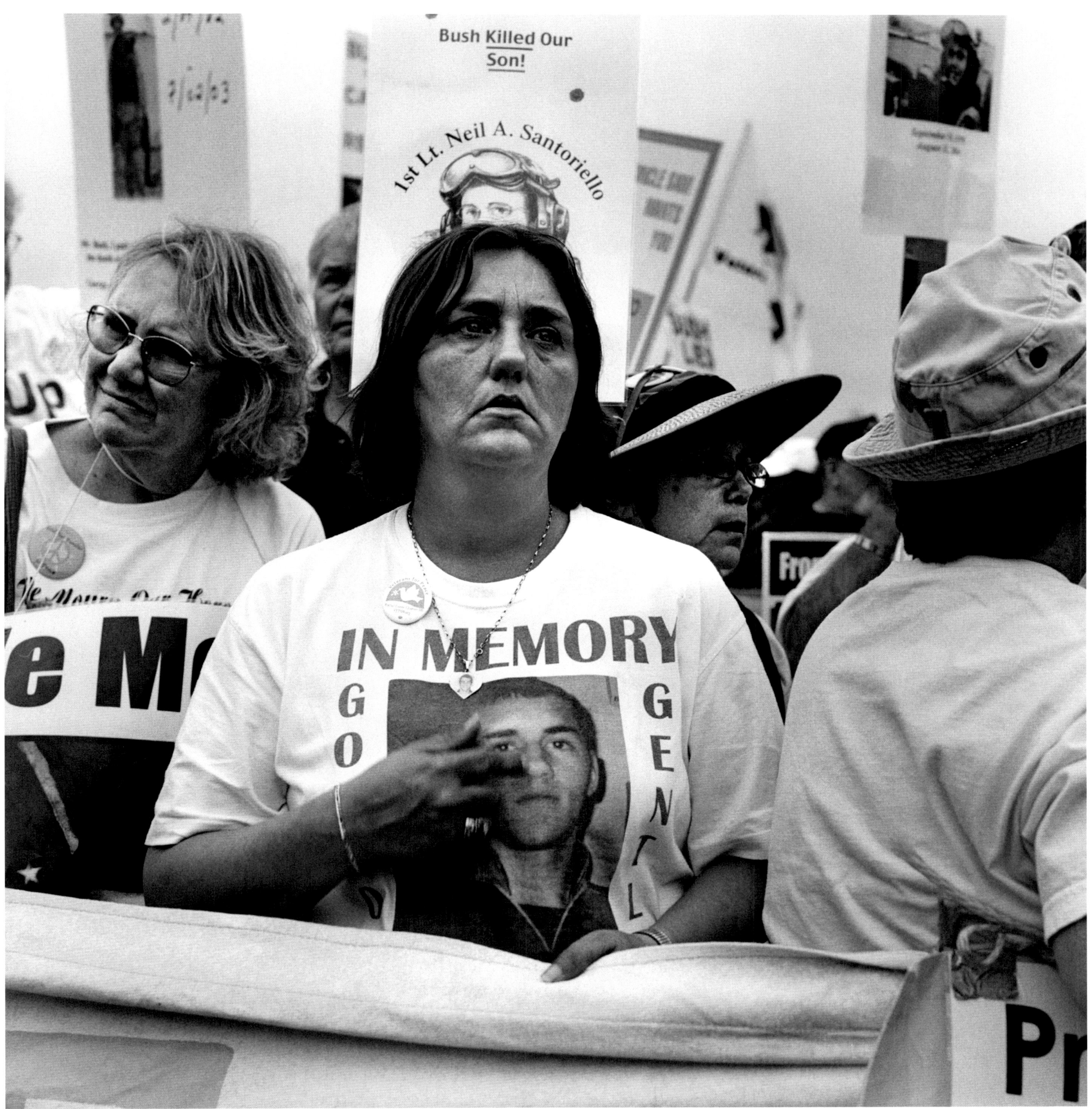
Bush Killed Our Son!
1st Lt. Neil A. Santoriello
IN MEMORY
GO GO GENTL

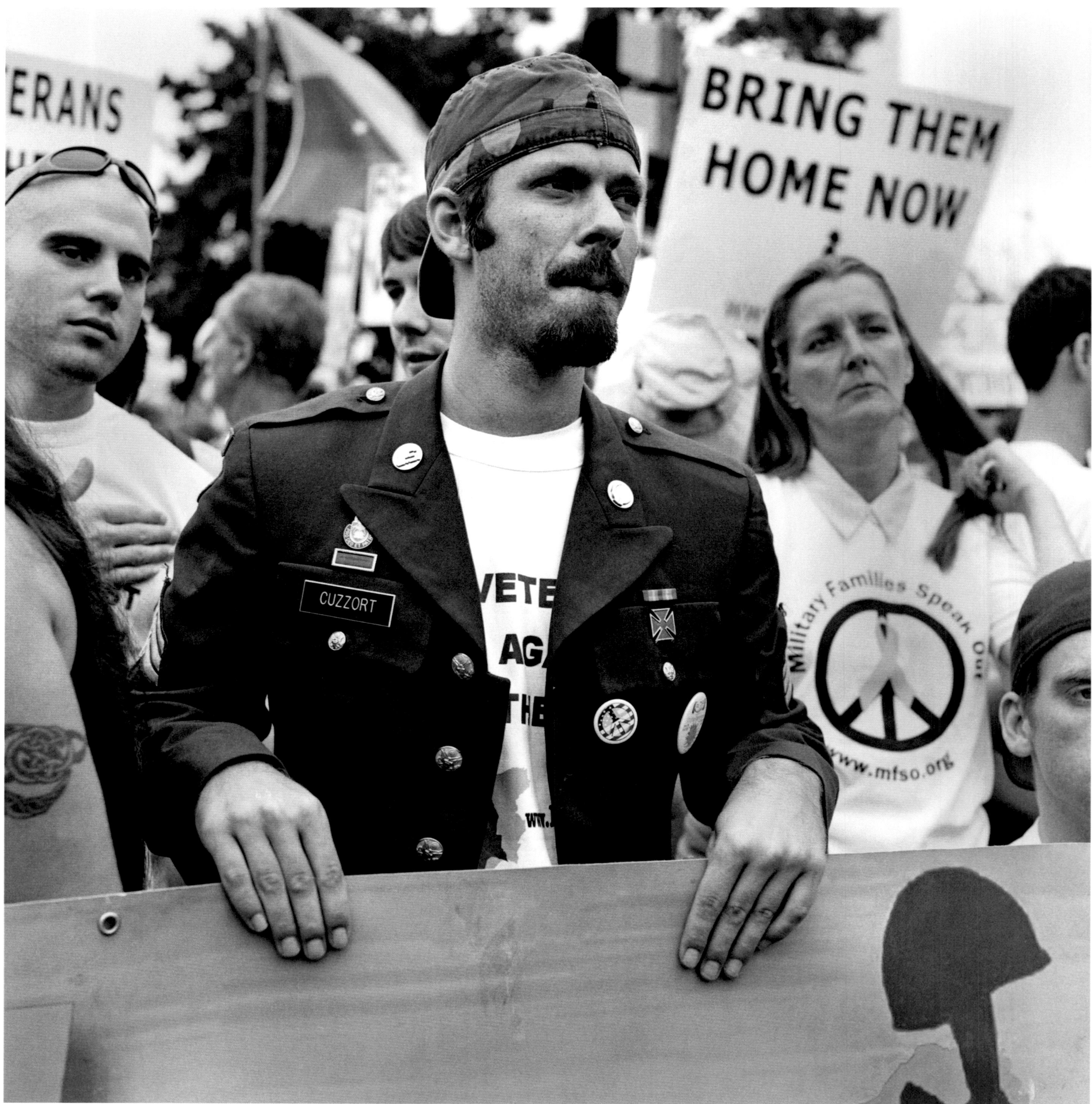
ERANS
BRING THEM HOME NOW
CUZZORT
Military Families Speak Out
www.mfso.org

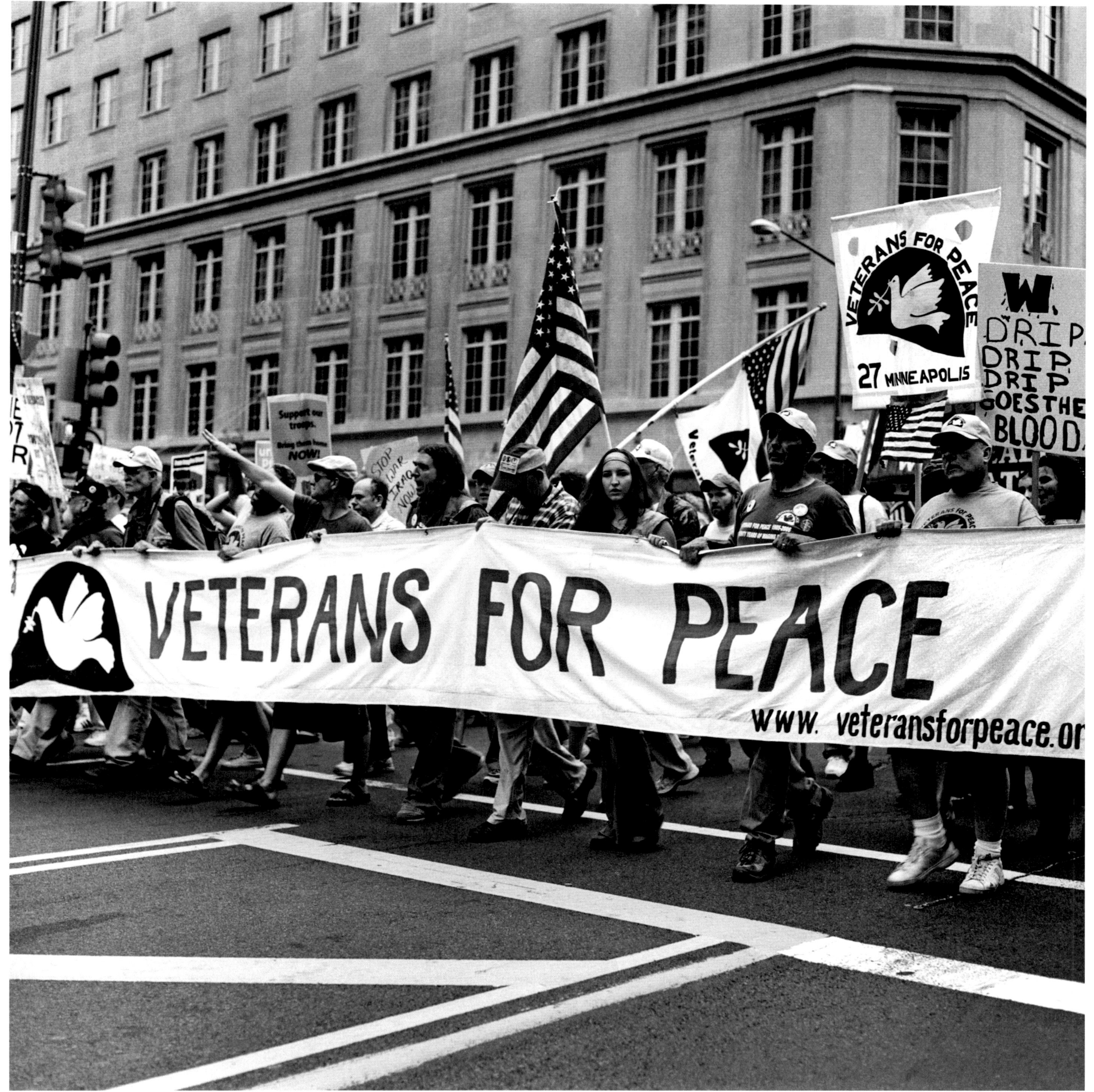
VETERANS FOR PEACE
27 MINNEAPOLIS
W.
DRIP
DRIP
DRIP
GOESTHE
BLOOD
Support our troops.
NOW!
VETERANS FOR PEACE
www. veteransforpeace.or

Rutland, Vermont, March 18, 2006

Peace Demonstration

A group of mostly older men and women gathered with their signboards on this cold Saturday in late winter, along Vermont Route 7 in downtown Rutland, to show their anger at President Bush, their opposition to the Iraq War, and their compassion for the Iraqi people and our servicemen and women. Almost half a century earlier, many of them had protested against the Vietnam War as well; some were veterans of that war.

The week earlier, an hour-and-a-half drive away in the village of Newfane, Vermont, during the annual town meeting, secret ballots revealed a vote tally of 121 votes to 29 votes in favor of impeaching President Bush.

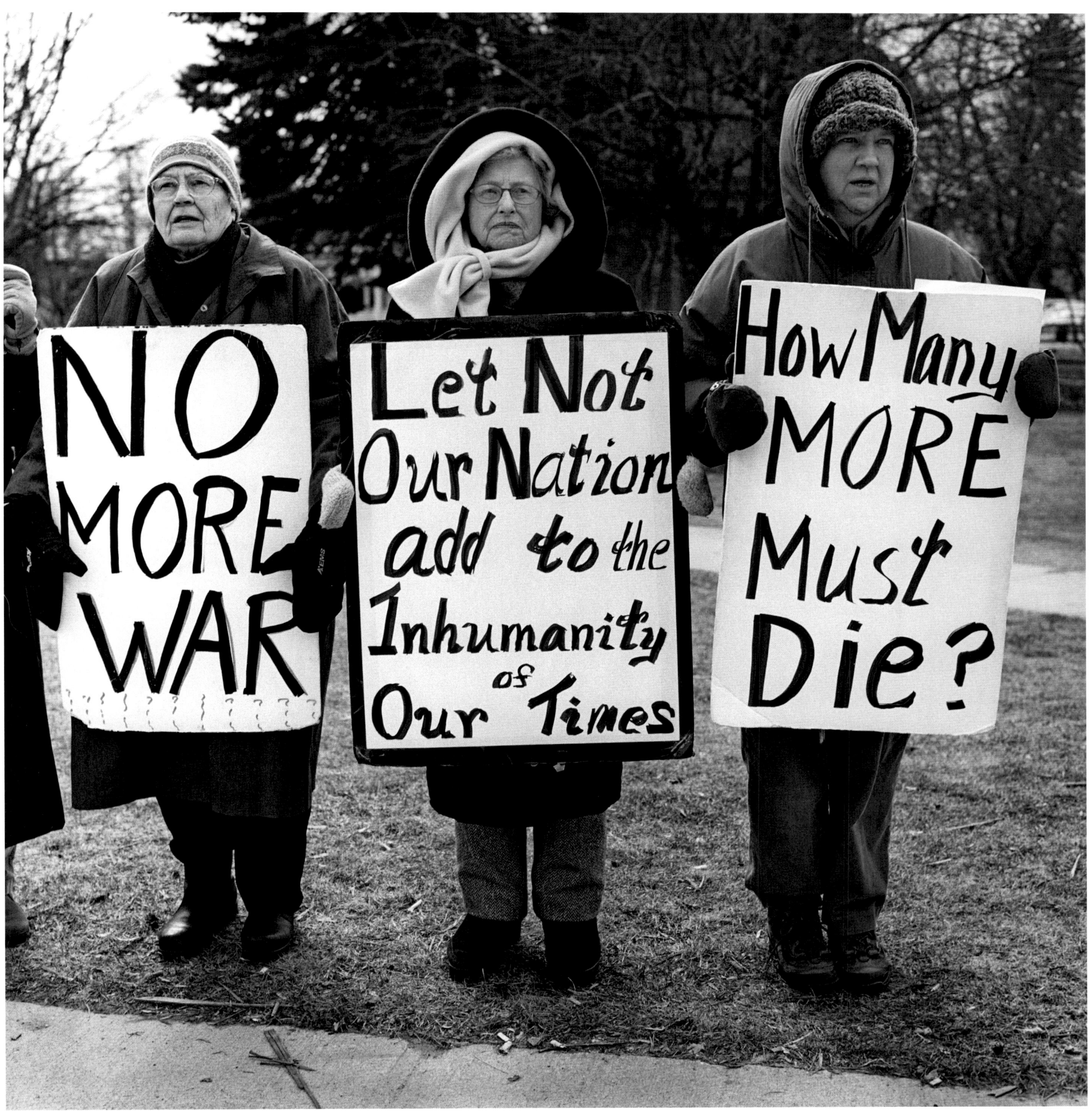
NO MORE WAR
Let Not Our Nation add to the Inhumanity of Our Times
How Many MORE Must Die?

Pittsfield, Massachusetts, July 4, 2006

Fourth of July Parade

Over the decades Pittsfield native Gordon Dunham has shown up each year as Uncle Sam in the Pittsfield Fourth of July parade, an annual tradition going back to 1812. In 2008, it was listed by *USA Today* as one of the top ten Fourth of July parades in the country. For the past 40 years the parade has been coordinated by a volunteer board of directors, and before that it was run by the Pittsfield Firemens' Muster.

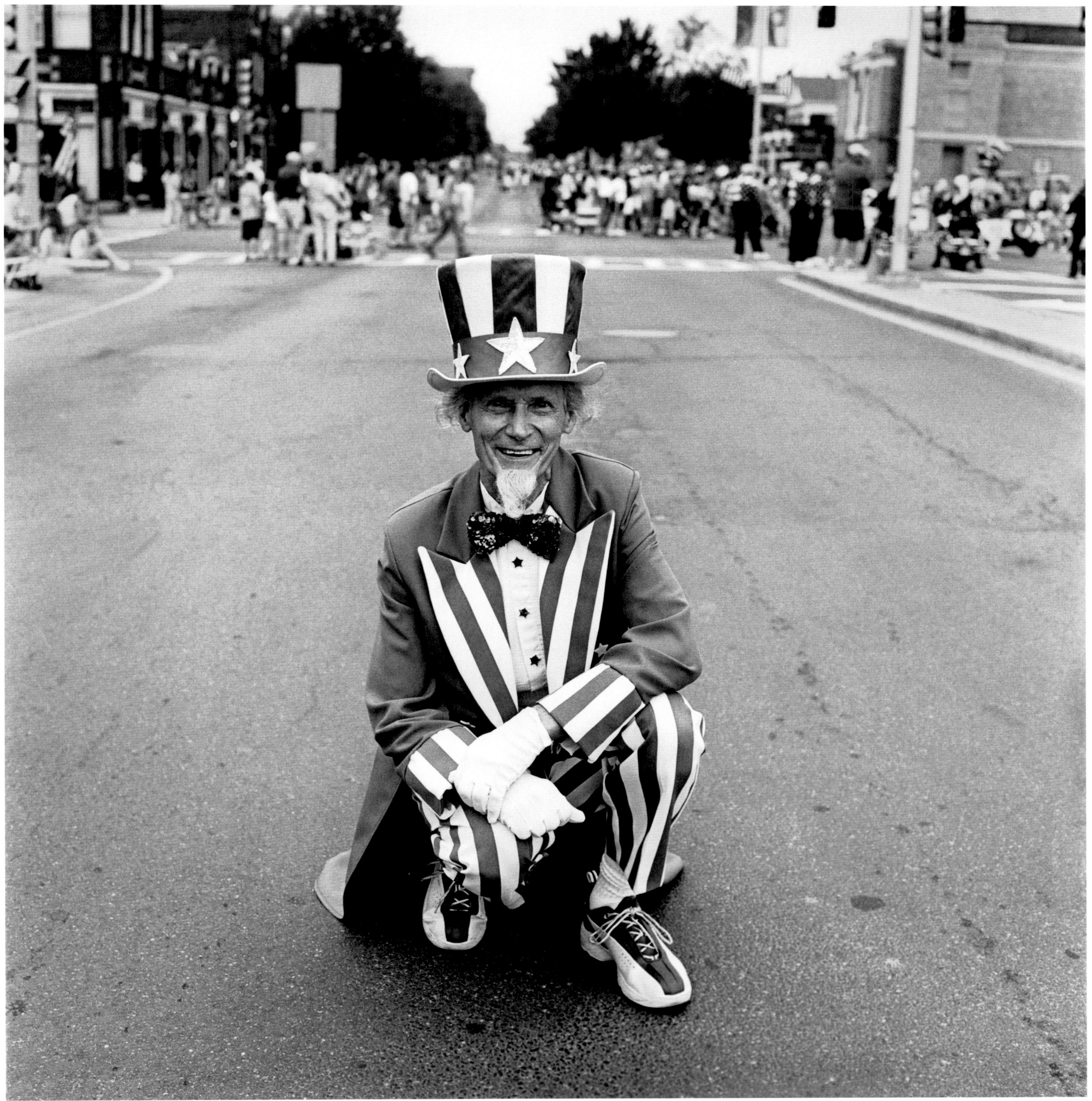

New York City, September 11, 2006

September 11 Anniversary Ceremony

A somber and orderly event in the morning united family members and friends of those who had lost their lives in the attacks five years earlier. Later in the afternoon, a large demonstration of activists promoting conspiracy theories congregated at the World Trade Center site and led a raucous march through Wall Street, unfurling banners asking who was really responsible for the September 11 attacks. Back at the World Trade Center site, the conspiracy theory activists were met by an equally large and vocal group of counter protestors yelling chants about Islamic fundamentalism. The afternoon's competing protests had a distinctly different feel from the solemnity of the morning's memorial.

The two demonstrations were emblematic of the larger political, economic, and spiritual division over the site and what would become of it. Ground zero was still an open wound, far from healed.

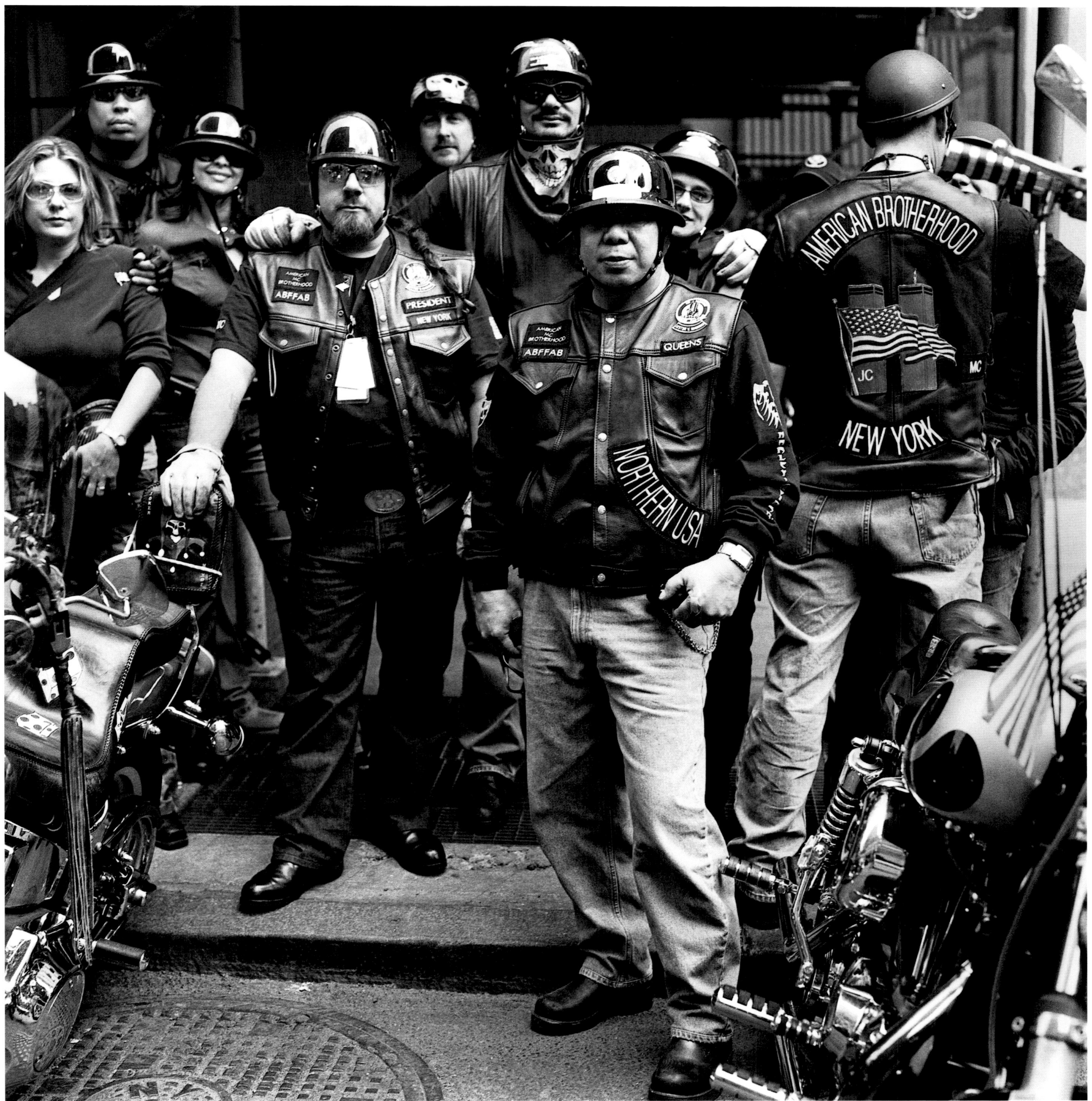
AMERICAN BROTHERHOOD
JC
MC
NEW YORK
NORTHERN USA
AMERICAN M/C BROTHERHOOD
ABFFAB
PRESIDENT
NEW YORK
QUEENS

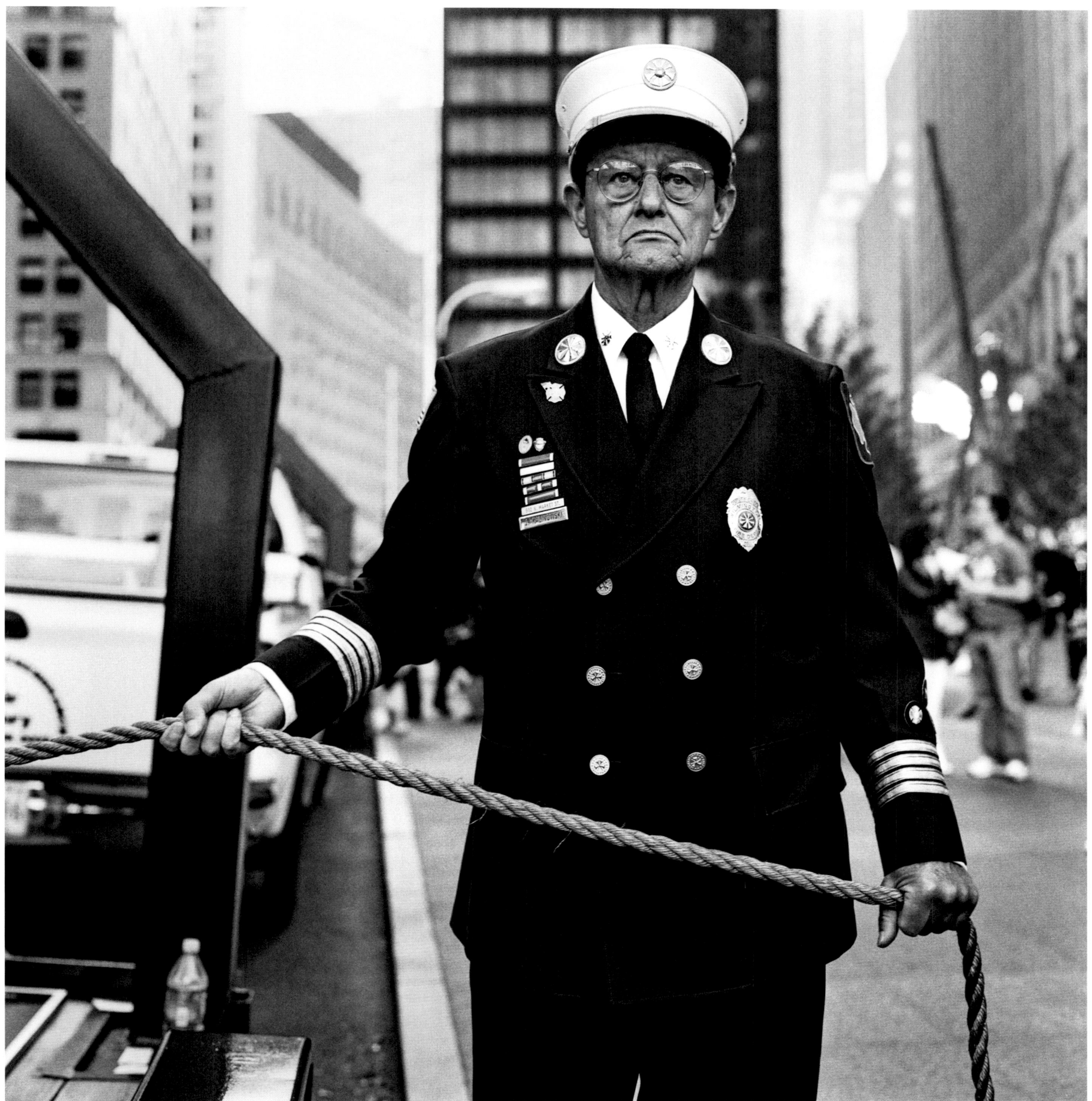

Bennington, Vermont, March 1, 2008

Obama Campaign Rally

For decades, the Greater Bennington Peace and Justice Center has led a Vigil for Peace at noon on the first Saturday of every month. Attracting other displays of hope for the future, this monthly meeting was infused with an energetic younger crowd throughout the 2008 presidential campaign, and their posters for Obama proliferated at Four Corners.

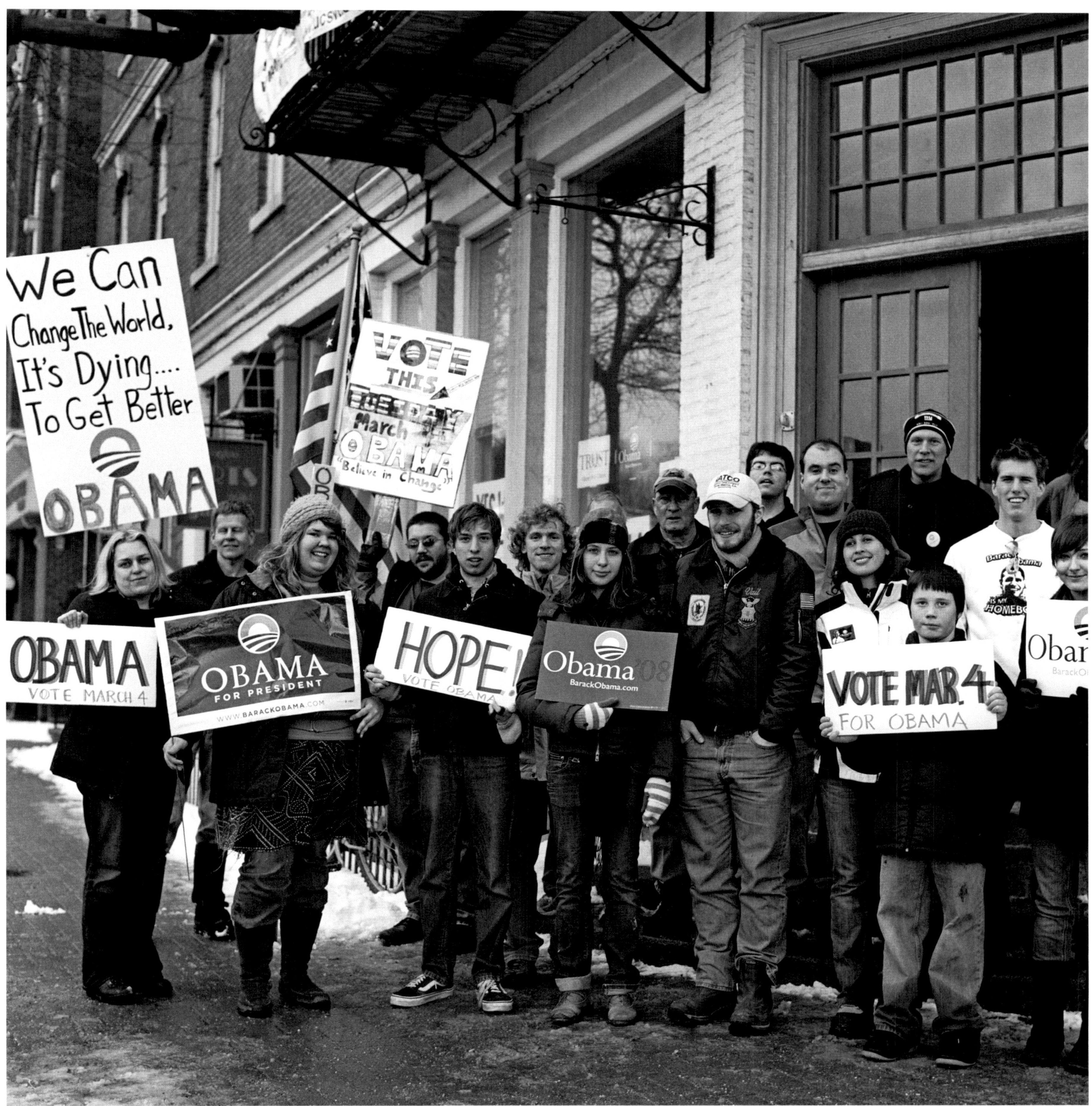
We Can
Change The World,
It's Dying....
To Get Better
OBAMA
VOTE
THIS
March
OBAMA
"Believe in Change"
OBAMA
VOTE MARCH 4
OBAMA
FOR PRESIDENT
WWW.BARACKOBAMA.COM
HOPE!
VOTE OBAMA
Obama '08
BarackObama.com
VOTE MAR. 4
FOR OBAMA

Washington, D.C., March 19, 2008

Fifth Anniversay of the Iraq War

Iraq Veterans Against the War were strong in numbers in Washington, D.C., on this fifth anniversary of the start of the Iraq War. They marched, they picketed, and they spoke publicly about the horrors they had witnessed. One young veteran, dwarfed amidst the monumental columns at the entrance to the National Archives, proudly waved a large upside down American flag, expressing his sense of emergency, national distress, and opposition to the war. Below him, at the bottom of the grand staircase, other veterans, young and old, chained themselves to railings as an act of civil disobedience.

Cree folk singer Buffy Sainte-Marie was there with her acoustic guitar leading the veterans in singing "Universal Soldier," her classic protest song that, along with the songs of Pete Seeger and others, helped galvanize peace advocates during the Vietnam War.

By late afternoon, scores of peace advocates marched silently up to Capitol Hill wearing white masks and placards around their necks with the names of Iraqi civilians killed by American bombs. They walked in single file, processing slowly and silently up to the Capitol. Under darkening gray skies and rain, they stepped across the security line near the Capitol building, where they were handcuffed and led by police officers to police vans that took them away.

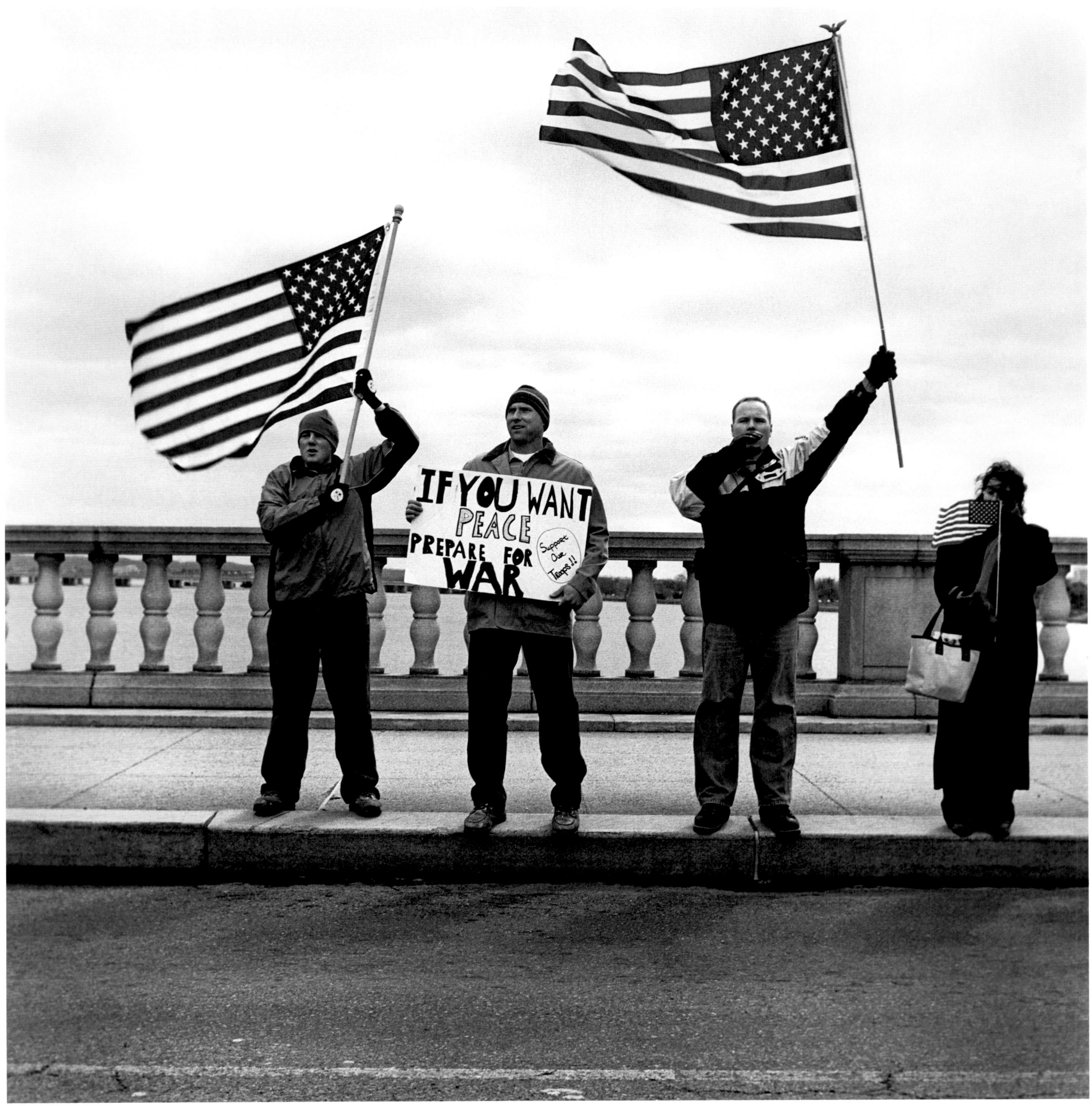
IF YOU WANT
PEACE
PREPARE FOR
WAR
Support Our Troops!!

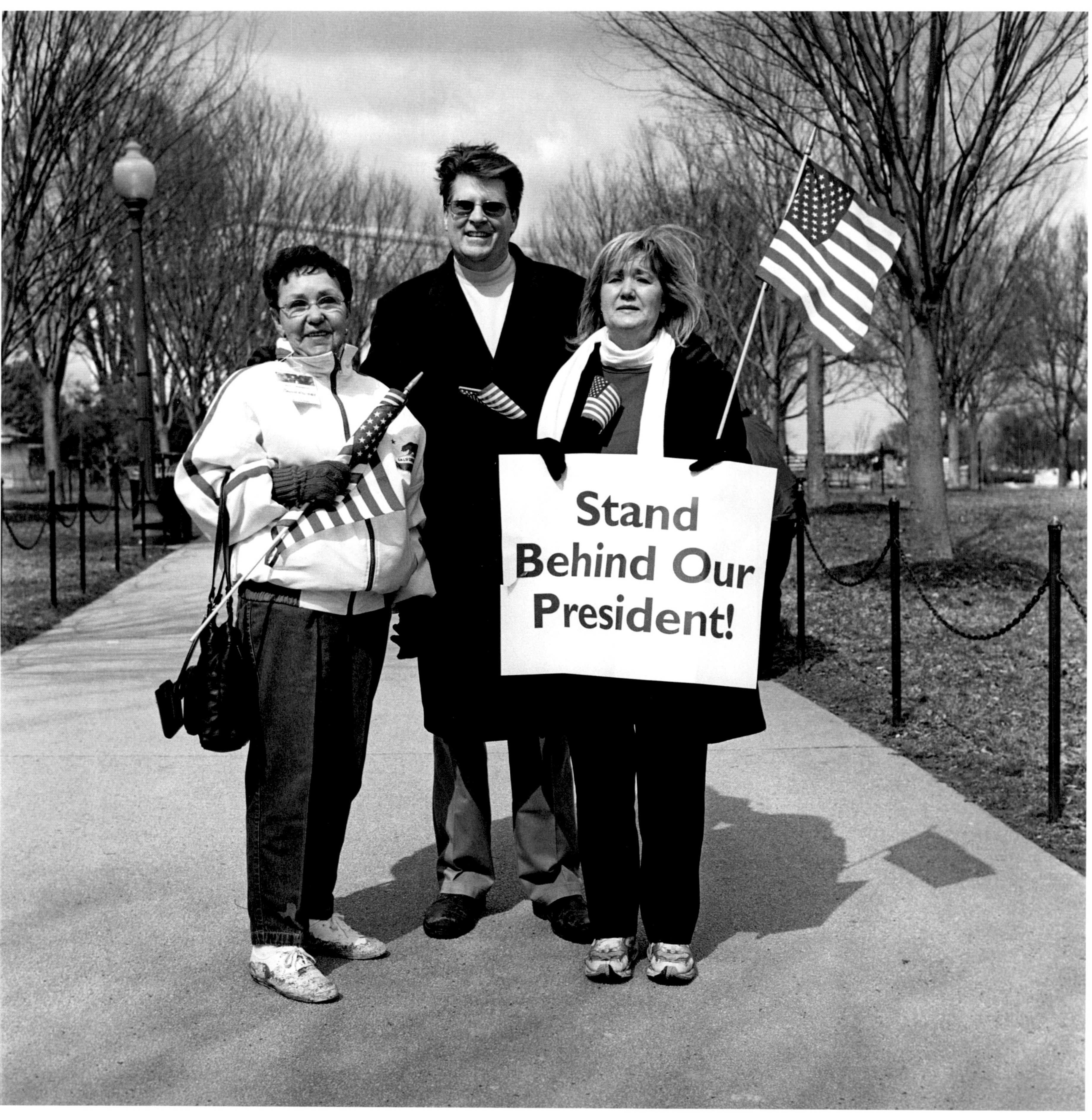
Stand
Behind Our
President!

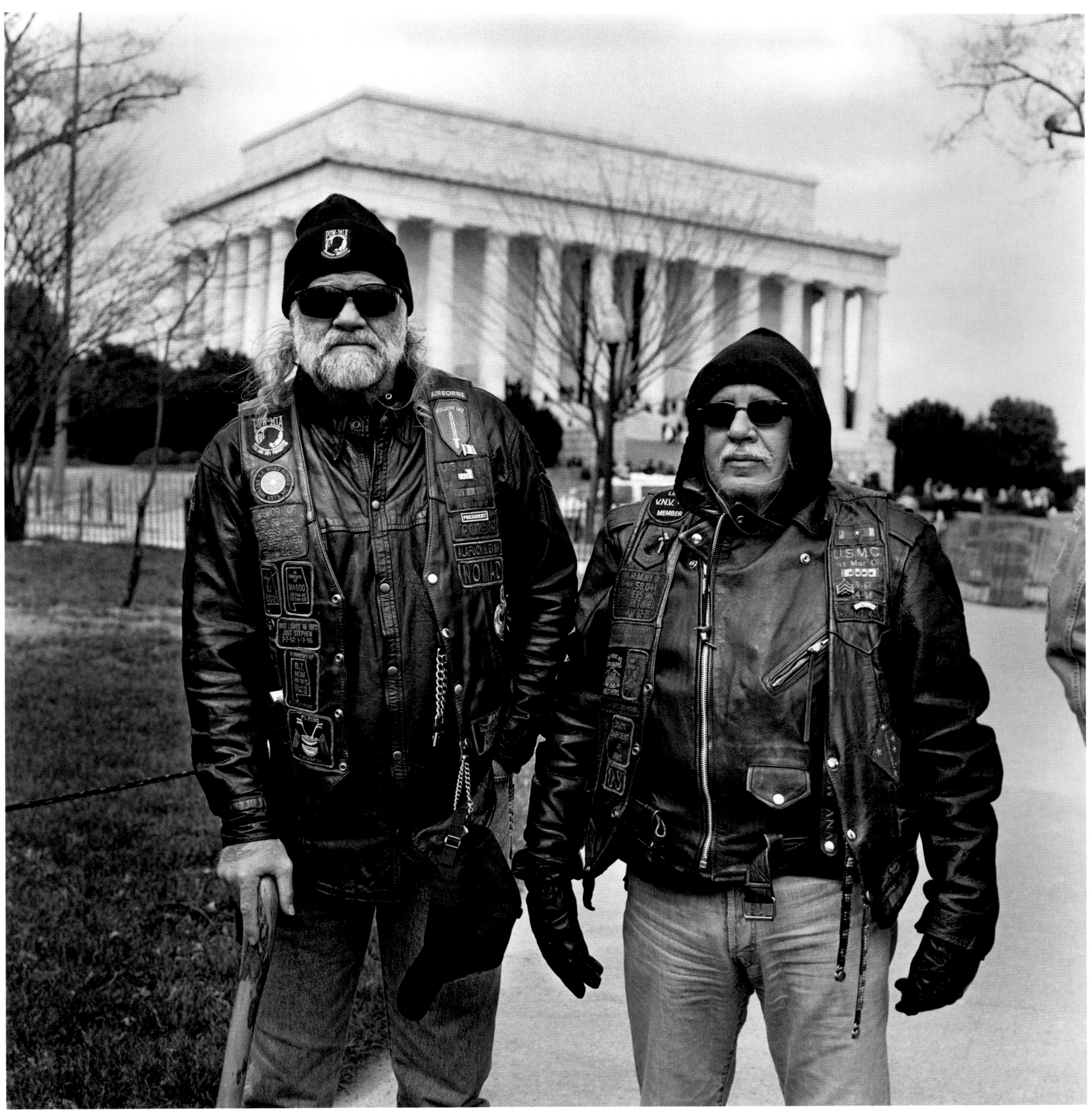
AIRBORNE
PRESIDENT
NOMAD
JUST STEPHEN
MEMBER
U.S.M.C

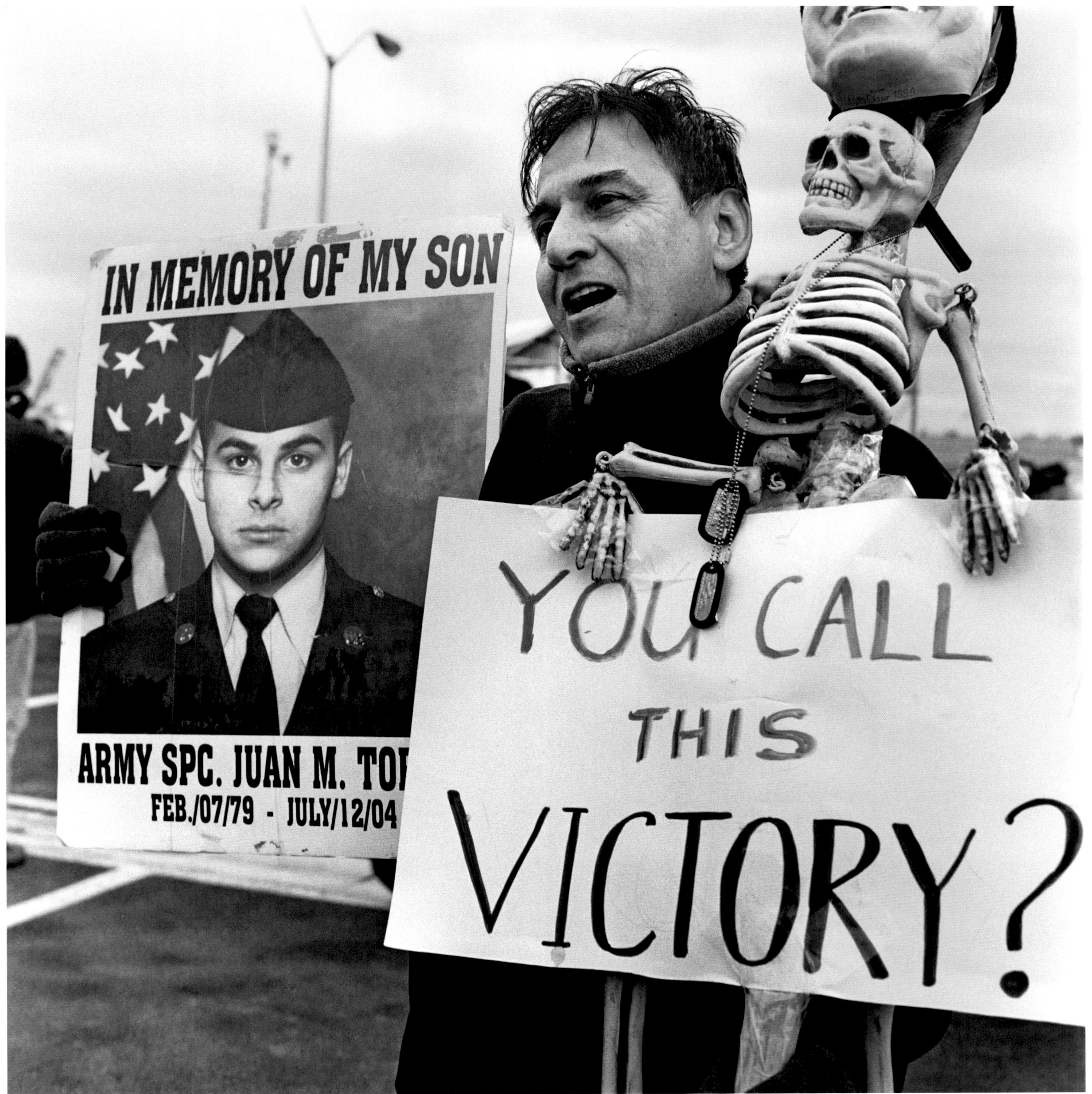
IN MEMORY OF MY SON
ARMY SPC. JUAN M. TO
FEB./07/79 - JULY/12/04
YOU CALL
THIS
VICTORY?

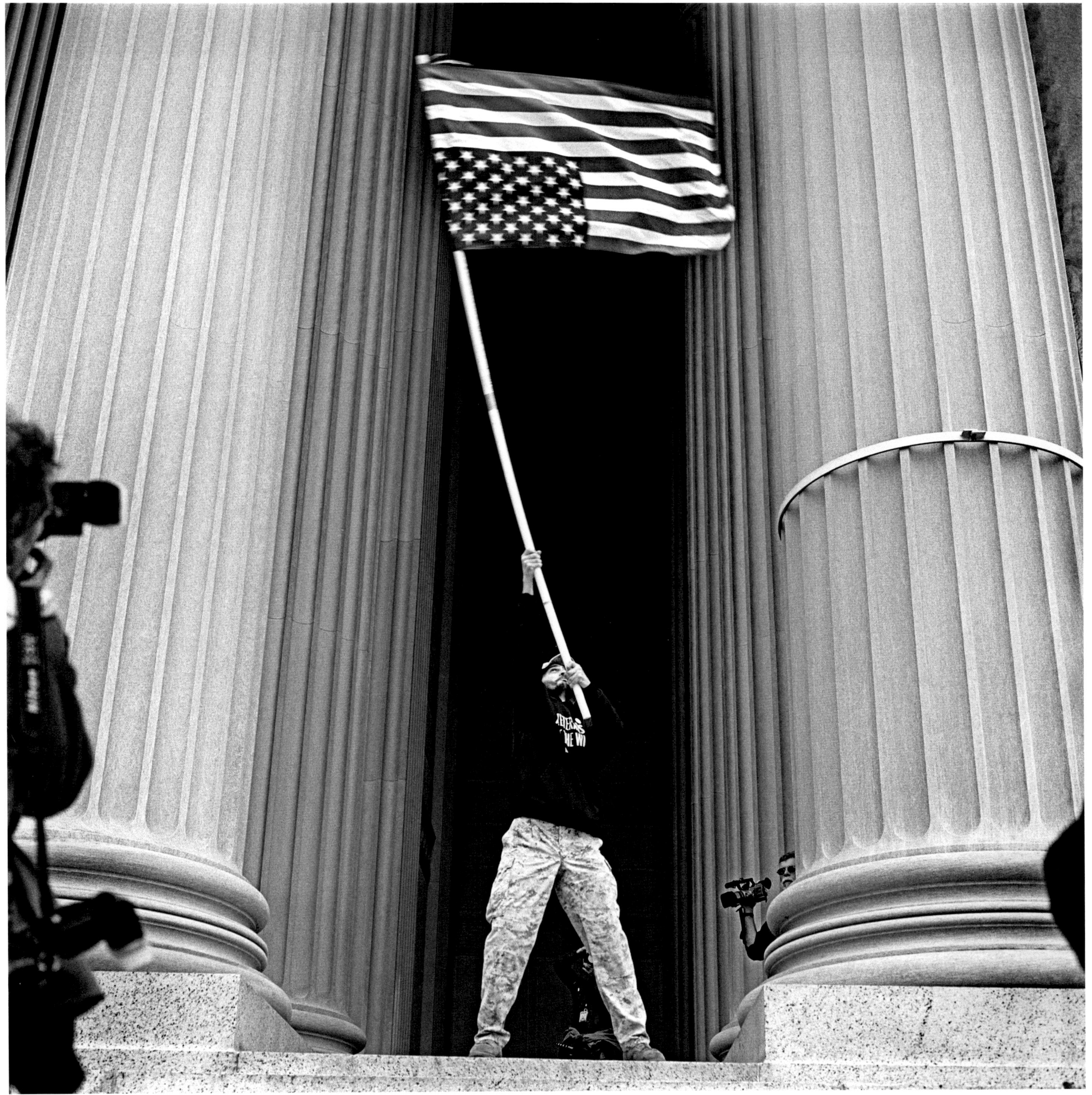

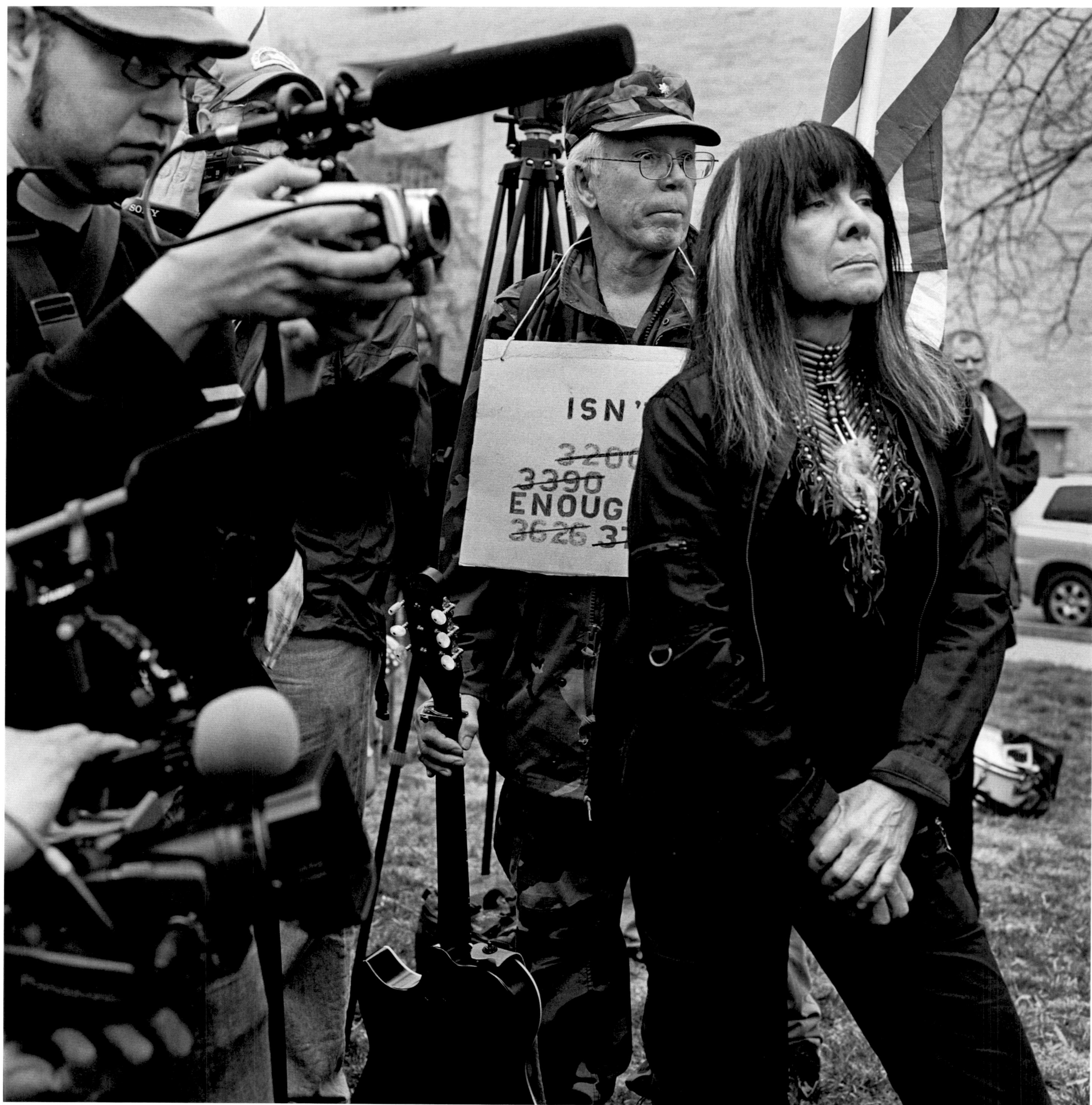
ISN'
3390
ENOUG
3626

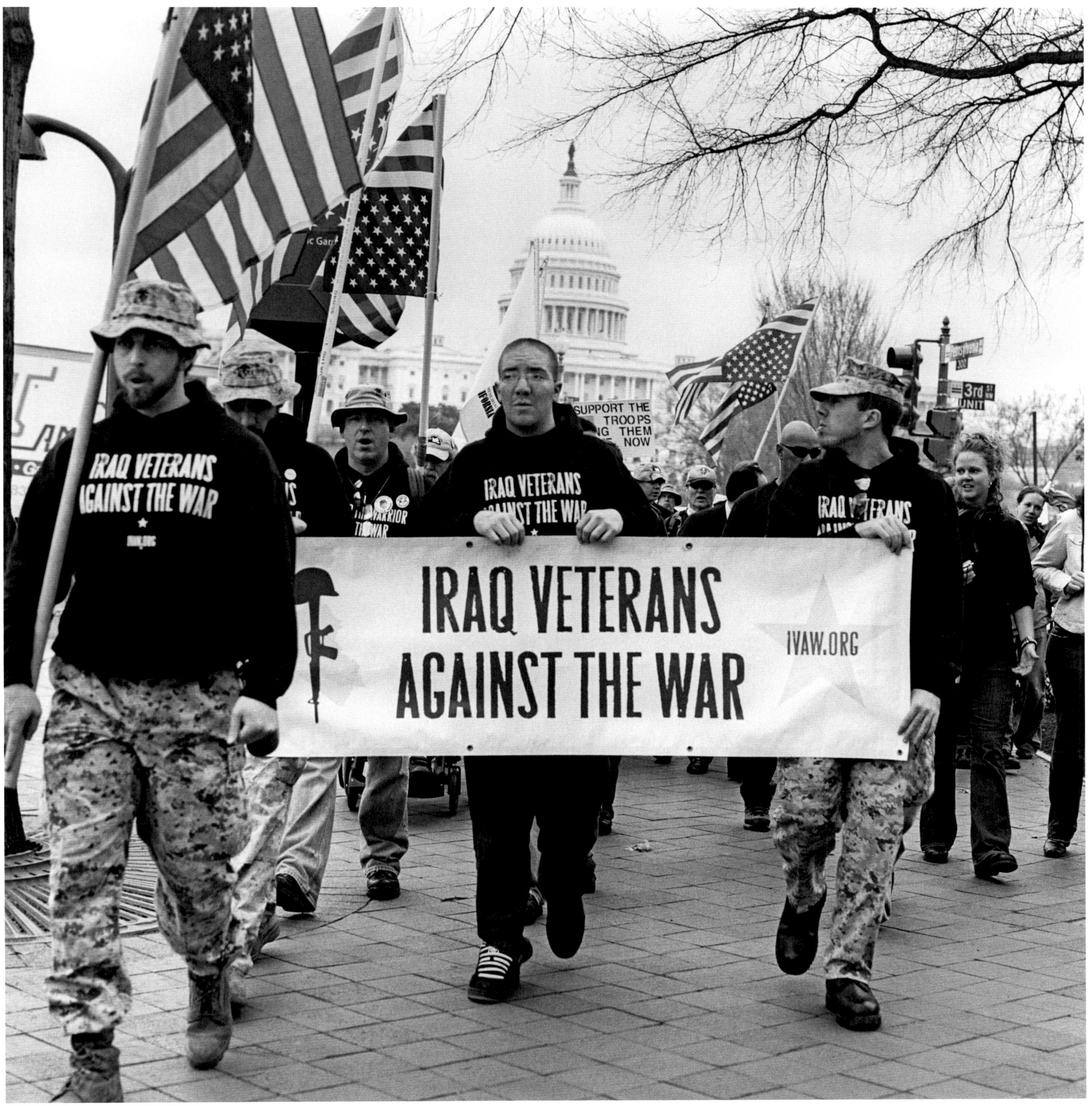
IRAQ VETERANS
AGAINST THE WAR
IVAW.ORG
IRAQ VETERANS
AGAINST THE WAR
IRAQ VETERANS
AGAINST THE WAR
SUPPORT THE
TROOPS
NOW
3rd

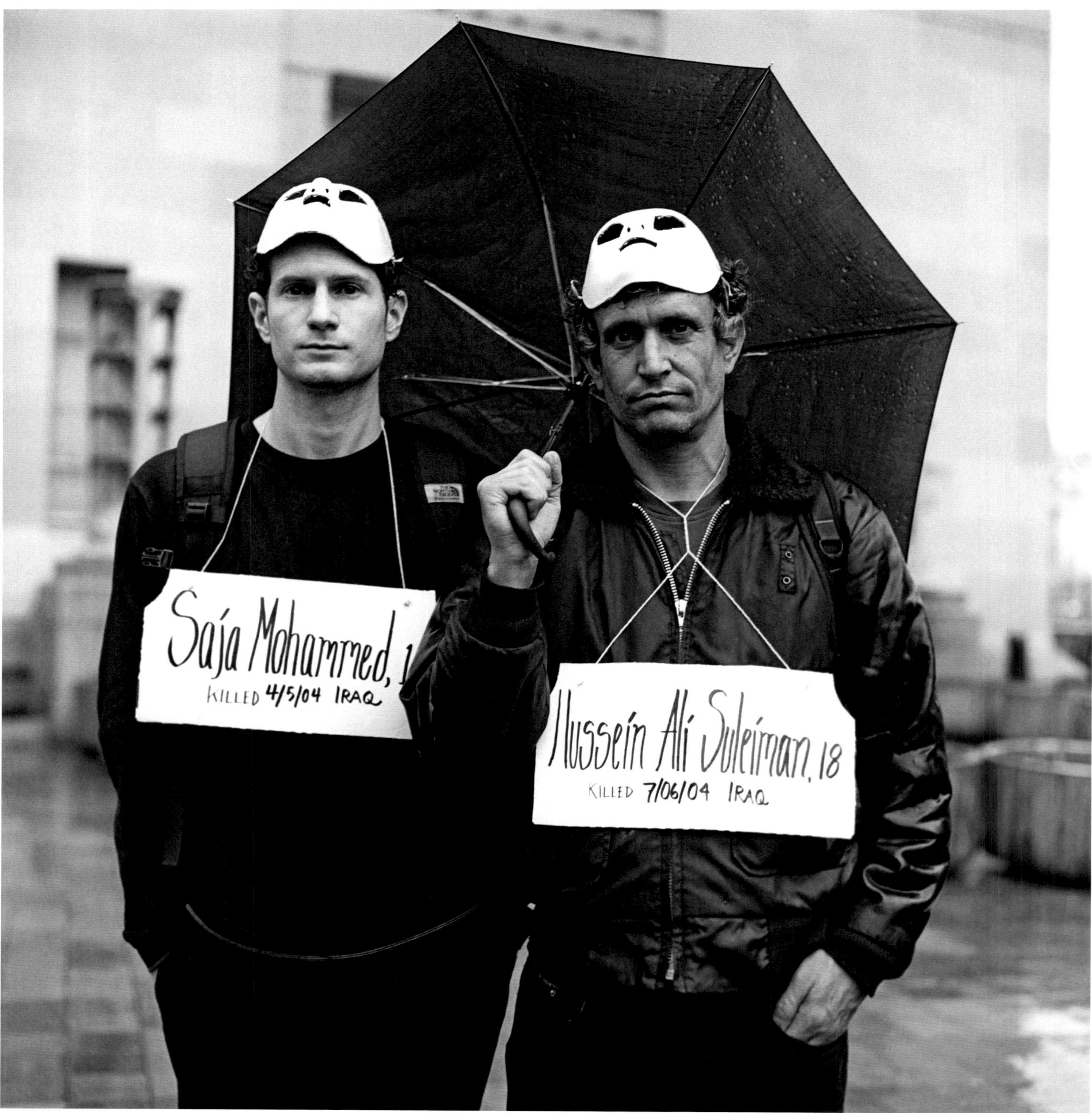
Sája Mohammed, 1
KILLED 4/5/04 IRAQ
Hussein Alí Suleiman, 18
KILLED 7/06/04 IRAQ

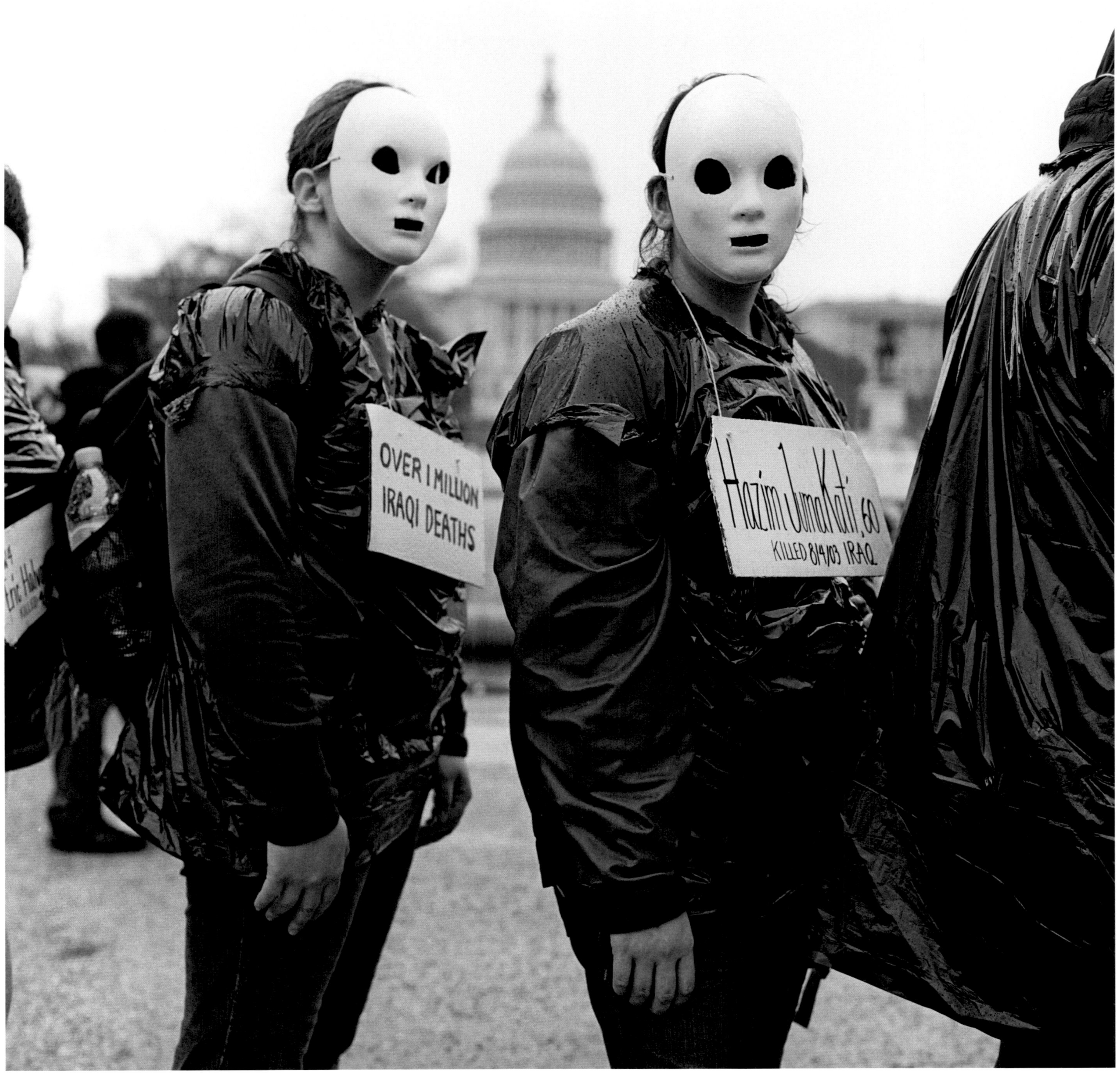
OVER 1 MILLION
IRAQI DEATHS
Hazim Juma Kati, 60
KILLED 8/4/03 IRAQ

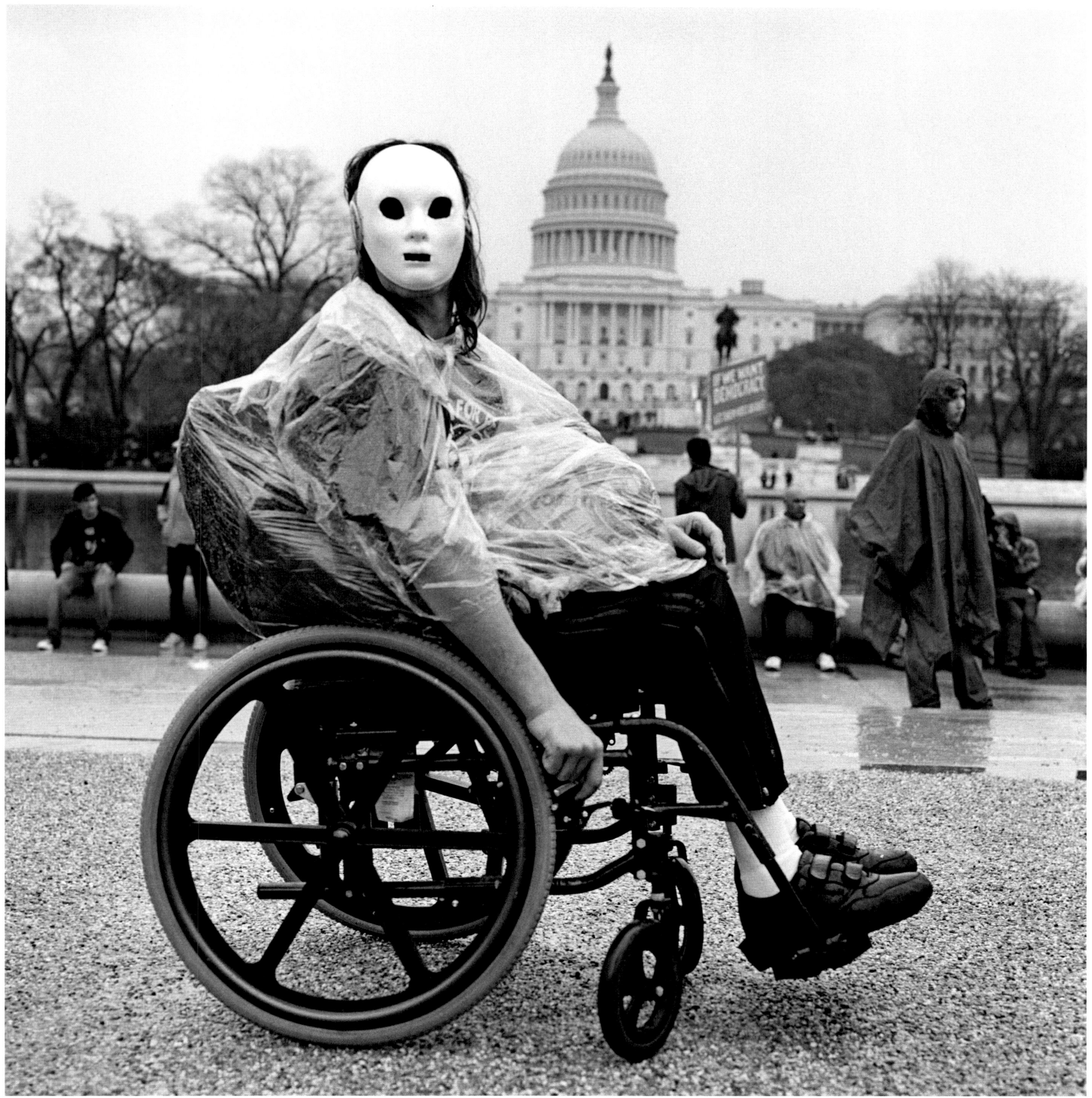

Washington, D.C., January 20, 2009

Inauguration of Barack Obama

On the morning of President Barack Obama's inauguration, the brilliant, crisp blue skies mirrored the optimism for the future held by the crowd gathered on the Mall—the largest inauguration crowd in American history. The day was marked by a palpable sense of hope, opportunity, and progress. From the Washington Monument to the Capitol, people joined together in celebration, despite the bone-chilling cold. Immediately after the inauguration ceremony, many took warm refuge in the Smithsonian Museums before long journeys home to all corners of the country.

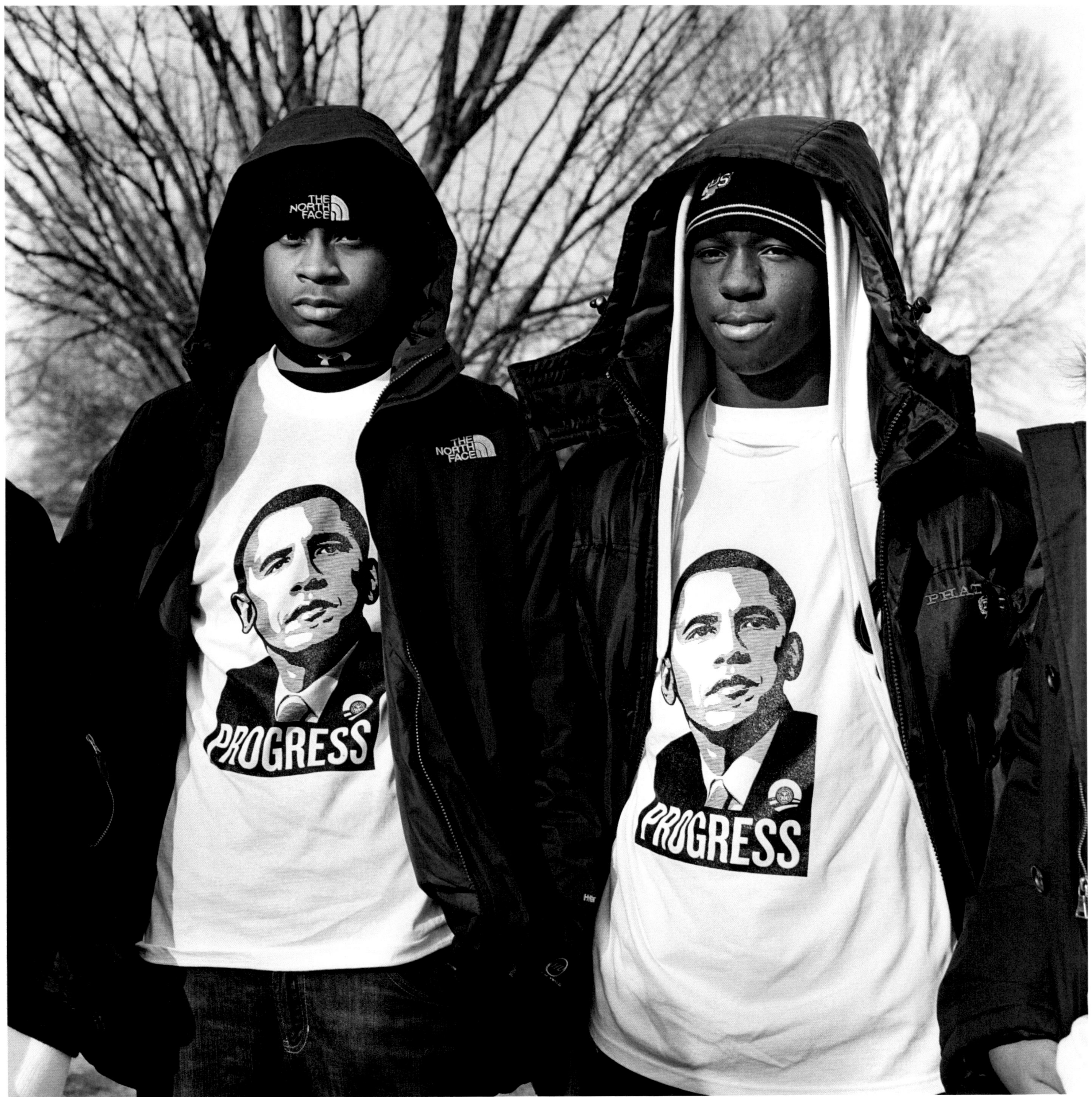
THE NORTH FACE
THE NORTH FACE
PROGRESS
PROGRESS

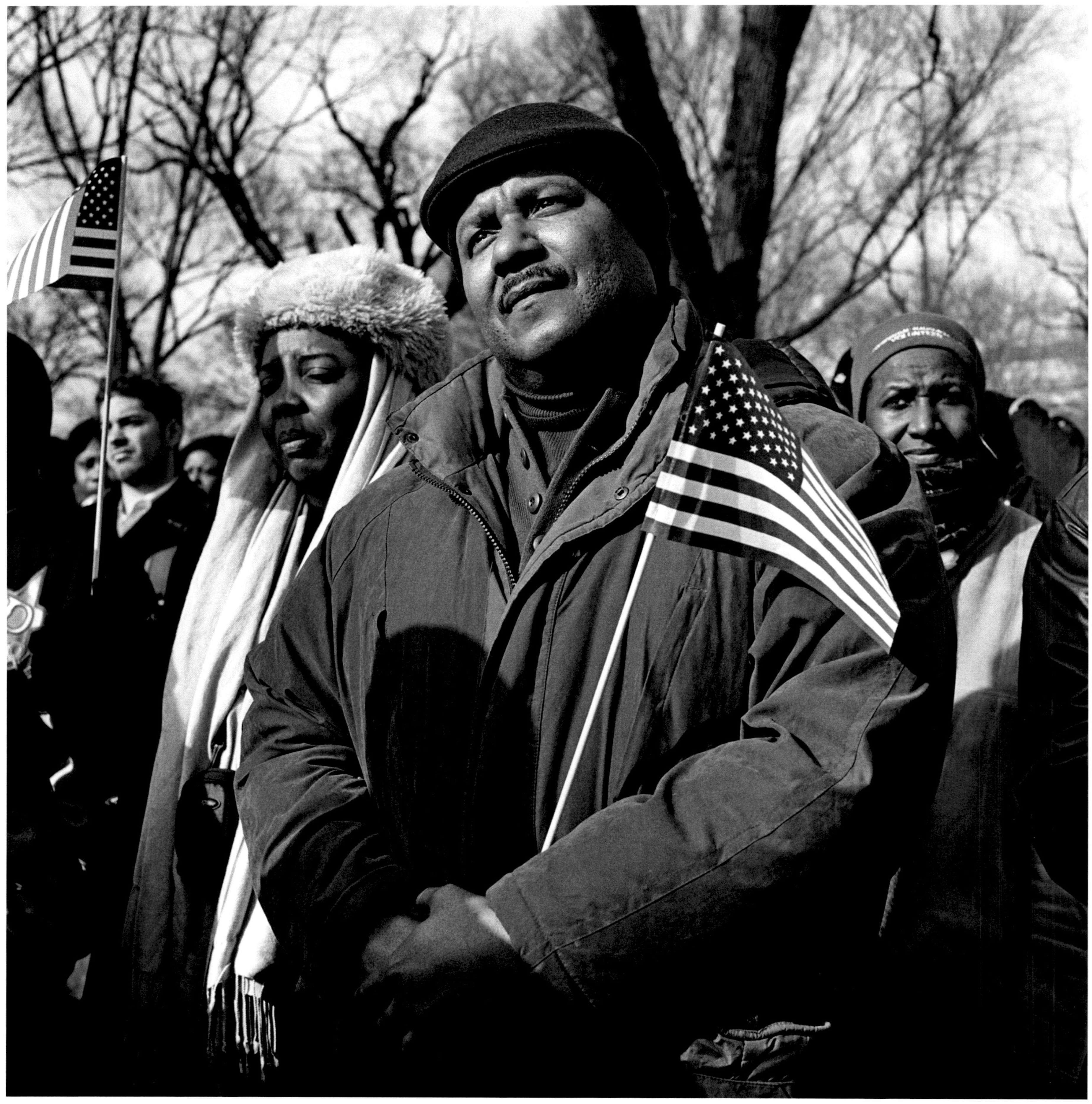

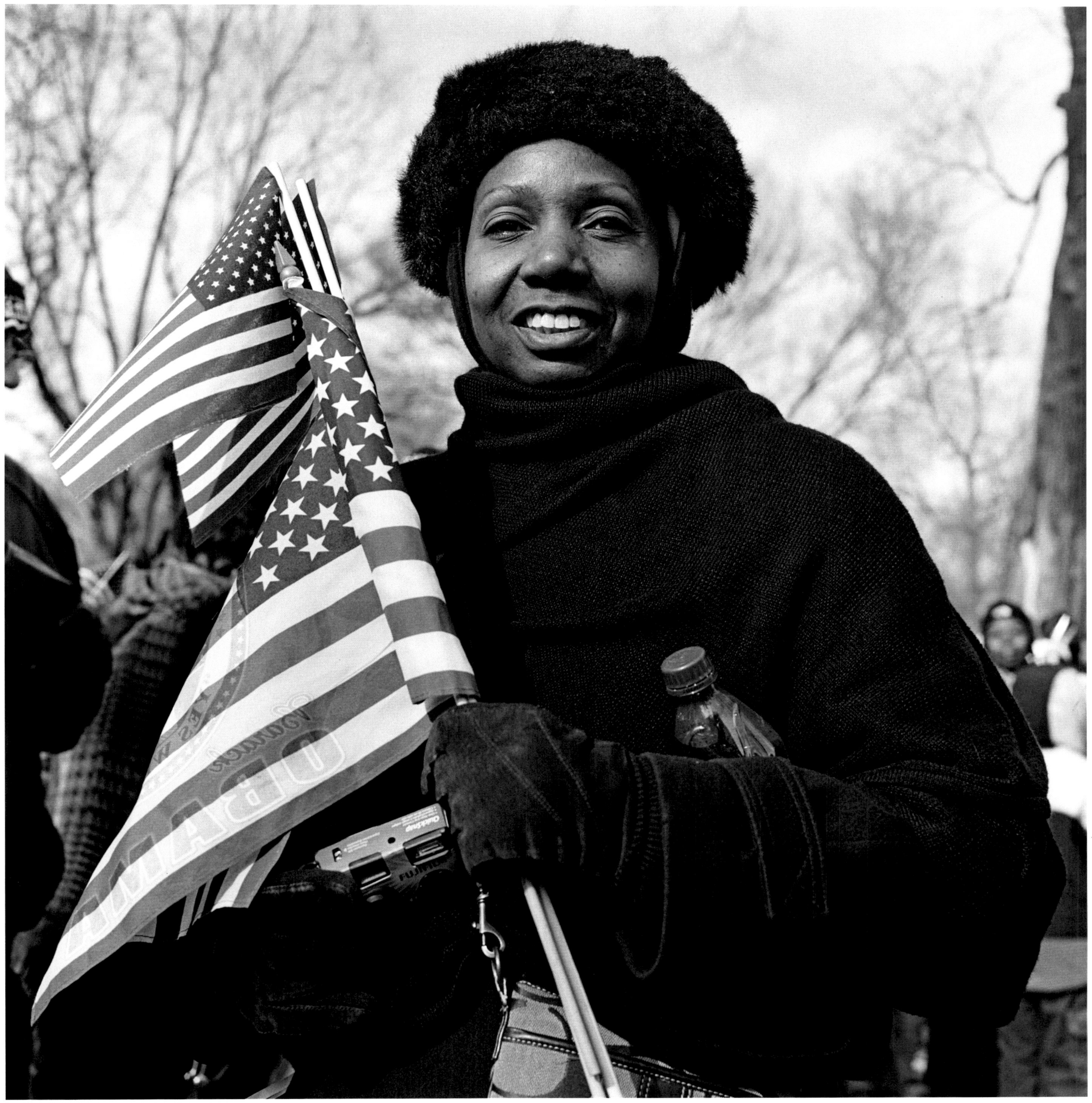

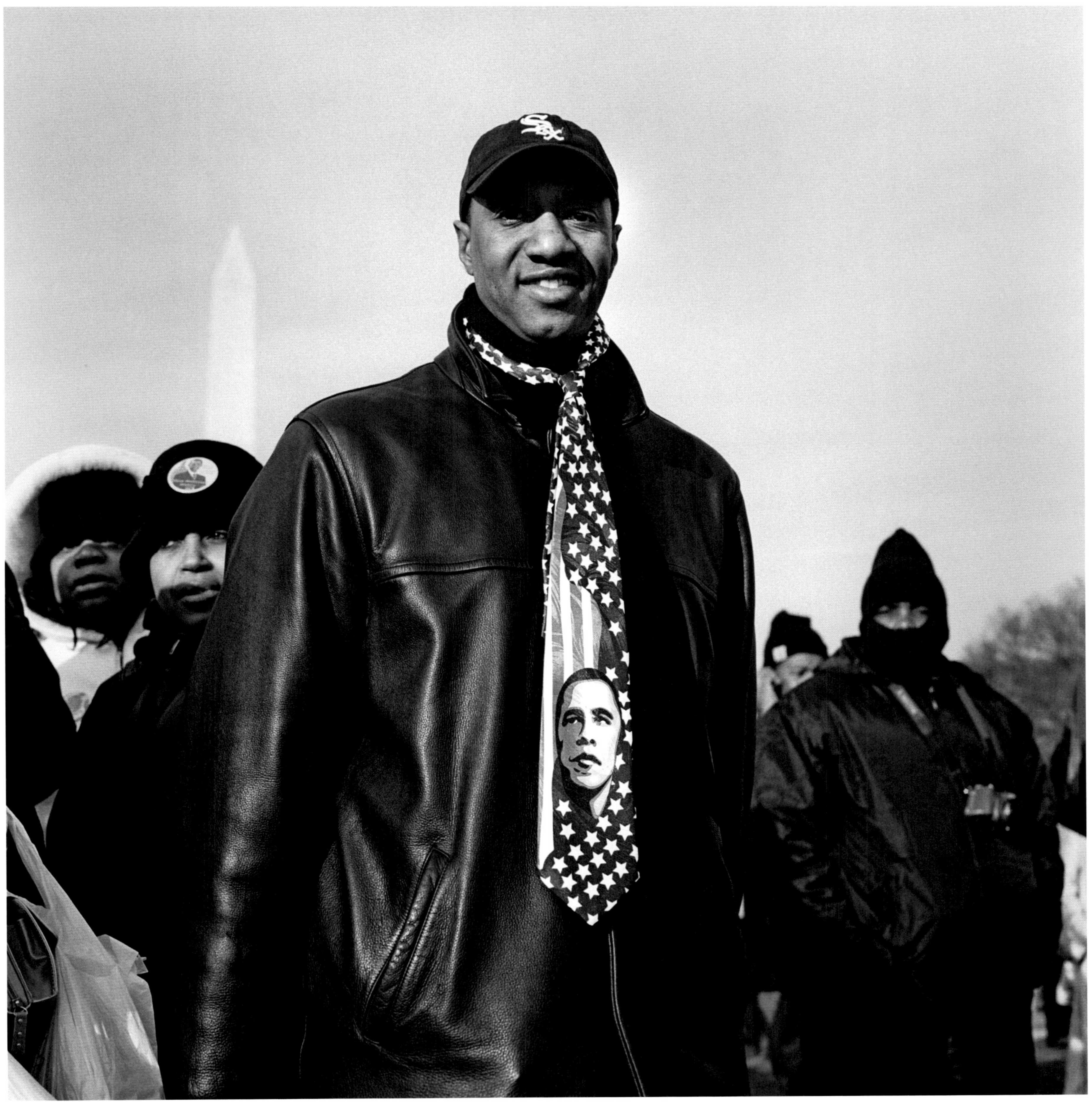

Burlington, Vermont, December 11, 2009

Vermont National Guard Deployment

Early in the morning, several hundred men and women in Vermont National Guard uniforms gathered with their friends and family in the University of Vermont's athletic field house. They were preparing to leave for training at Camp Atterbury, Indiana, part of a 1,500-strong contingent of Vermont National Guard members headed to Afghanistan. Home-baked cookies and other treats were shared; selfies and family portraits were snapped. A call to order ushered an immediate separation of the troops away from families and friends as the formalities of the deployment ceremony began. Immediately following the ceremony, the soldiers met awaiting buses ready to take them to Camp Atterbury. After training they would briefly return home for Christmas and then depart for Afghanistan.

The Vermont National Guard deployment totaling 1,500 from across the state was part of President Obama's order to send 30,000 additional troops to Afghanistan. Watching the deployment ceremony, one couldn't help but imagine all the families the soldiers would soon leave behind, dependent on the support of their hometown communities.

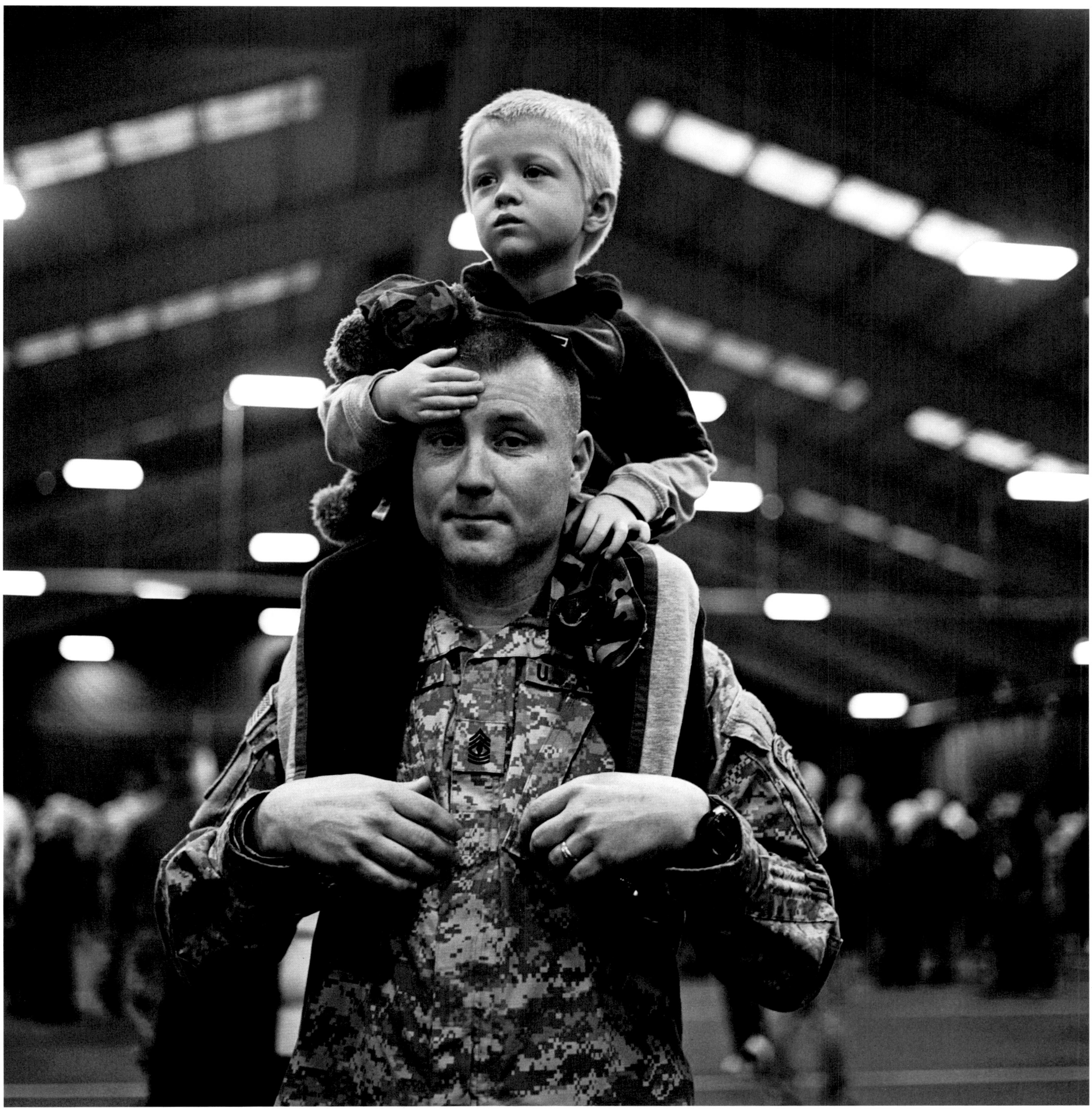

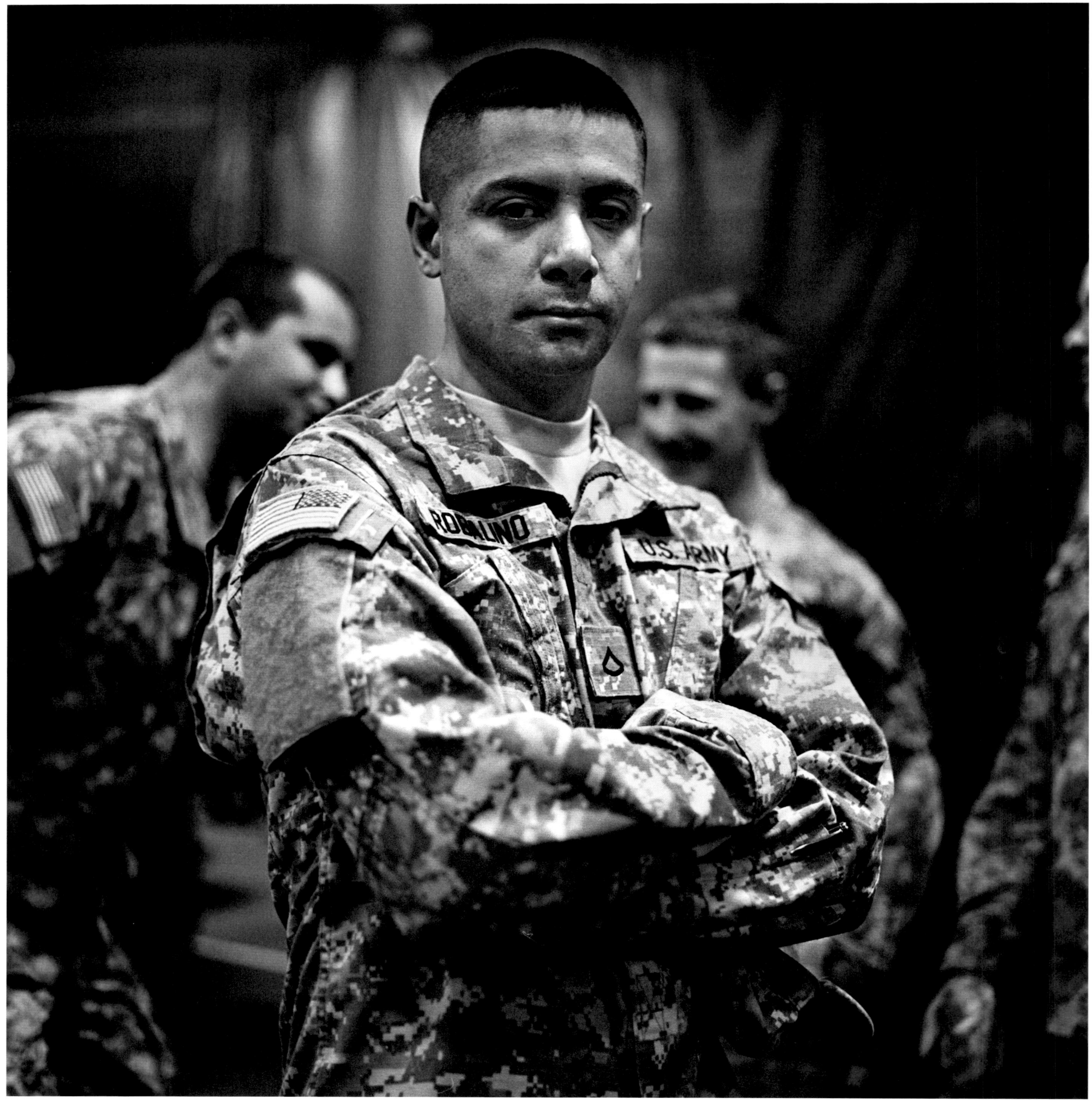
ROBALINO
U.S. ARMY

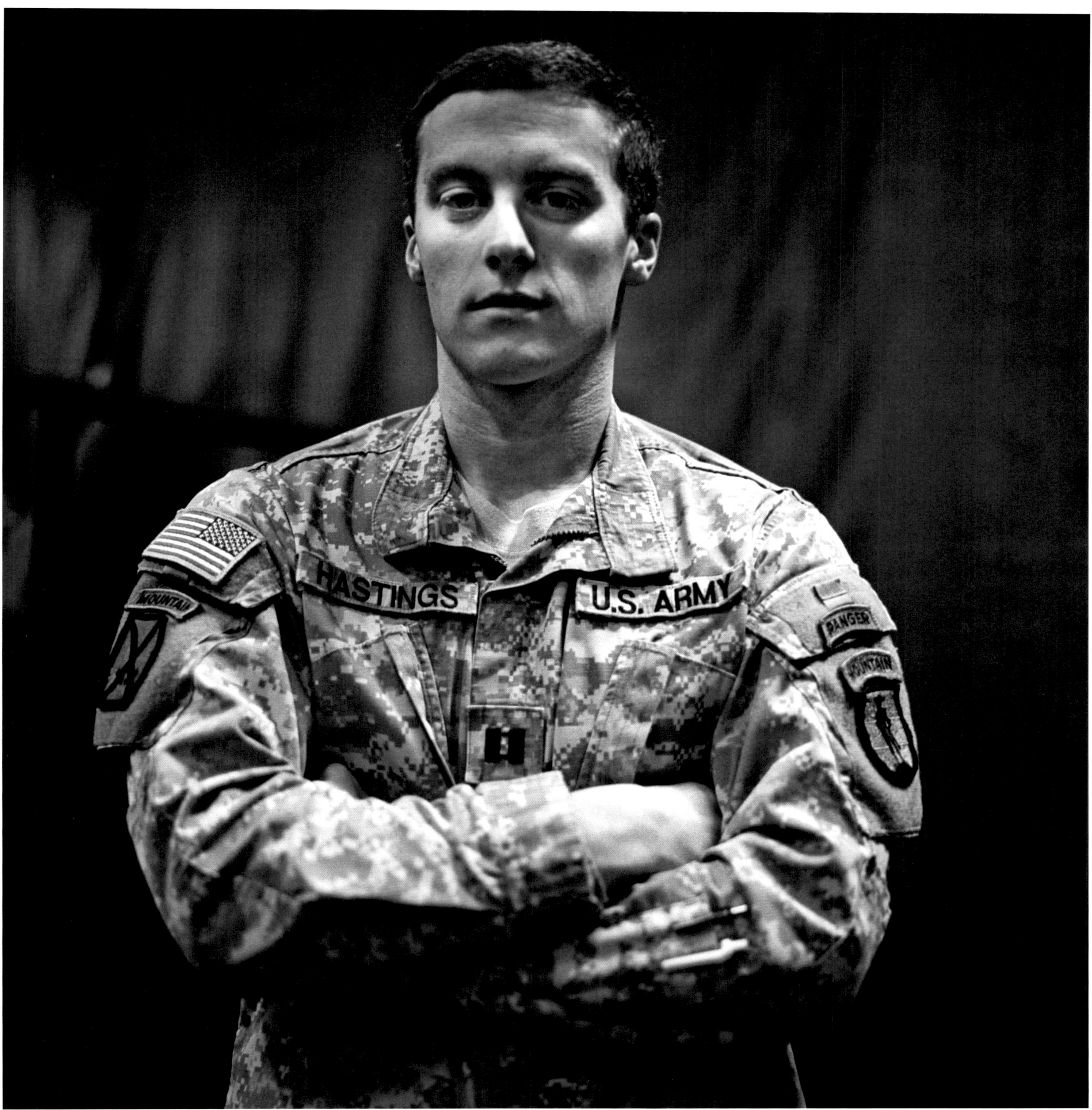
HASTINGS
U.S. ARMY
RANGER

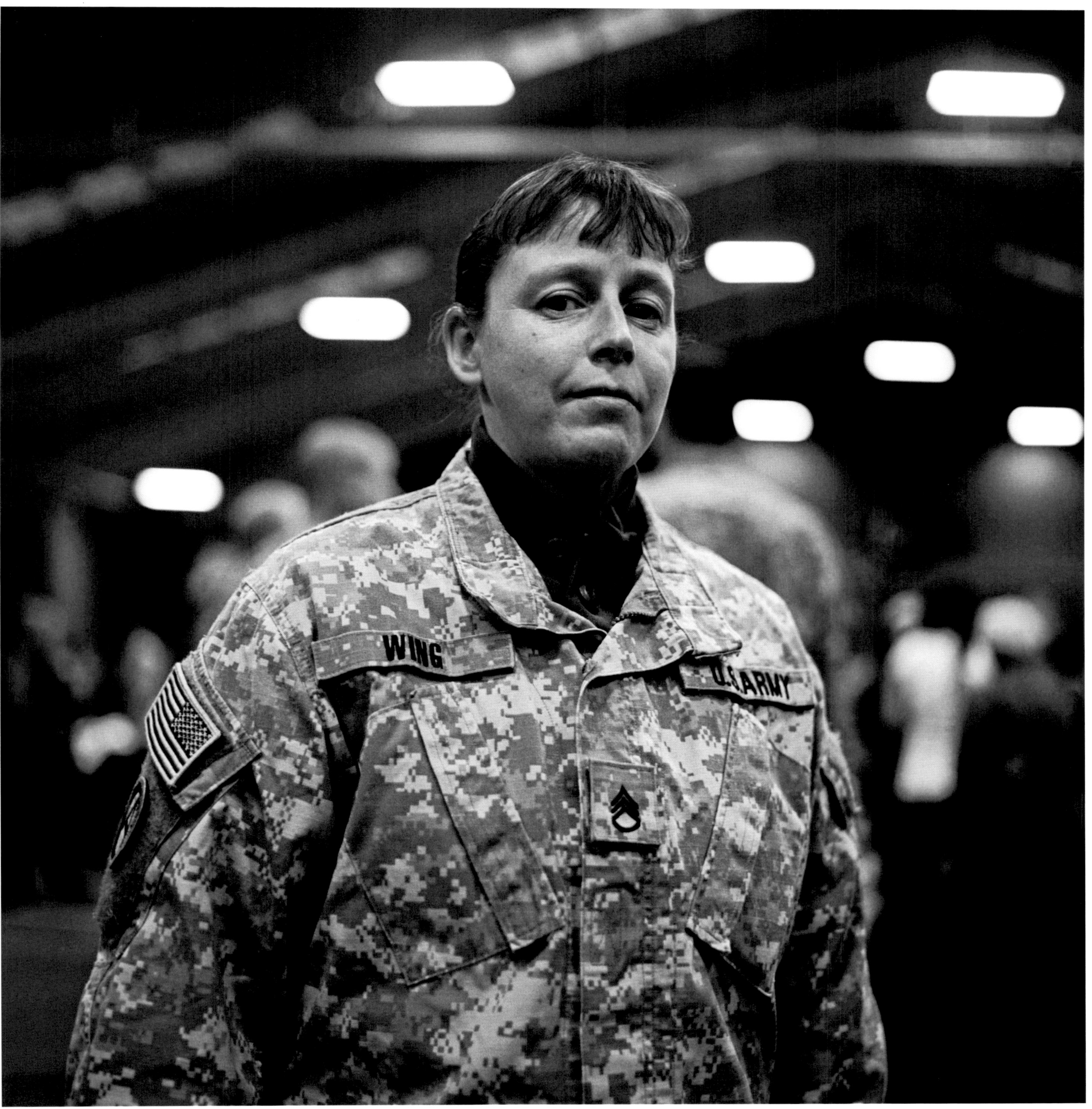
WING
U.S. ARMY

New York City, September 11, 2011

September 11 Anniversary Ceremony

The tenth anniversary of the September 11 attacks fell on a Sunday, and, indeed, ground zero in lower Manhattan felt reverent and church-like in its silence. The reflective glass surfaces of the not-yet-completed One World Trade Center building brilliantly amplified the sunshine and rich blue sky. The National September 11 Memorial & Museum opened to the public the following morning: the original towers' footprints transformed into two large pools with hypnotic waterfalls cascading down their vertical walls. Cut into the wide metal perimeter surrounding the two pools are the names of all the victims of the attacks.

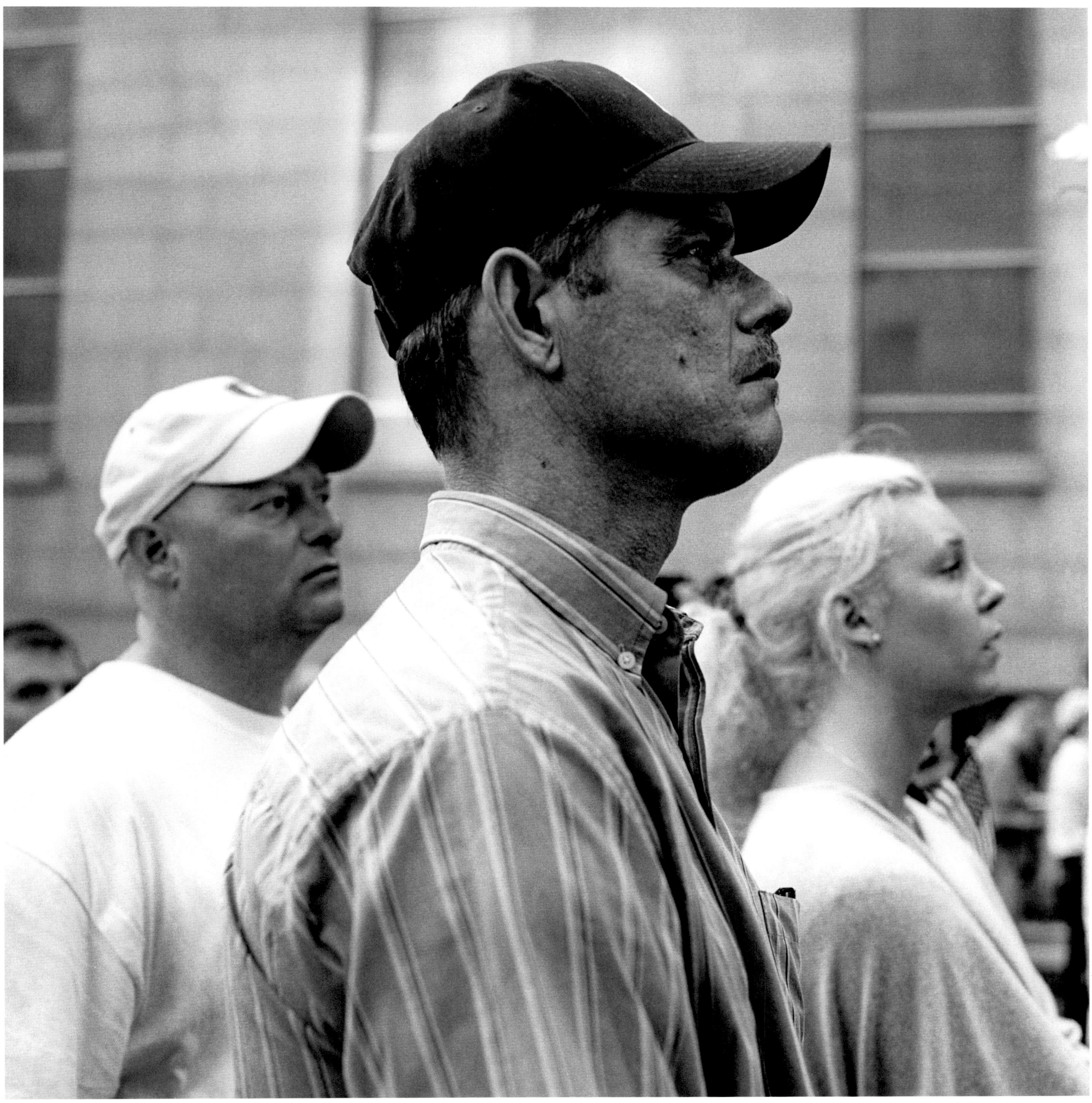

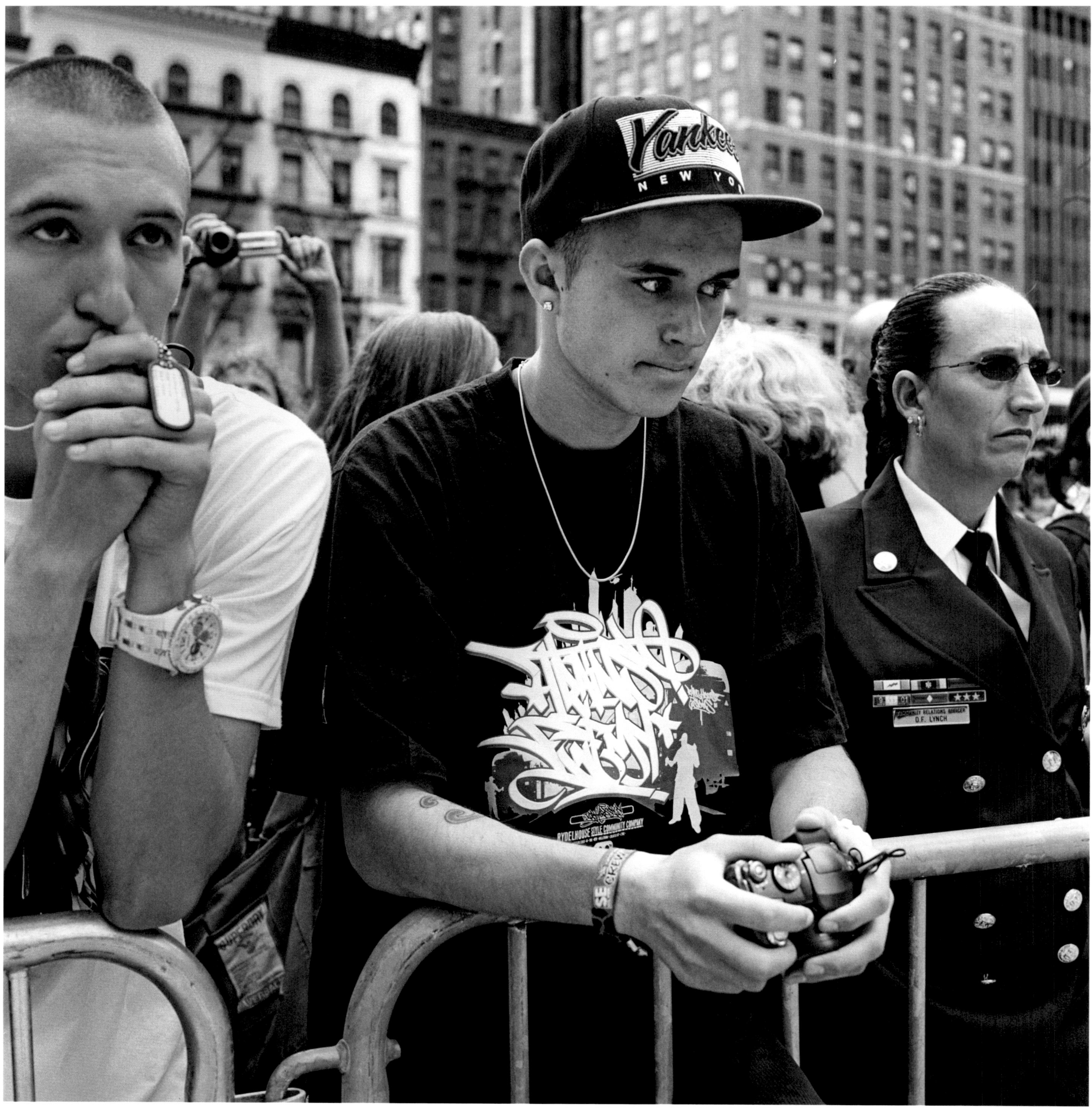
NEW YO
RYDELHOUSE STYLE COMMUNITY COMPANY
RELATIONS
D.F. LYNCH

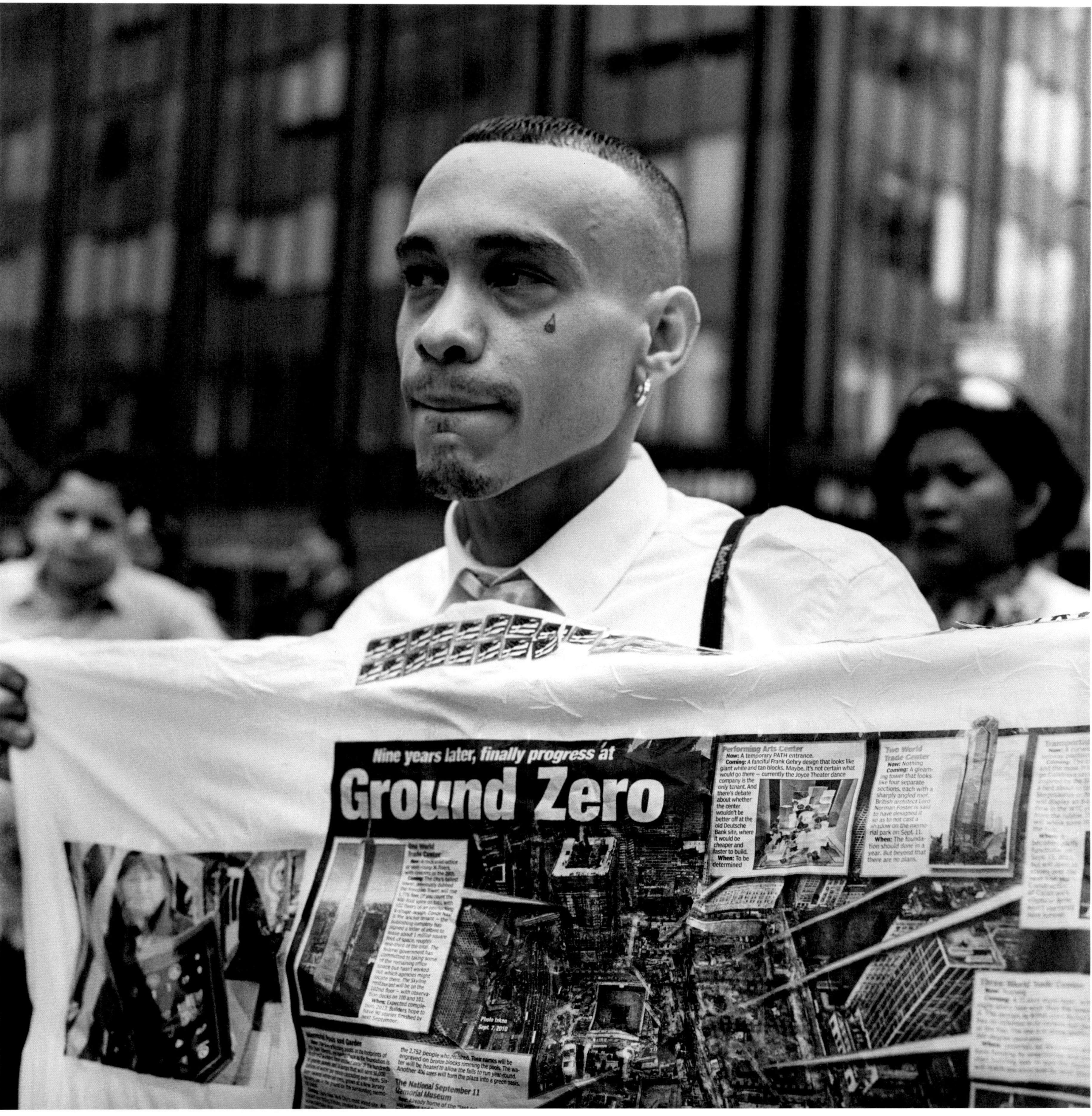
Nine years later, finally progress at
Ground Zero
Performing Arts Center
Now: A temporary PATH entrance.
Coming: A fanciful Frank Gehry design that looks like giant white and tan blocks. Maybe. It's not certain what would go there — currently the Joyce Theater dance company is the only tenant. And there's debate about whether the center wouldn't be better off at the old Deutsche Bank site, where it would be cheaper and faster to build.
When: To be determined
Two World Trade Center
Now: Nothing
Coming: A gleaming tower that looks like four separate sections, each with a sharply angled roof. British architect Lord Norman Foster is said to have designed it so as to not cast a shadow on the memorial park on Sept. 11.
When: The foundation should be done in a year. But beyond that there are no plans.
Photo taken Sept. 7, 2010
the 2,752 people who perished. These names will be engraved on bronze blocks rimming the pools. The water will be heated to allow the falls to run year-round. Another 400 trees will turn the plaza into a green oasis.
The National September 11 Memorial Museum

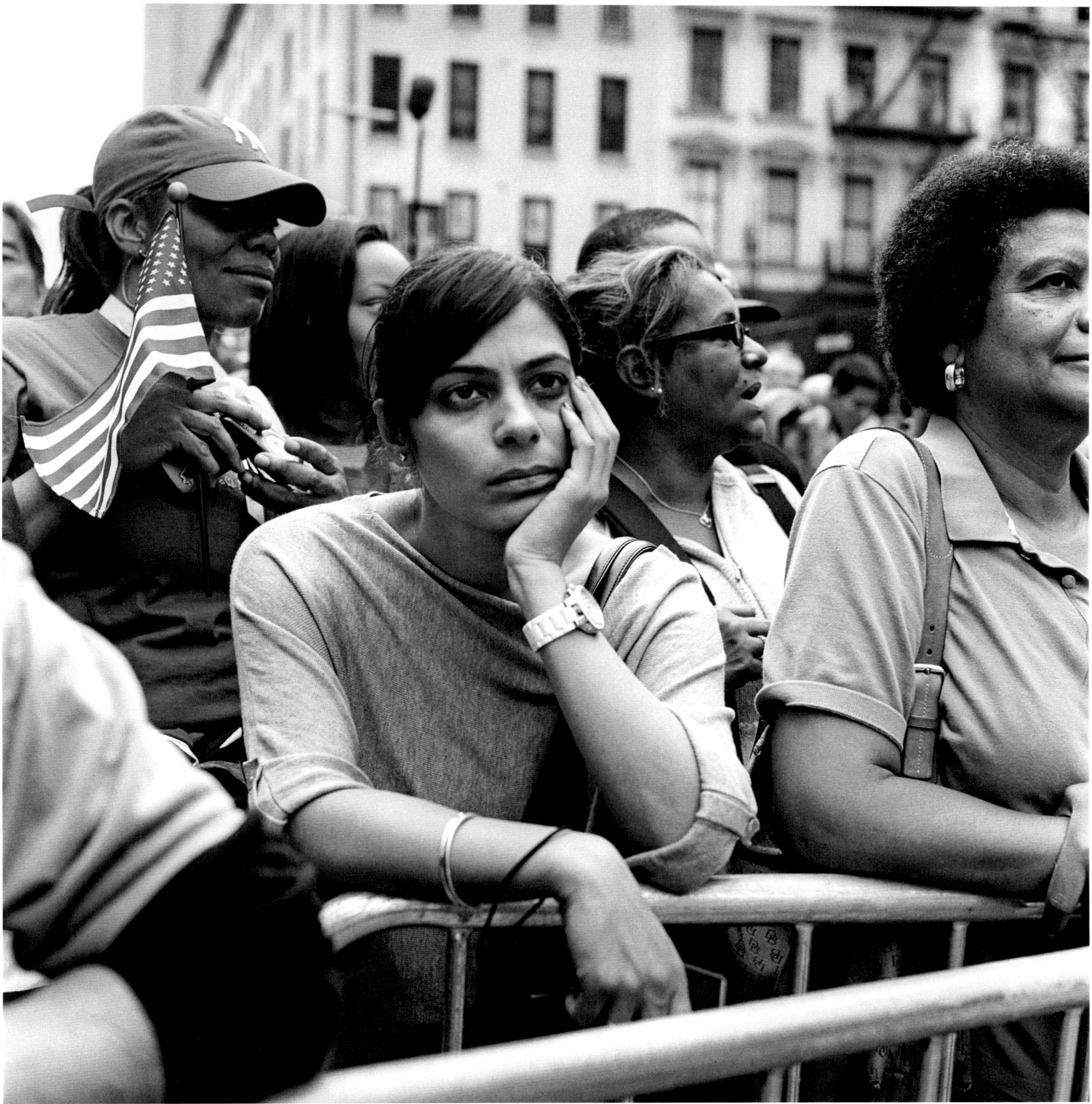

New York City, October 10, 2011

Occupy Wall Street

The Occupy Wall Street movement was a powerful political phenomenon of civil disobedience that captured media attention around the world and spurred occupations across the country. The movement and occupation of Zuccotti Park began on September 17, 2011 as a demonstration against the economic and political hegemony of Wall Street money and corporate power, and a defense of the human and civic rights of all people. This was a young and leaderless movement, anti-authoritarian, and anti-discriminatory in its orientation, without specific objectives or official demands. Its general intent was to advocate for the 99% of the American population against the 1% that holds half the wealth of the country—and its symbolism and idealism proved powerful.

On October 10, 2011, then-mayor Michael Bloomberg announced that as long as the protesters camping in the park obeyed the laws of the city they would not be arrested or removed. Three days later, on October 13, the mayor told demonstrators that they needed to clear Zuccotti Park for it to be cleaned and that the encampment and sleeping equipment could not remain. After weeks of threats, the occupation of Zuccotti Park ended the night of November 15 when Mayor Bloomberg ordered the New York Police Department to clear the Park. By early December any evidence of the months-long occupation of Zuccotti Park had been entirely erased. Only through memories, stories, and photographs could one recall the visceral power of the occupation.

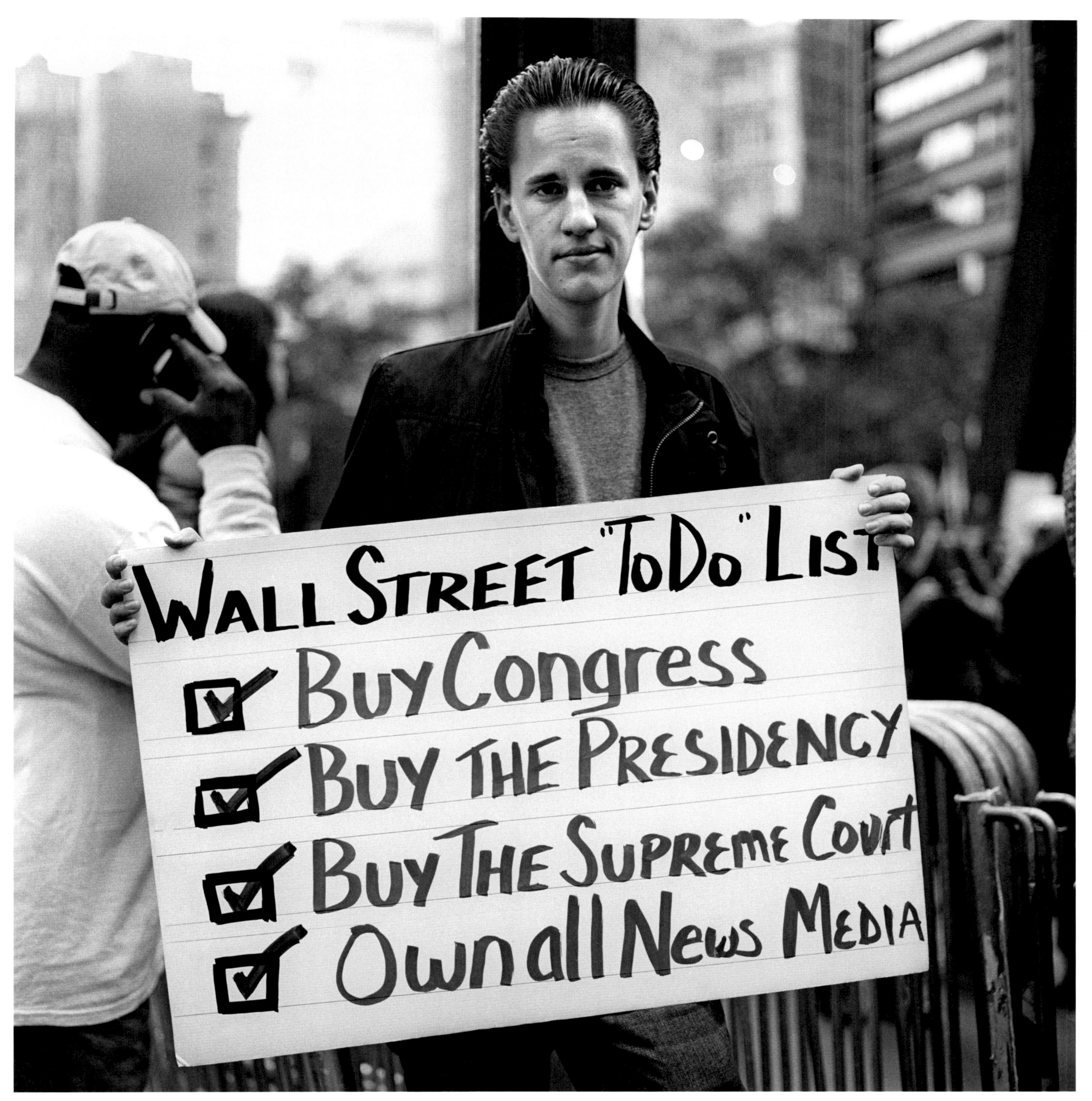
WALL STREET "TO DO" LIST
BUY CONGRESS
BUY THE PRESIDENCY
BUY THE SUPREME COURT
OWN ALL NEWS MEDIA

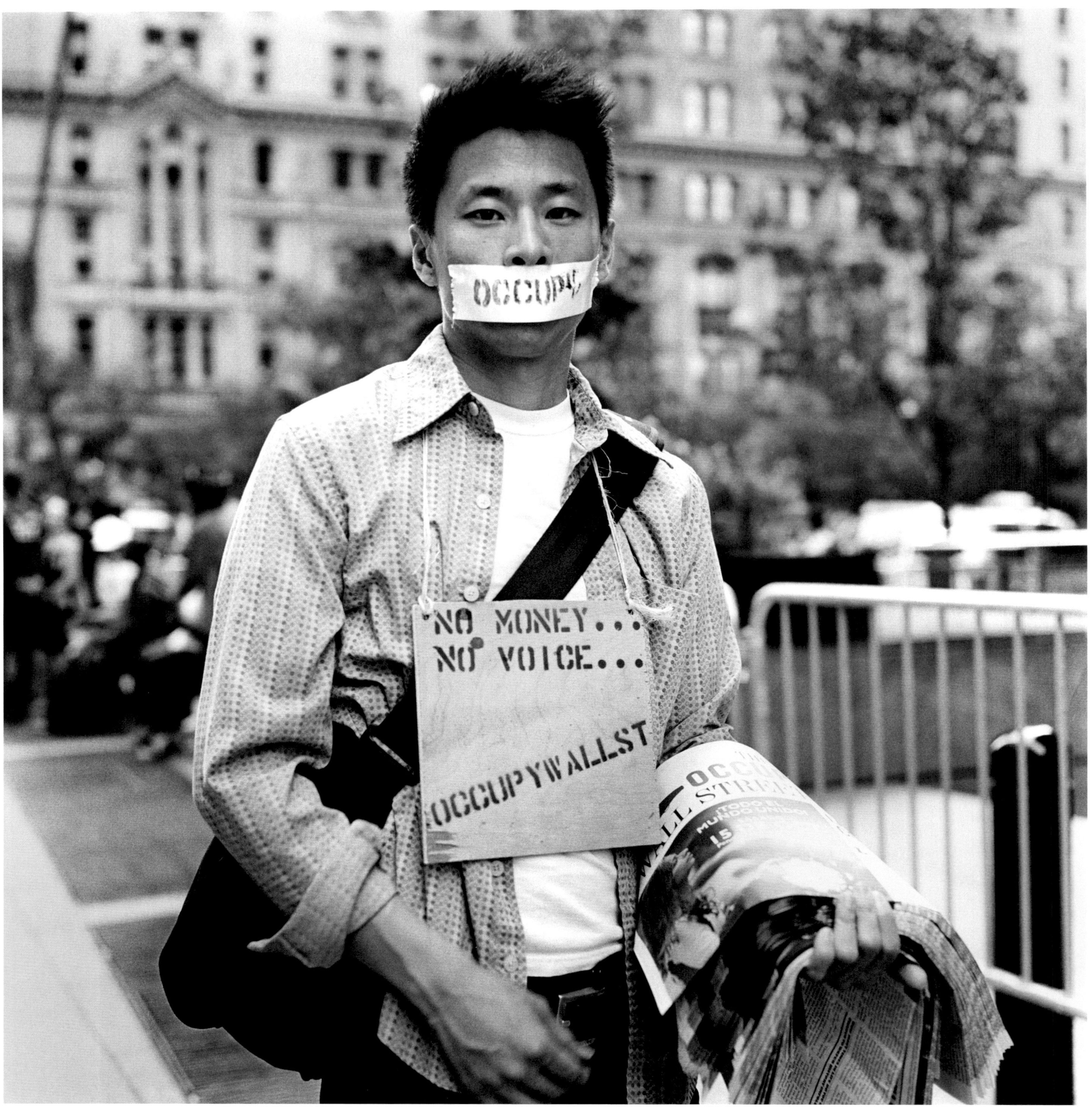
NO MONEY...
NO VOICE...
OCCUPYWALLST

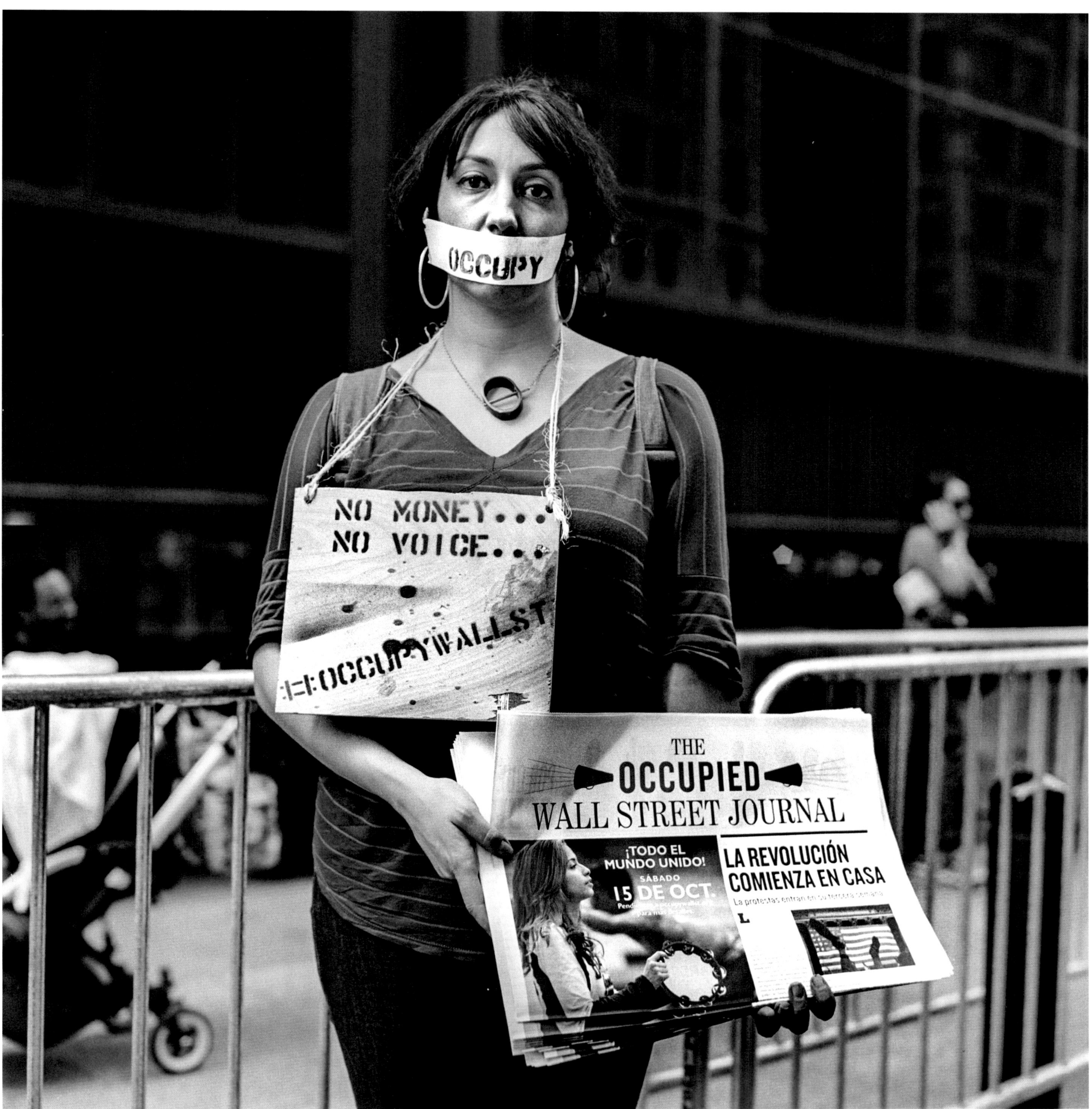
OCCUPY
NO MONEY...
NO VOICE...
#OCCUPYWALLST
THE
OCCUPIED
WALL STREET JOURNAL
¡TODO EL
MUNDO UNIDO!
SÁBADO
15 DE OCT.
LA REVOLUCIÓN
COMIENZA EN CASA

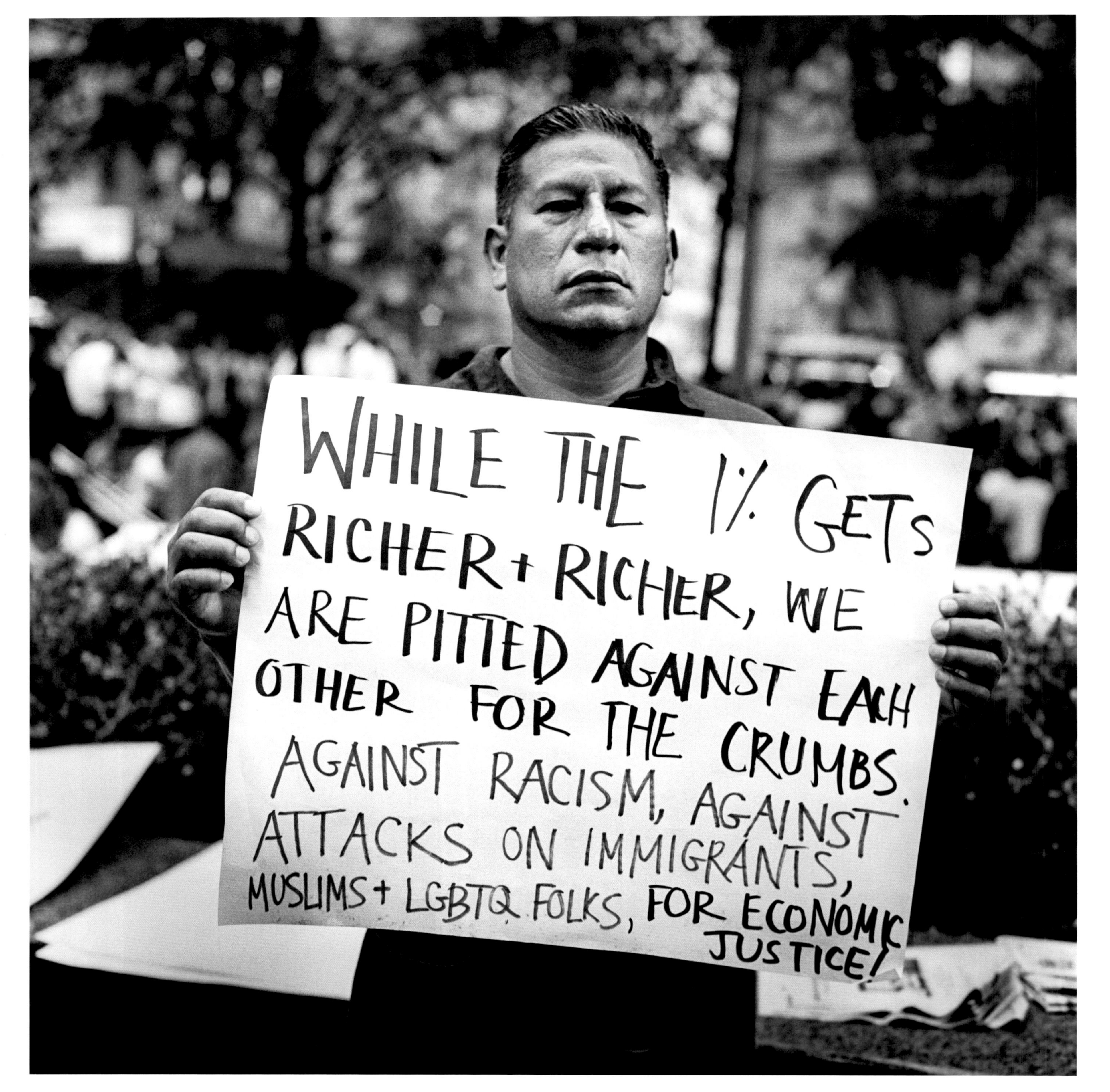
WHILE THE 1% GETS
RICHER + RICHER, WE
ARE PITTED AGAINST EACH
OTHER FOR THE CRUMBS.
AGAINST RACISM, AGAINST
ATTACKS ON IMMIGRANTS,
MUSLIMS + LGBTQ FOLKS, FOR ECONOMIC
JUSTICE!

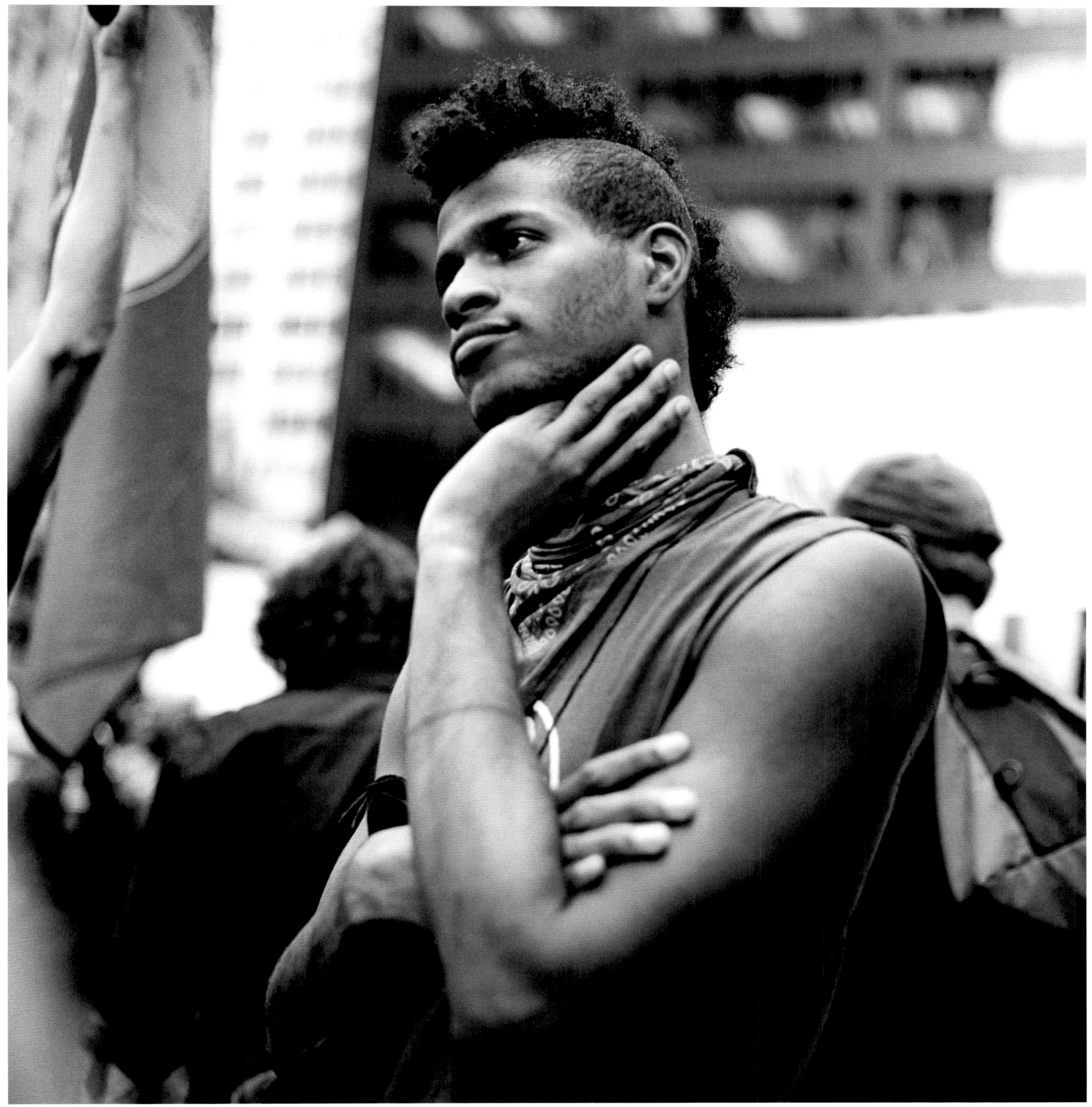

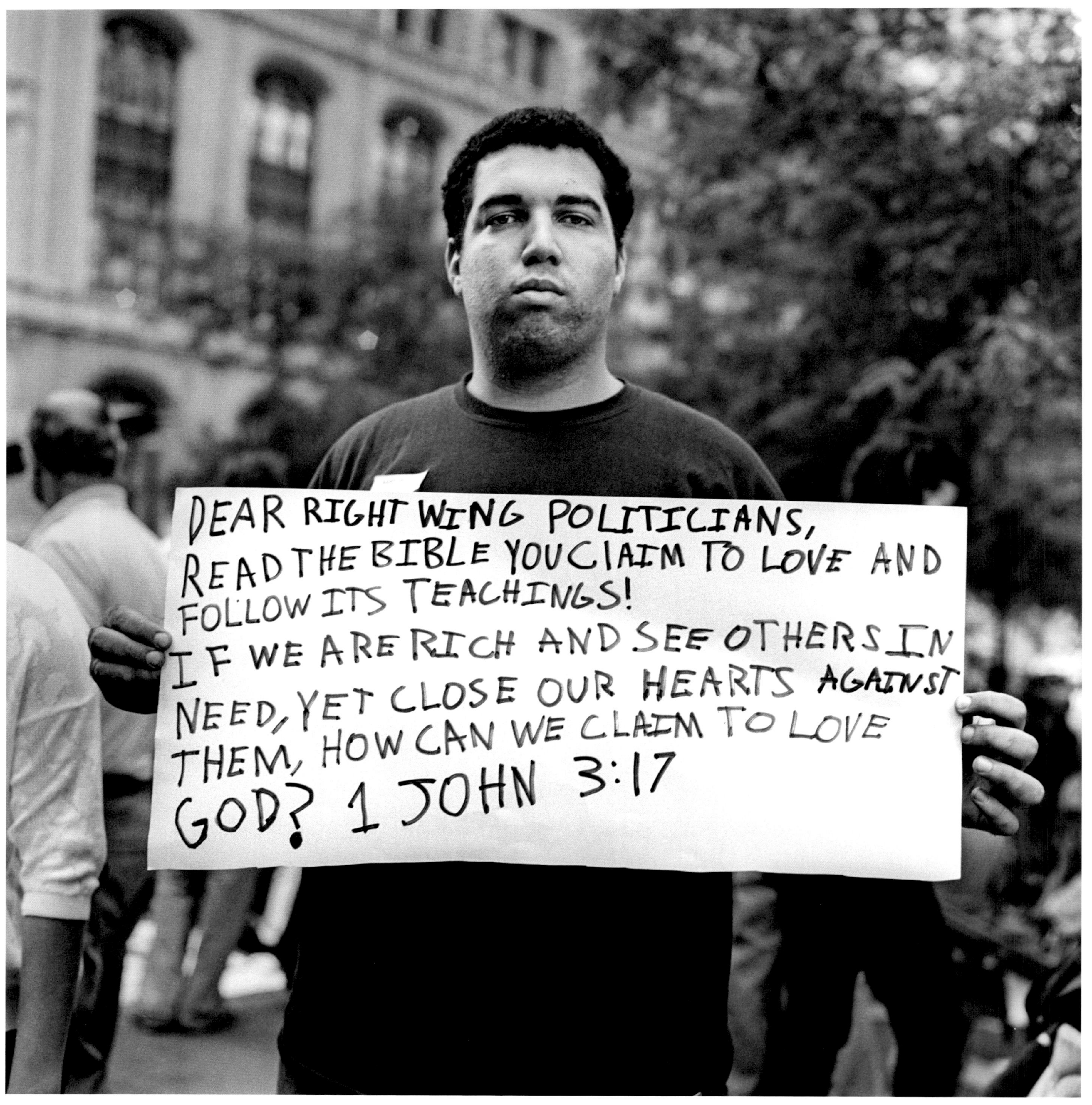
DEAR RIGHT WING POLITICIANS,
READ THE BIBLE YOU CLAIM TO LOVE AND
FOLLOW ITS TEACHINGS!
IF WE ARE RICH AND SEE OTHERS IN
NEED, YET CLOSE OUR HEARTS AGAINST
THEM, HOW CAN WE CLAIM TO LOVE
GOD? 1 JOHN 3:17

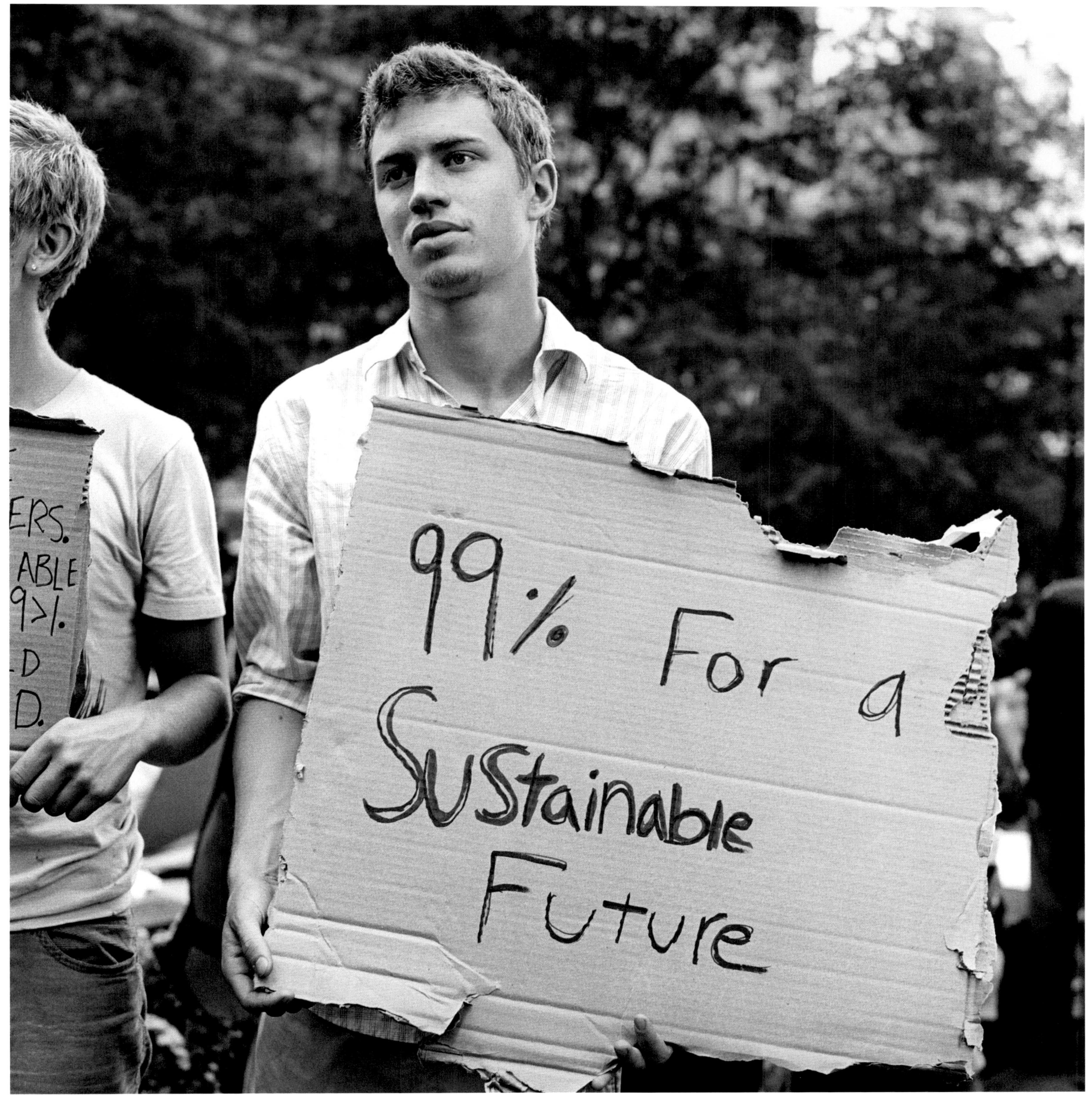
99% For a
Sustainable
Future

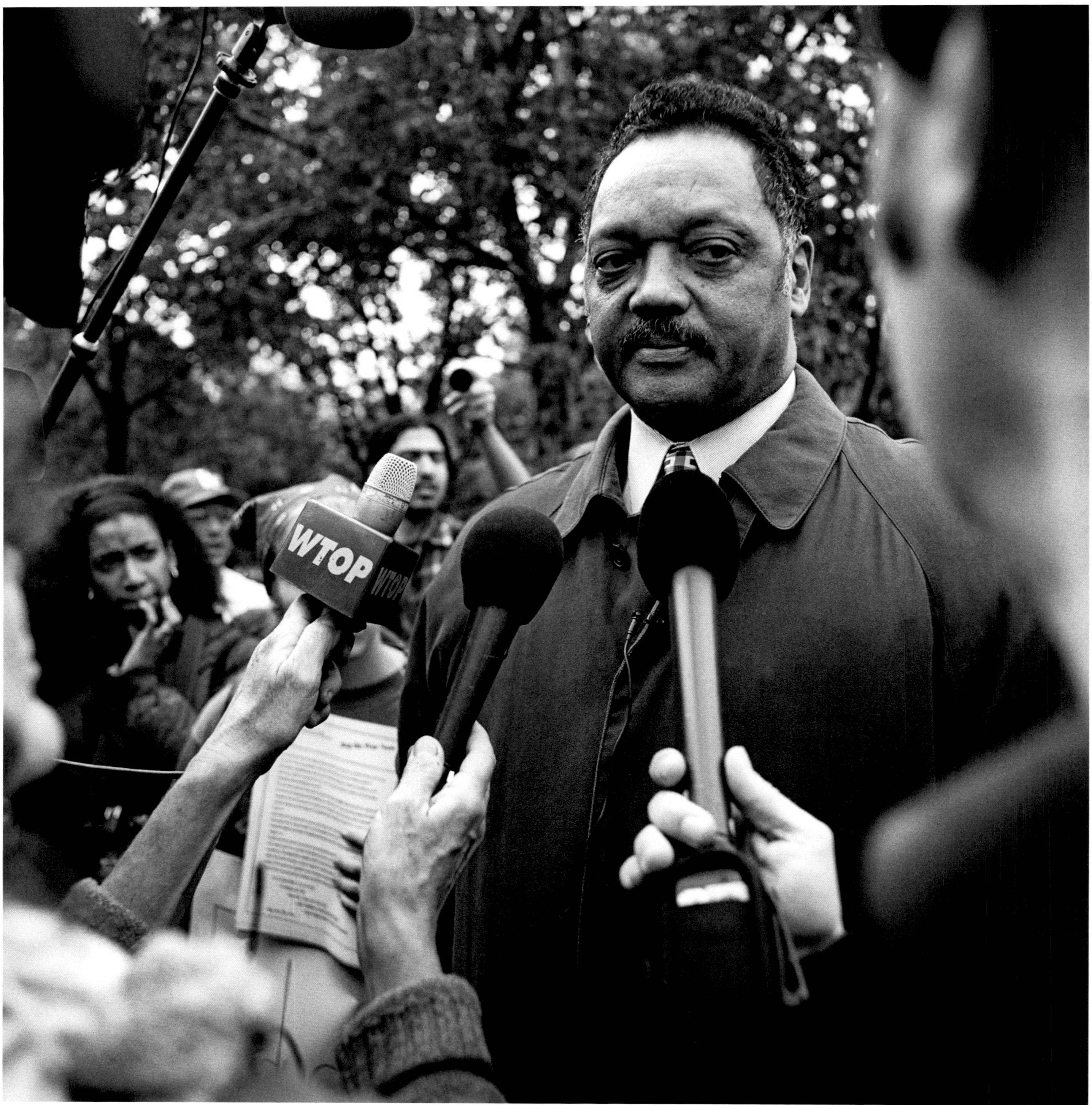
WTOP
WTOP

Afterword

HOWARD ZINN

When a gifted photographer like Kevin Bubriski turns his attention, not to a random selection of images in a visual world infinitely varied, but rather to those scenes of American life which speak to his social conscience, we have a special work of art.

We are living in a world so beleaguered by war, sickness, poverty—from which even the privileged population of the United States cannot escape—that every contribution to social change must be welcomed. Artists can make a special contribution, because they can use their talents to awaken the conscience of people who may live in a cocoon of comfort, far from zones of trouble, but who can be confronted with a reality they cannot ignore.

Artists,whether they are poets, musicians, actors, painters, or photographers, may present us with the beauty of the world, in a way that can suggest to us, however troubled we are, what life can be like at its best. But they can do more than that. They are more than artists, they are citizens and human beings, and they can use their art to help transform a world that badly needs transformation. There is a special gift that artists have—they can not only imagine the kind of world tranquil and beautiful, which we all want to live in; they can use language or images to present the reality of the world as it is, but in such a way that moves us to compassion, perhaps even to action. We all can remember lines of poetry, or scenes of a novel, or photographs in a newspaper, that awakened us to a new understanding of something we knew nothing about, or were aware of only vaguely.

In the years of the Vietnam War, the people of the United States were gradually becoming aware of what our bombing was doing to innocent people, living in the villages of that small country. But when certain photographs appeared in the press, we were startled, shocked into an awareness of the reality of the war that had escaped us. There was the photograph of the Vietnamese girl running along a road, her skin shredded by napalm, her face revealing shock and pain. There were the photos of the My Lai Massacre, showing U.S. soldiers pouring automatic rifle fire down into trenches where terrified mothers huddled with their children.

We live now again in a time of war. Once again, there is an atmosphere in which criticism of the war, criticism of government policy is looked upon as "unpatriotic." There is a mistaken notion, deliberately propagated by the government, and too often not challenged in the press, that patriotism means unquestioning support of whatever the political leaders decide. But our greatest Americans—from the revolutionaries of the Boston Tea Party, to Henry David Thoreau protesting the Mexican War, to Mark Twain denouncing our massacre of Filipinos at the start of the twentieth century—were dissenters. They understood that true patriotism, true love of country, means being true to the ideals of peace and justice, and not to the policies of the government.

It is a time when we need our artists to prod our consciences, to show us a reality we may only dimly have perceived, to inform us soberly, to move us emotionally. Kevin Bubriski's *Our Voices, Our Streets*, joins the long line of art throughout history that has played a part, modest but crucial, in the struggle for a better world.

HOWARD ZINN, JUNE 2006

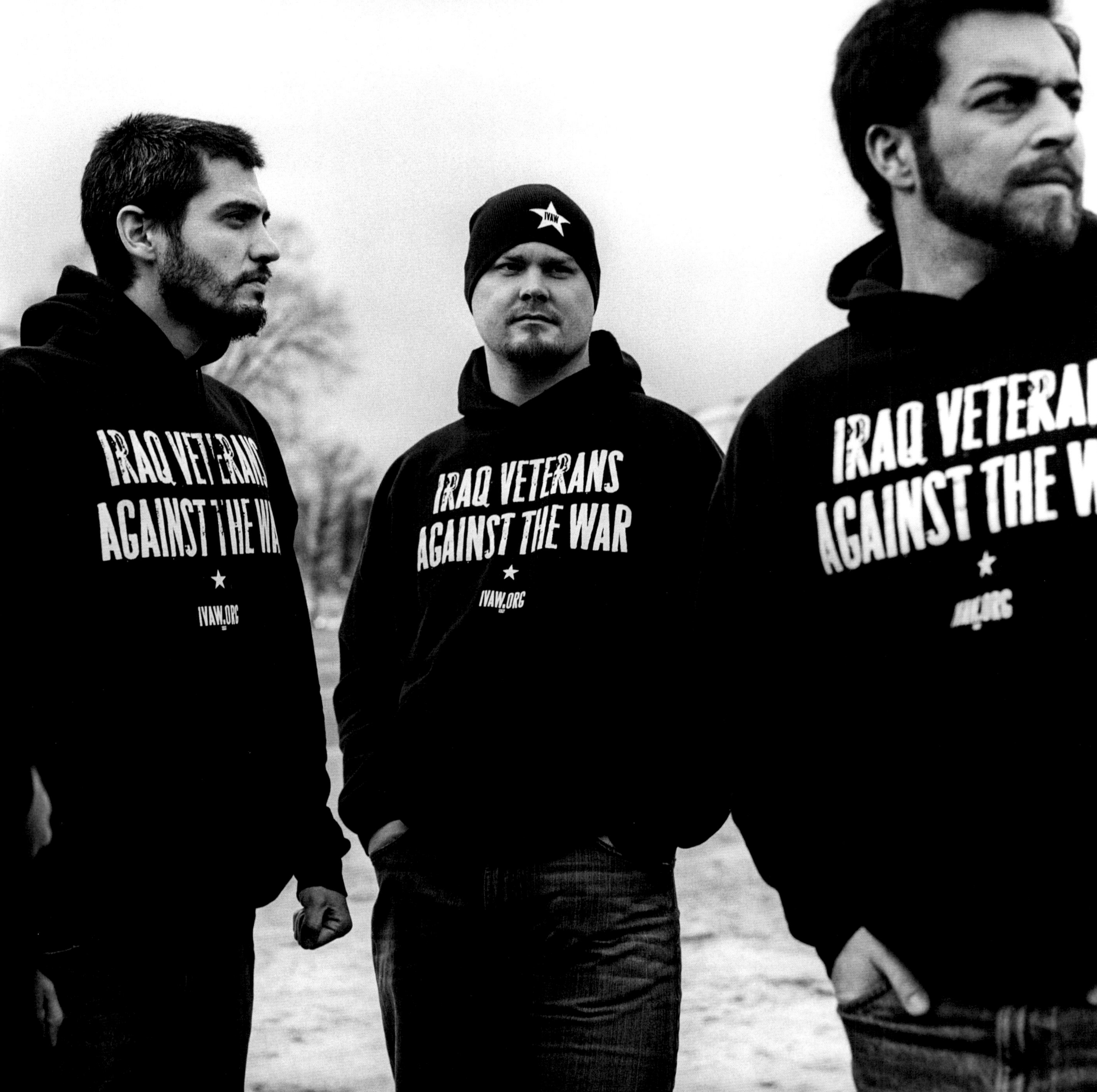
IVAW
IRAQ VETERANS
AGAINST THE WAR
IVAW.ORG

Acknowledgements

My thanks to my wife, Laura, my daughter, Tara, and son, Ryan, for their love and support. Thank you, Laura, for always inspiring me, encouraging me, and believing in the images.

This book would not have been possible without the very generous support of the William and Salomé Scanlan Foundation. Thank you to the J.M. Kaplan Fund: Furthermore Grants in Publishing for their very early support of this book. My thanks also to my brother, Peter Bubriski, and dear friends Michael McKeon and Carolyn Williams for their support of this book.

Howard Zinn's thoughtful and empathetic afterword is a powerful reminder to us all that our democracy and political destiny require our constant attention and active participation. Lucy McKeon's clear and radiant words bring us into a deeper engagement with the images and contemporary moment.

My Vermont neighbors Dorothy Halvorsen, Ricky Greene, Andrew Shoerke, Rosemarie Jakowski, and Nathan Wallace-Senft contributed their powerful and expressive words. Sincere thanks to the people from all walks of life and of various political persuasions who are represented here in the photographs. We should never take for granted our constitutional and legal rights, which allow us to be in the streets, to exercise the freedom of speech, and to tell our stories.

My thanks to Megan Williams for creating the first design of this book in 2006, and to Nick Costantino, my steadfast assistant over many months, for scanning negatives, editing images, and laying out the initial sequence of the book. David Skolkin has brought his very fine eye to the design of this book and masterfully handled its production. Thanks to John Vokoun for the pre-press preparation of the image files, and to powerHouse Books and EBS for bringing the images to life in ink and paper.

Our Voices, Our Streets: American Protests 2001–2011

Published in the United States by powerHouse Books,
a division of powerHouse Cultural Entertainment, Inc.
32 Adams Street, Brooklyn, NY 11201-1021
e-mail: info@powerHouseBooks.com
website: www.powerHouseBooks.com

First edition, 2020

Library of Congress Control Number: 2019957027

ISBN 978-1-57687-947-4

Designed by David Skolkin
Printed by Editoriale Bortolazzi Stei srl, Verona

10 9 8 7 6 5 4 3 2 1

Printed and bound in Italy